JANET H. HOWARTH is Emeritus Fellow of St Hilda's College, Oxford, special-
ising in the history of the women's movement and the history of education in
modern Britain.

'A century of change and continuity in women's lives is masterfully narrated by Janet Howarth in this excellent book. We grasp the myriad meanings of being a woman in twentieth-century Britain through the words of politicians and policy makers, feminists and agitators, social investigators and sociologists, novelists and poets, and we hear women's own voices in every key. Howarth's selection of texts offers a tantalising flavour of the rich resources available for exploring women's history, covering every subject from motherhood and work to politics and sexuality. Prefaced with a superb essay by the author synthesising major themes in the recent scholarship, *Women in Britain* is highly recommended for anyone teaching or studying this intriguing and capacious subject.'

Helen McCarthy, University Lecturer in
Modern British History, University of Cambridge

'This comprehensive collection of original sources on women in Britain from 1914 to the millennium is an invaluable asset for students studying contemporary British history. Informative and timely, it portrays the rich diversity of women's lives during this period.'

June Purvis, Professor of Women's and
Gender History (Emerita), University of Portsmouth

'This is an excellent resource for staff and students and will rapidly become a "go-to" book for students of history undertaking assignments on women in twentieth-century Britain. The comprehensive introduction contextualises the primary sources brilliantly, also providing very useful historiographical insights. The documents are well chosen and very wide ranging offering readers a masterly survey of this important topic which is essential for any serious historian of the social history of modern Britain.'

Sue Bruley, Reader in Modern History,
University of Portsmouth

'Extracts from writings and statements by women of all classes, different races and supporters and opponents of gender equality bring to life diversity and change in women's experiences through the twentieth century. Reminding us that, even in the 1970s, the BBC believed that women lacked the "authority, consistency and reliability" to read the news, it provokes questions about what has and has not changed.'

Patricia M. Thane, Research Professor in Contemporary
British History, King's College, London

Women in Britain

Voices and Perspectives from Twentieth-Century History

JANET H. HOWARTH

I.B. TAURIS

LONDON · NEW YORK

Published in 2019 by
I.B.Tauris & Co. Ltd
London • New York
www.ibtauris.com

ISBN (HB): 978 1 85043 455 9
ISBN (PB): 978 1 85043 456 6
eISBN: 978 1 78672 424 3
ePDF: 978 1 78673 424 2

A full CIP record for this book is available from the British Library
A full CIP record is available from the Library of Congress

Library of Congress Catalog Card Number: available

Typeset by Riverside Publishing Solutions, Salisbury, Wiltshire
Printed and bound in Great Britain

Contents

List of Illustrations and Maps

Acknowledgements

This book was originally commissioned as a 'Reader', a collection of documents on twentieth-century women's history, and has evolved over the years in response to developments in the secondary literature on women's history, gender history and contemporary British history. In the processes of thinking out, researching and writing it I have incurred many debts.

A book of this kind could not have not have been completed without the commitment and expertise of editors at I.B.Tauris, and above all Tom Stottor's tireless, patient and effective work in – among other essential tasks – tracking down and negotiating with copyright owners. Its publication has been made possible by a grant from the Scouloudi Foundation in association with the Institute of Historical Research. I am most grateful for this support, and also for the generosity of the many authors and rights holders who have allowed me to reproduce their work for a nominal fee, or no fee at all.

I must acknowledge, too, the invaluable help and advice I have had from librarians and archivists at the institutions in which the book was researched: the Bodleian Library, The Women's Library at the London School of Economics and its predecessor the Fawcett Library, the British Library, Balliol, Somerville and St Hilda's Colleges.

Many former colleagues (not all of them historians) and students, graduates and undergraduates, will recognise in the book (if they read it) the various ways in which their work has contributed to it, both in outline and in detail. Ross McKibbin, whose approach to the writing of history has had a formative influence, read a draft of the book with a critical eye and provided much needed encouragement. Warmest thanks are due to all of them. Any mistakes or shortcomings in the final version are of course my responsibility alone.

Finally, thanks go to my family and friends for their forbearance and support over the years in which 'the book' has been a preoccupation.

Introduction

Fifty years ago it was still necessary to make a case for 'writing women in' to narratives of national history. That is no longer true; and yet it is often far from straightforward to work out *how* to place women in canonical versions of history. The aim in this book is therefore to provide an anthology of printed sources on women in Britain in the 'short twentieth century' – that is between the beginning of World War I and the millennium. It is not an exercise in separatist women's history but a contribution to the work of incorporating women into an inclusive history of modern Britain.

In the twentieth century, women's lives were profoundly affected both by upheavals in what was still a predominantly male political domain – above all, World Wars I and II – and also by autonomous, unforeseen and sometimes radical processes of demographic, economic and cultural change. This was the century in which British women achieved equal citizenship but their experience of, and perspectives on, change and continuities over a life-cycle could be significantly different from that of their male contemporaries. Ultimately historians may be able to offer a comprehensively gendered account of Britain's development in the past century. Much progress towards that goal has already been made, especially in writing on World Wars I and II and the interwar years. In the meantime, those who take the long view of contemporary British women's history debate patterns of continuity and change, how far change in the modern world represents 'progress' or not, and in what directions it might be leading, how women have figured in the experience of 'modernity'. The choice of sources here reflects these themes in the secondary literature, but the underlying purpose has been to explore ways of thinking about the changing place of women in British society and politics.

The book is primarily aimed at students of contemporary British history, in the hope of encouraging them to exploit the full range of sources on women available to them. The wealth of source material available to the twentieth-century historian is of course already unprecedented and expanding rapidly, as oral history and Mass Observation projects tap into new bodies of evidence and digitisation creates new means of accessing and analysing it.[1] Yet it is also as true of the twentieth century as of any other period that women and issues of gender figure much more prominently in the contemporary literature than in most secondary histories. Many of the sources in this anthology are out of print; others – such as *Hansard* – are voluminous and not altogether easy to search; others again, are simply unlikely to figure on history student reading lists. That said, I would not want to claim – for several reasons – that the selection of extracts included here is in any way authoritative. Anyone who has taught on a Women's Studies course learns to mistrust the whole idea of a 'canon'. Historians of all periods take it as read that perspectives will differ, and change over time, and that histories are never definitive. But there is a particular hazard in constructing an anthology of twentieth-century sources. Much of the material one might wish to use is in copyright. Permission to reproduce it cannot always be obtained or the fees afforded. For all these reasons, the reader – whatever his or her range of interests – will certainly find that the selection of texts and images here is less than ideal. If she or he is prompted to go and look for source material to fill the gaps, redress the bias and open new lines of enquiry, so much the better.

I have divided the book into two sections. The first five chapters are thematic, dealing with patterns of regional, social class and ethnic diversity, and with four areas in which women have had some common gendered experience of change in the past century: the balance between family and work, education, sexualities, and ideas about feminism and femininity. The second is chronological and illustrates the place of women in national life in five periods between 1914 and 2000. This introductory chapter offers an overview and contextual material by way of background.

Class, Region and Ethnicity

To speak of 'national' life makes sense only if we acknowledge the diversity of cultures and communities within the nations that make up Great Britain. This is a theme that runs throughout the book, but Chapter 1 includes a range of sources on regional, class and ethnic differences and ways in which women have experienced them.

Regional and ethnic aspects of diversity became more marked in the second half of the century, with the rise of Welsh and Scottish nationalism and patterns of immigration that turned many English cities – Greater

London especially – into multi-cultural communities. But from the standpoint of gender, Wales and Scotland had distinctive histories of their own, featuring patriarchal religious traditions – the Calvinist Protestantism of the Welsh chapels or the Presbyterian Kirk – and national archetypes such as the 'Welsh Mam' and the male-voice choir, or Scotland's regiments and hard-drinking football fans. These were low-wage economies dominated by mining, heavy industry and more or less depressed agriculture. Except in the textile and clothing industries and the jute factories of Dundee there was little industrial work for women in Scotland, still less in Wales before World War II. In South Wales during the depressed 1930s, malnutrition caused exceptionally high levels of maternal mortality. Nowhere in Britain was housing as overcrowded as in Scotland. Only in the remote Shetland Islands have historians found an oral tradition that celebrates the economic role of women, hand-knitters and crofters in communities where the men spent long months at sea fishing.[2]

If living standards were somewhat higher for the English, gender regimes in working-class families throughout the British Isles were shaped by local labour markets. In mining communities and in most agricultural districts, where the workforce was by the early twentieth century overwhelmingly male, daughters were sent away when they left school, mainly into domestic service, and those who returned to marry had large families. A different pattern prevailed in regions where local industries traditionally employed women – such as the textile towns of Lancashire and Yorkshire or the Staffordshire potteries – and increasingly in cities, and in the prosperous South East, which offered a range of commercial and industrial jobs for women. Fertility fell faster, school-leavers of both sexes normally stayed at home and contributed from their earnings to the family income until they married. Local labour markets also affected the gendered impact of interwar depression, and of the longer drawn-out processes of deindustrialisation and patchy reindustrialisation that began again in the 1960s. The change in lifestyles these might bring was foreshadowed in J. B. Priestley's picture of 'three Englands' in the 1930s: 'Old England, the country of the cathedrals and minsters and manor houses and inns, of Parson and Squire'; 'the nineteenth-century England, the industrial England of coal, iron, steel, cotton, wool, railways'; and the new, Americanised England that was emerging in London and the Home Counties, with its 'filling stations and factories that look like exhibition buildings' and its egalitarian mass consumer culture.[3]

To Priestley 'this new England' seemed 'as near to a classless society as we have got yet'. For a while in the middle decades of the century it looked as if class distinctions might be eroded by rising real wages and consumerism. In terms of social structure, the middle classes expanded at the expense of the working class, slowly between the wars but rapidly in the 1960s and after, reflecting the growth of the service sector and decline of manufacturing. The proportion of manual workers in the workforce fell from 72 per cent in 1921 to 38 per cent in 1991.[4] Historians and sociologists continue to debate the shifting perceptions of class that accompanied these changes.[5] Yet social surveys continued to show that class awareness was a fact of British life: when asked to place themselves in a social class all but a tiny minority of the population – 6 per cent in the British Election Study of 2005 – still did so.[6] Social class continued to affect life-chances significantly: rates of infant mortality and life expectancy, levels of educational achievement, patterns of sexual behaviour. In the 1990s the likelihood of having a child outside marriage was two-and-a-half times as great for a woman from a manual working-class family as for a woman from a non-manual background.[7] By the millennium the coming of a classless society seemed less likely than it had 50 years earlier. From the 1980s a trend towards greater inequality of incomes set in. Women played a part in that process. On the one hand, they were recruited to fill low-paid, mostly part-time jobs in manufacturing and the service sector, as deindustrialisation accelerated, labour markets were deregulated and male unemployment rates rose. On the other, opportunities for qualified women opened up in the professions and commerce, boosting the income of dual-career middle-class families. Traditionally it was usual to assign women to a social class on the basis of the occupation of their father or husband – the male head of the household to which they belonged. By the 1980s this practice had become anomalous: more women had their own occupational identity and they were clearly contributing (willingly or not) to the reshaping of class hierarchies.

What can we say about women's distinctive experience of social class? 'The social round in England is very complicated, very intricate', wrote Stevie Smith, describing the 'extremely class conscious' suburban world of North London where she lived with her aunt in the 1930s.

> Everybody is always trying to be the next step up [...] given a slight increase in income and ordinary luck, and a wife that is quick at noticing, there you are, you'll be one step up as soon as sneeze.[8]

There were many ways in which wives and mothers might contribute to a family's social position. Manners and appearances were important at all levels of society. As managers of the family lifestyle, deciding who to interact with and how, monitoring boundaries, there was some common ground between the 'lady' and the 'respectable' working-class woman. In both cases certain conventions would be enforced, if not created, by women. Rules of behaviour and gradations of status for the genteel and upwardly mobile might be codified in publications like the various editions of Lady Troubridge's *Book of Etiquette* (see Chapter 1). Nancy Mitford's mid-century guide to distinctive upper and upper-middle class usages – 'U' as opposed to 'non-U' – did the same thing for language.[9] But gossip also played its part. Agatha Christie, author of many country house mysteries, recalled how in her lifetime the shifting criteria for admission to county society had been discussed in drawing-room small-talk.

> Three phases have succeeded each other [...] In the first the question would be: 'But who *is* she dear? Who are her *people*? Is she one of the *Yorkshire* Twiddledos? Of course, they are badly off, very badly off, but she was a *Wilmot*.' This was to be succeeded in due course by: 'Oh yes, of course they *are* pretty dreadful, but then they are terribly *rich*' [...] The third phase was different again: 'Well, dear, but are they *amusing*?' 'Yes, well of course they are not well off, and nobody knows where they came from, but they are very *very* amusing.'[10]

The 'old queens' of Salford, Lancashire matriarchs remembered from his childhood by Robert Roberts, played a similar role in registering standards and status within the local working-class community. They were 'guardians, but not creators, of the group conscience and as such possessed a sense of social propriety as developed and unerring as any clique of Edwardian dowagers'.[11]

How far there could be genuine sympathy between women of different social classes was unclear to Virginia Woolf, as she mulled over impressions of a Women's Co-operative Guild Congress in Newcastle just before World War I. 'One could not be Mrs. Giles of Durham because one's body had never stood at the wash-tub; one's hands had never wrung and scrubbed and chopped up whatever the meat may be that makes a miner's supper.'[12] Yet conditions of life for working-class women were the main concern of early twentieth-century social feminists. They were documented in a flourishing

literature of social observation and, increasingly, by public health profession-
als. The clinics that provided ante- and post-natal medical care, for example, revealed both poor standards of general health and low expectations of
well-being among mothers. Commenting on the results of a 1930s survey,
the medical officer Dame Janet Campbell wrote:

> We find that the expectant mother is often mal-nourished; she
> is frequently anaemic; indigestion and constipation are accepted as a
> matter of course; varicose veins and dental caries pass almost unnoted
> except perhaps when pregnancy accentuates the aching and weari-
> ness of her legs, or causes a more rapid decay of defective teeth [...]
> Unfortunately, it is a much more difficult task to persuade a mother to
> seek or accept post-natal advice for herself than to induce her to ask
> for guidance in infant management.[13]

At the most basic level the experience of family poverty was still a stage in
the life-cycle for working-class mothers with more than the average number
of children. And that really was a gendered experience. Mothers had the job
of making ends meet, went hungry in order to feed the breadwinner and
children, worked to maintain the extended family links that could secure
help in hard times, represented the family in encounters with welfare authorities and social workers, and bore much of the blame when lifestyles did not
come up to scratch. The price of failure in the 1960s – homelessness, children
taken into care – was the theme of the powerful television drama directed
by Ken Loach, *Cathy Come Home* (1966). Incomes rose over the decades, but
some persistent features of working-class cultures – a more authoritarian
style of child-rearing for example – continued to reflect mothers' strategies
for coping with limited resources.

At the other end of the social spectrum, there was what Anne Summers
has termed the 'domestic service paradigm'.[14] Having at least one resident
domestic servant was, at the start of the twentieth century, the hallmark
of a middle-class family. It was not until World War II that domestic
help became unusual, except in the form of a daily cleaner or charwoman.
Domestic service was on the whole an unpopular occupation, rarely chosen
where there was an alternative of factory or office work. The mistress–servant
relationship could be positive, even affectionate, but it tended to encourage
in middle and upper-class women an assumption that authority was conferred by social position and a manner that could, in public or professional

life, cause deep resentment. This was, according to one Bradford housewife, among the reasons why girls were reluctant to join the women's auxiliary armed services in World War II:

> It is unfortunate that so many of the officers have loud, unfriendly, patronising voices and speak what they think is King's English with so much affectation and over-emphasis. Neither the King nor the Queen show any sign of this affectation. The officers seem to think that if a girl speaks with a Northern accent she is uneducated, uncouth, insensitive [...] and proceed to treat her as if she were a kitchenmaid being interviewed by an ill-bred duchess. As very few self-respecting girls in the West Riding would dream of going into domestic service (they look on it as degradation), they resent the haughty, patronising ways of the ATS officers.[15]

By the middle decades of the century, domestic service (except perhaps for a 'daily' cleaner) was beyond the means of the ordinary middle classes, surviving only in the grander upper or upper-middle class household. Linda Blandford, researching girls' public boarding schools in the 1970s, was told:

> You can always tell a grammar school girl who has married well by the fact that she's a fraction too familiar with her servants and rather uncomfortable with yours.[16]

For a brief period middle and working-class housewives had the common experience of doing their own housework, with more or less help from the new household technology. When demand for paid domestic help revived, chiefly in dual-career business and professional families in the 1980s and after, it was met mainly by non-resident cleaners and nannies.

To the Fabian socialist Mabel Atkinson in 1914 it had seemed inevitable that the women's movement would divide on class lines on some issues, so profoundly different were the situations of middle and working-class women. In the 1980s the notion of feminist solidarity was challenged by black British women such as Hazel Carby from the standpoint of race, not class. They represented the New Commonwealth immigrants, mostly Afro-Caribbean or South Asian, of the post-1945 era. (Not much had been heard from women of previous generations of ethnic minority immigrants; the records we have of the voices of Irish and Jewish women, for example, are mostly a product of later oral history projects.) Cultural differences associated with ethnicity often took gendered forms: a high incidence among Afro-Caribbeans and a very low incidence among Indians of lone mothers with dependent children; much lower workforce participation rates among Muslim women.[17] Cultural influences of a different sort were, however, behind the angry protests of the 1980s against the patronage of white feminists. They reflected chiefly the realities of racist discrimination in post-colonial Britain. For many black women the enemy was not patriarchy but racism – shown by the police and other representatives of the state as well as ordinary citizens. Yet there were also feminist groups, such as the Southall Black Sisters, who defended women against violence of all kinds: among their targets were culturally specific forms of patriarchy – notions of 'honour', for example, that might victimise women who attempted to leave violent husbands. Integration proceeded unevenly and took various forms. Individuals from ethnic minorities made their mark in many fields, including sport, the media, literature and the arts, politics and trade unionism. By the turn of the century girls from black or Asian families were more likely to get to university than girls from the white working class; and an opinion poll of 2001 showed that anxieties about immigration – which were shortly to rise sharply in the wake of terrorist incidents – had subsided to a low level.[18] The extracts from ethnic minority women in this volume speak

1. Valerie Amos, Baroness Amos of Brondesbury, born in Guyana in 1954, was to become in 2003 the first black woman to serve in a British Cabinet, as Secretary of State for International Development. Her parents, who were teachers, moved to England when she was nine. With degrees from the universities of Warwick, Birmingham and East Anglia and experience in London local government, she was appointed chief executive at the Equal Opportunities Commission (1989–94). Tony Blair made her a life peer in 1997.

of cultural difference and of racist rejection, but also of experience shared as women and within communities defined primarily by class.

Family and Work

Family structure and the gendered division of labour within families changed dramatically in the course of the century. Marriage and the male breadwinner/female homemaker family were the norm for all social classes until the early 1970s. A mid-twentieth-century 'marriage boom' brought a fall in the proportion of women who never married from about 15 per cent in the inter-war years to about 5 per cent of those born in the years after 1945.[19] But, after 1972 marriage rates fell. The trend was now towards a more diverse pattern of family forms and multiple-earner households, with growing acceptance of divorce, cohabitation and the lone parent family (the latter in about nine out of ten cases headed by the mother). There is no general agreement on how to interpret these late twentieth-century changes. On the one hand they amounted to a return to earlier patterns of family life and household economy: single mothers were freed from the stigma imposed on them by the 1834 Poor Law; couples could choose, as in the eighteenth century, to cohabit without the forms of marriage; both partners would as a rule contribute to household income. But they also reflected contemporary values – individualism and a rejection of stereotyped gender roles.

One must be careful not to exaggerate how much had really changed by the end of the century. Most children born to unmarried couples were still registered by both parents (78 per cent in 1995).[20] Single mothers often went on to form stable partnerships, even marry. And lone parent families had a long history. In the past, when life expectancy was lower, many marriages were cut short by bereavement: the chances of divorce within 25 years of marriage in the late twentieth century were about the same as the chances a century earlier of being widowed within 25 years of marriage.[21] As for the family economy, in practice men never had been the only breadwinners. A study published in 1921 estimated that a third of female wage-earners were (partially or in a few cases wholly) responsible for supporting dependants.[22] And in the 1990s men still earned more than women, one reason being that over 40 per cent of female employees were part-time workers.[23] Nevertheless change in the norms of family life was real enough, and rapid. The divorce rate for England and Wales increased more than six-fold between 1960 and 1995 (from 2 to 13.6 per 1,000 married people).[24] Lone parent families were 8 per cent of all families with dependent children in 1971, 22 per cent by 1995.[25]

One in ten married women was listed as employed in the 1931 census; by 1961 nearly 30 per cent of wives went out to work; by 1991 more than half (53 per cent), and 72 per cent of those aged 35–54.[26]

The focus in Chapter 2 is on women's work, both inside and outside the home. Opportunities for women's employment expanded in interwar Britain – clerical and shop work, production-line work in the new consumer goods industries where employers were looking for a docile, non-unionised workforce. For educated women, there were limited professional openings in the higher civil service, law and medicine as well as the more established career fields in teaching, nursing and social work. World War II propaganda and advertising paved the way for the claim that modern women had 'two roles', in the labour market as well as at home. Welfare reform in the 1940s and after created more jobs in the caring professions. But throughout these decades women's presence in the workplace could create unease and friction of various kinds. Evelyn Sharp, later to become the first woman permanent secretary, had problems as a junior civil servant in the 1920s both with colleagues who made unwelcome advances and a boss at the Ministry of Health who prided himself on treating her 'exactly as he would have treated a man in her place':

> He took her to lunch at the 'Escargot' in Soho, gave her port to drink and told her risqué stories, and he sent her alone to represent her ministry at a meeting of a Midlands town council [...] 'The Town Clerk,' she told [her friend Alix Meynell], 'said he could not take the responsibility of introducing me as the Minister's Representative; he thought it must be some kind of joke. 'Very well', I said. 'I'll introduce myself', and I pushed open the door of the Council Chamber [...] There was a shocked silence until the Chairman said, 'We didn't expect a lass but you're very welcome', and pocketed the large cigar lying beside the place [...] reserved for the Minister's Inspector'.[27]

Even in the Yorkshire woollen industry, where women's factory work was traditional, there was discomfort around the sexualised banter that went on in a mixed workforce. The sociologist Dennis Marsden commented in the 1960s that some Huddersfield 'mill girls':

> had developed a fixed, slightly hard facial expression and a facility with back-chat which hinted at a growing insensitivity in their relations with other work-people.

2. Clementine Churchill with her husband in 1915: the 'incorporated wife' in politics. Recent biographies record her crucially important role in supporting Winston throughout his long career, but especially as war-time Prime Minister 1940-5.[i]

One man told him, 'I wouldn't like my girl friend to have to work here: not from t'work point of view, but from what they have to put up with and t'language they have to hear'.[28] The persistence of masculinised work cultures is, in fact, a theme that recurs at the end of the century, despite equal opportunities legislation and the opening of new fields of employment, including high-earning posts in the commercial and financial sectors. 'Superwoman' fund managers, such as Nicola Horlick and her role model at S. G. Warburg & Co., Carol Galley, could now find a place in the City of London.[29] Yet Linda McDowell's research on city banks in the early 1990s found that, especially in trading and dealing rooms:

> exaggerated versions of men behaving badly were acceptable modes of
> everyday social interactions in the workplace. Often unbuttoned and
> in shirtsleeves, men (and these occupations remained almost entirely
> male dominated) shouted, sweated, bawled into phones, indulged in
> forms of verbal and visual sexual denigration of women – both in gen-
> eral and of their few female colleagues and greater numbers of female
> support workers – as well as in school-boyish antics and pranks.[30]

A more traditional role for women was support of a husband's profession or occupation as what has been termed the 'incorporated wife'; the survival of that role in many fields, from diplomacy and the church to the rural police, was analysed by social anthropologists in the 1980s.[31] Opportunities for unpaid public work, moreover, expanded: the magistracy was opened to women in 1919 and by the late 1940s nearly a quarter of all magistrates were women.[32] For much of the century, though, the dominant view was that married women, and above all mothers of young children, ought not to take paid work outside the home. Between the wars it was a common requirement that women should leave their jobs on marriage. The 'marriage bar' for teachers and civil servants ended in the 1940s; in the diplomatic service, which was first opened to women in 1946, resignation on marriage remained the rule until 1973. But social disapproval of working mothers (even if in practice it did not extend, as Wendy Webster points out, to immigrant women) continued for some time.[33] Many factors contributed to it. The Labour movement wanted to protect men's jobs and their claim to be paid a 'family wage'. Interwar stereotypes of the 'modern housewife' romanticised women's domestic roles. So did the image of the working-class mum, 'the pivot of the home' as Richard Hoggart described her.[34] And public concern for the traditional family drew on more than sentiment. Between the wars there were eugenic nightmares of 'race suicide', encouraged by a falling birth rate. In the postwar decades the psychiatrist John Bowlby stressed the importance for a young child of:

> a warm, intimate, and continuous relationship with his mother (or permanent mother-substitute – one person who steadily 'mothers' him) in which both find satisfaction and enjoyment.[35]

Bowlby's warnings about the long-term effects of 'maternal deprivation' on mental health and delinquency were influential. Steeply rising rates of juvenile crime and, in the later twentieth century, high rates of welfare dependency were blamed on the collapse of traditional family life. Margaret Thatcher increasingly took that view in her years as prime minister in the 1980s:

> All the evidence – statistical and anecdotal – pointed to the breakdown of families as the starting-point for a range of social ills, of which getting into trouble with the police was only one.

Hence her resistance to proposals for tax relief or subsidies for child care which, she felt, would have 'swung the emphasis further towards discouraging mothers from staying at home'.[36]

Meanwhile women themselves tended to endorse the breadwinner/homemaker ideal. The economic historian Deidre McCloskey locates the 'ideological change' in favour of married women's work in the years 1965–80: now 'women decided they were market workers. So did their husbands'.[37] Yet oral history testimony and social surveys show that women's attachment to their primary role as housewives often lingered on, even when they had jobs. This may in part explain why they continued to carry a 'double burden': a 1992 survey showed that in two-thirds of relationships where both partners worked full time, it was the woman who was mainly responsible for the housework.[38] Feminists, following Olive Schreiner in her influential critique of 'sex parasitism', had for some time tended to take a different line: it was a woman's right – even a duty – to work for the market.[39] The notion that housework was demeaning and that women deserved liberation from it gained support in the 1970s. Those who did not share that view sometimes complained that it was feminists who forced wives out into the labour market. But increased workforce participation by women in the second half of the century was an international trend and influenced by structural as well as cultural factors: increased life expectancy and smaller families, labour shortages, growth in the service sector at the expense of manufacturing, and – perhaps crucially, as Jan de Vries suggests – changing patterns of household consumption in Western Europe and North America.[40] There was more that money could buy to enhance a family's lifestyle and family welfare became less dependent on household labour. With the steep increases in house prices and rents that began in Britain in the early 1970s, moreover, two incomes were increasingly needed to provide basic necessities. By the twenty-first century the 'new capitalist mother', whether an immigrant or a native of Great Britain, would expect to share the role of breadwinner.[41] The unemployed housewife – especially the lone mother – was associated with family poverty, and policy-makers of all parties were devising ways of getting her into paid employment.

Education

Britain's education system in the early twentieth century was shaped by social class as well as gender. Schooling up to the age of 14 was free and compulsory for both sexes, with a gendered curriculum in the (mostly mixed) elementary schools that catered for working-class children: needlework and domestic science for girls, extra arithmetic for boys. Secondary education, which except in Scotland was traditionally provided in single-sex schools, became free to all only after the Butler Education Act of 1944. In England before that it was largely confined to the middle classes, although by 1914 there was a narrow scholarship ladder for elementary schoolchildren. Many of these – girls especially – would go on to teacher training colleges, qualifying there to teach in elementary schools or the 'secondary moderns' which gradually took over schooling for the less academic child over the age of 11. Academic girls' schools took various forms: grammar or 'High' schools (which might be independent – like the schools of the Girls' Public Day Schools Trust – or run by the local education authority), convent schools, a very few academically ambitious independent boarding schools such as

3. Higher Education and Academic Recognition for Women: slow progress before the 1970s.

3i. Queen Mary (1867–1958). Neither George V's wife nor their daughter Mary, the Princess Royal, had much formal education, but Queen Mary's commitment to philanthropic work included women's higher education. She became, in 1921, the first woman to receive an honorary DCL at Oxford. © Library of Congress, Prints & Photographs Division [reproduction number, e.g. LC-B2-1234].

3ii. Beatrice Webb (1858–1943). The eminent social scientist and, with her husband Sidney, co-founder of the London School of Economics Beatrice Webb was elected in 1932 as the first woman Fellow of the British Academy.

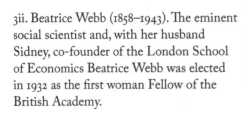

3iii. Dorothy Garrod (1892–1968). Archaeologist and prehistorian Dorothy Garrod, pictured here between two fieldwork colleagues, became in 1939 the first woman to hold an Oxbridge chair. Her election as Disney Professor of Archaeology at Cambridge has been described as 'a milestone in the struggle to gain access to higher education for women in England'.[ii]

3iv. Dorothy Hodgkin (1892–1968). The chemist and crystallographer Dorothy Hodgkin on the platform at the opening in 1967 of a new building at her Oxford college, Somerville, with the Principal, Barbara Craig, and the university's Chancellor, Harold Macmillan. In 1964 she became the first British woman scientist – and the only one in the twentieth century – to win a Nobel prize. Press reports of her achievement described her as an 'affable-looking housewife' and 'mother of three'.[iii] Courtesy of the Principal and Fellows of Somerville College, Oxford.

Cheltenham Ladies' College, St Leonards, St Andrews or Roedean. But on the whole the sharpest contrast between the education of boys and girls for much of the century was found in the upper or upper-middle class families whose sons went to exclusive public schools and Oxford or Cambridge.

Parents tended to economise on the cost of educating daughters, whose fortunes in life would mostly depend on making a good marriage. They might be educated by a governess at home, or sent to a boarding school or private day school, which though socially select did not give high priority to academic education. A year at finishing school, often on the continent, supplied polish before a girl 'came out' as a debutante. Rich and well-born girls were much less likely than in the United States to go to college.

Women's higher education – associated as it was with the women's movement and the *fin de siècle* image of the 'New Woman' – had nevertheless made significant progress. By 1920 all British universities were open to women (although at Cambridge they were not admitted to the MA degree and full membership of the university until 1948). Attendance at university was admittedly low for both sexes – under 2 per cent of the age group; but the proportion of women among full-time students – nearly one in four – was at that stage high by comparison with continental Europe. These early women graduates made an important contribution to professional and public life. But for girls the half-century after 1914 brought little further progress. The proportion of women students in British universities actually fell slightly between the 1920s and early 1960s. The reasons for this are complex, but overt discrimination certainly played its part. The single-sex tradition in elite education was defended tenaciously. London's medical schools succumbed to pressure to admit women students in wartime but most excluded them in the 1920s, and in the 1950s and 1960s they kept numbers down by restrictive quotas.[42] Oxford and Cambridge also introduced quotas for women students in the 1920s, encouraged by the Asquith Commission's recommendation that 'Cambridge should remain mainly and predominantly a "men's University" though of a mixed type'.[43] The women's colleges at these ancient universities – three at Cambridge, five at Oxford by the mid-twentieth century – remained in any case too poor to expand much, and it was not until the 1970s that the men's undergraduate colleges began to go mixed. The Board of Education also discriminated against women: after 1930 more of the means-tested State Scholarships that funded the ablest students went to men.[44] In state secondary education, too, boys had preferential treatment. Under the 1944 Education Act, framed to promote equality of opportunity, children competed by examination for grammar school places. Girls outperformed boys in the '11 plus' examination, yet there were never as many grammar school places for girls as for boys. This was justified on the grounds that girls matured earlier and boys overtook them in the later stages of secondary school.

The case for equality in education was bound to struggle for credibility in a period still dominated by the male-breadwinner ethos. Even in the 1920s, when marriage rates were low and the surplus number of women in the population at record levels, educationists urged that girls' education should be less academic than boys', in view of their destiny as housewives. Ironically in the circumstances, women were by that stage a large majority in the teaching profession (206,000 to 89,000 men in 1931).[45] But the treatment of women teachers by the state and by the local authorities which employed them underlined their inferior status as workers. Most were subject to the marriage bar, and those forced to resign on marriage mostly lost pension rights along with the job. The Board of Education provided four-year grants to finance the cost of university education, for those who took the 'pledge' to teach for (usually) five years: that meant postponing marriage, and posts in schools were hard to find in the depressed 1930s. Failure to redeem the pledge meant that the grant had to be repaid. Meanwhile the self-supporting single women of the National Union of Women Teachers fought a long drawn-out battle for equal pay, finally achieved only in 1961. For a well-to-do family, incentives to invest in a daughter's education remained low well into the second half of the century. Some believed that a university degree might actually damage a girl's chances of marrying well. Except for the few who became headmistresses, or made careers in medicine, the civil service, law or academic life, it rarely paved the way to a well-paid job.

Demographic trends after World War II seemed if anything to strengthen the case for differentiation in the school curriculum. Against a background of rising marriage rates, a book on *The Education of Girls* by the progressive young chief education officer for Hertfordshire, John Newsom, argued that the aim should now be 'to teach girls how to grow into women and to re-learn the graces which so many have forgotten in the past thirty years'.

> [The] vital influence of women as women [is to] civilize men and thus preserve civilization [...] This mission of women is a far greater one than can ever be fulfilled by attaining the minor political or professional successes, which in the past generation they have imitatively adopted from men as a criterion of social usefulness.

Newsom claimed that in his experience 'almost all intelligent women agree [...] and that those who do not, however able and intelligent they may be, are normally deficient in the quality of womanliness'.[46] An account in the *Oxford Dictionary of National Biography* of Newsom's influential career as an educationist – he was knighted in 1964 – describes these views as 'unfashionable'. But in the 1950s the claim that university was not the best preparation for married life was heard even from some women graduates. Predictably, there were also those who maintained that a degree was wasted on women who married. The need to adjust to demographic change and the realities of a gendered labour market is a central theme in the Crowther Report (1959) on the schooling of 15–18 year olds. Girls were marrying younger – and at a younger age than boys: they needed a curriculum that prepared them for married life. Those who stayed on at school after 15 with a view to gaining qualifications were more likely than boys to be preparing for non-graduate jobs. Recruitment to teacher training colleges increased rapidly in response to the postwar baby boom; and – like training for nursing and secretarial work – it did not require the same 'A Level' qualifications as universities.

The educational scene for women was transformed in the later twentieth century. That was an era of sweeping change in the sector, driven by the need to push up standards but also by increased demand for higher education and access to university for students from all social classes. A shift towards comprehensive education in state secondary schools, with a higher school-leaving age and, from the 1980s, pressure for better performance in public examinations; the coming of mass higher education and absorption of teacher and nursing education within universities – these new developments coincided with a remarkable improvement in the educational achievement of girls. By 2000, girls were achieving more 'A' grades than boys at both GCSE and A Level. In universities women overtook the number of men students from 1996. By the early twenty-first century they outnumbered men even in medical schools. Carol Dyhouse, in her book *Students: A Gendered History*, has analysed the dynamics of this transformation. It was foreshadowed in the 1960s when the Robbins Report (1963) argued for more university places for girls, and new 'plate-glass' universities such as Sussex began to offer attractive interdisciplinary arts courses. But a series of crucial changes came in the 1970s. The 1975 Sex Discrimination Act forbade the use of quotas and encouraged the opening of Oxbridge colleges to women. The sharp fall in the birth rate meant that there would be fewer schoolchildren: numbers of places in teacher training institutions fell by over two-thirds between 1974 and 1982.[47] New business and professional opportunities opened up for qualified women; the age at first marriage rose; and families increasingly required two incomes to sustain a middle-class lifestyle. University education for women now became fashionable even in the upper classes. The quality of education available to girls in the independent sector improved dramatically and they were now more likely to join their brothers in elite higher education institutions. Numbers of women undergraduates from independent schools at Oxford and Cambridge increased threefold between 1970 and 1990, and there was a five-fold increase (1972–92) in numbers of women from these schools studying medicine and dentistry at English and Welsh universities.[48] As for state schools, it seems that anti-discrimination policies introduced in these years were more effective in combating disadvantage based on gender than on ethnicity or social class. A report commissioned by the Equal Opportunities Commission in the 1990s found – to the surprise of the authors – that 'Equal Opportunities policies which included gender (81 per cent primary and 93 per cent secondary) were claimed by most schools responding to our survey'. The schools inspectorate OFSTED encouraged these initiatives and there was now 'much more media coverage of equal opportunities issues'.[49] State-educated girls also benefited disproportionately from policies that had been primarily intended to drive up educational standards, such as the introduction in the 1980s in England and Wales of a National Curriculum to which all pupils must have access.

A controversial feature of these changes was the spread of coeducation. In England and Wales, where single-sex schooling had been the norm for state secondary schools, that remained the case in grammar schools, but by 1975 most local education authorities were rapidly replacing selective schools with comprehensive schools, and 87 per cent of the latter were mixed.[50] As for the public schools, the admission of girls to Headmasters' Conference Schools began only in 1968 when Marlborough opened its Sixth Form, but in the following decades the trend towards coeducation gathered pace, putting many independent girls' schools out of business.[51] Both coeducation and single-sex education had their champions: it was impossible to show conclusively which produced the best results because mixed and single-sex schools catered in practice for different ranges of pupils, in terms of both social class and academic ability.[52] But the spread of coeducation coincided with a reaction against the differentiation of the school curriculum by gender – and there was evidence that in mixed schools girls were less likely to opt for science subjects and boys less likely to study languages.[53] Still more disturbing was the evidence from both state and independent schools of harassment, bullying and abuse of girls by boys, and a tendency for boys to receive more classroom attention from teachers.[54] In Oxford and Cambridge, the transition to co-residential colleges was apparently smoother, yet disturbing features included a widening gender gap in the 1980s between the proportion of men and women getting Firsts.[55] There was also very slow progress in appointing more women to tenured and senior academic posts. Here Oxbridge was not alone. Official statistics showed that in 1999 'male professors still outnumbered female professors by ten to one'.[56] The ethos of equal opportunities can however be seen in various initiatives, official and unofficial, to counteract gender bias. By the end of the century, after the Dearing Report, they had backing from funding bodies.

By the 1990s there was concern about the under-achievement of boys in secondary schools. But that 'gender gap' was much smaller than the continuing social class gap in achievement.[57] The underlying causes for that have been much debated: how far does it reflect the inhospitable attitude of the more academic schools and universities towards working-class cultures? How far the material and cultural disadvantages of working-class children themselves? Proposals for pre-school nursery education to compensate for such disadvantages were adopted only patchily, even in the late twentieth century.[58] In earlier years, when post-elementary education depended on a scholarship ladder, scholarship girls as well as boys were at risk of losing friends and of bullying as they made their way home in school uniform. As an East Londoner from Bethnal Green put it, recalling her grammar school days in the 1930s:

> I was more or less ostracised by the other girls in the street. They made fun of us secondary school girls. They would shout out something about being stuck up or 'swank pot'.[59]

The Liverpool playwright Willy Russell gives another version of the pressures on working-class pupils, this time in a 1970s comprehensive school, in *Educating Rita*:

> 'studyin' was just for the geeks and the wimps, wasn't it? See, if I'd started takin' school seriously then I would have had to become different from my mates; an' that's not allowed [...] By y'mates, y'family, by everyone. So y' never admit that school could be anythin' other than useless an' irrelevant. An' what you've really got to be into are things like music an' clothes an' gettin' pissed an' coppin' off an' all that kind of stuff.'[60]

Rita gets a second chance as a mature student in higher education: and increasingly by the end of the century working-class girls did find encouragement to go to university, though with options often restricted by family circumstances, such as the need to live at home while studying.

Indications of a different sort that things really were improving for schoolgirls can be found in a West London ethnographic study of 1972, repeated in 1991, which asked girls to say whether they would rather be a girl or a boy.[61] Perhaps unsurprisingly, there was a marked contrast between responses from white and Asian girls: in 1972, 25 per cent of white girls but as many as 80 per cent of Asian girls would have preferred to be a boy, the latter citing 'the greater freedom afforded to boys in their religion (regardless of whether they are Sikh, Hindu or Muslim)'. But by 1991 the proportion who preferred to be girls had gone up in both cases, to 84 per cent of white and 44 per cent of Asian girls.

> For everyone, the reasons for choosing to be girls in 1991 [...] illustrated an increased range of positive attributes: as a girl you can potentially do everything a boy can, as well as be able to wear a wide variety of clothes; feel free to show your emotions; get away with more; etc.

The experience of education was not the only influence at work here but it had no doubt made a contribution.

Sex and Sexualities

Nowhere was talk of contrasts between the 'Victorian' and the 'modern' more common in the early twentieth century than in discussions about sex. In an essay on 'Modern Love', written during World War I, the Anglican feminist Maude Royden denounced:

> the horrifying superstition [...] that a woman, at least, should love without physical desire, and that a really refined and civilized woman should not only be indifferent to, but perhaps actually repelled by, the physical side of marriage.

'The young lovers of today are changing all this', she claimed.

> To the modern, 'physical' does not mean base, and to say that the love of sex is 'partly physical' is not to say that it is 'partly vile', but

rather that it is very whole and sane. We live in bodies, and find in them the temple of the spirit.[62]

Marie Stopes's bestseller *Married Love*, published the following year, echoed the message: modern women should view sex – that is, heterosexual relations within marriage – positively and expect to enjoy it.

How far modern attitudes now affected the experience of sex is hard to say. The term 'sex appeal' came into use in the 1920s. There was more freedom of association between young women and men: the chaperone belonged to the Victorian past. After the *Well of Loneliness* trial of 1928 there was also more awareness of lesbianism – although as Rebecca Jennings notes even after World War II 'same sex desire between women [...] was shaped and defined by silence'.[63] Among artists and intellectuals of the Bloomsbury set and the 'bright young things' of London Society there were uninhibited subcultures, well documented in literary sources, as in an exchange between society mothers on the subject of 'the Younger Generation' in Evelyn Waugh's *Vile Bodies* (1930):

> 'What I always wonder, Kitty dear, is what they actually *do* at these parties of theirs. I mean *do* they?'
> 'My dear, from all I hear, I think they do.'
> 'Oh, to be young again, Kitty. When I think, my dear, of all the trouble and exertion which we had to go through to be even moderately bad [...] those passages in the early morning and mama sleeping next door.'
> 'And yet, my dear, I doubt very much whether they really *appreciate* it all as much as we should [...] young people take things so much for granted. *Si la jeunesse savait.*'
> '*Si la vieillesse pouvait*, Kitty'.[64]

Jill Tweedie's memories of her Swiss finishing school in the 1950s point however to a rather different conclusion: among the girls there, sex was certainly 'a school obsession' but peer-group opinion was against 'going all the way'.

> We knew the saying 'nice girls don't' and we dismissed it as the usual adult rubbish. Who cared about niceness? Our rule was much more down to earth and effective: pretty, smart, popular girls didn't and plain, dumb girls did [...] For the observable fact was that since

a man would sleep with anyone if he got the chance, it was no testimony to a girl's attractions and, besides, once he'd done it he'd cast you off. What incentive was that for going all the way? Pregnancy, the adults' direct threat, was unreal [...] compared to the lively certainty of losing the man while being ridiculed behind your back by the girls.[65]

Historians differ as to how far sexual behaviour really did change in the first half of the century outside certain privileged circles. Did a Victorian 'culture of abstinence' actually last, as Simon Szreter has suggested, until the 1960s?[66] Fertility fell steeply between the 1870s and the 1930s; and except in wartime recorded births outside marriage – 'illegitimacy' – hovered around the very low rate of 4–5 per cent of live births until the sixties.[67] No wholly dependable method of contraception existed before the introduction of the oral contraceptive pill (1962). Until 1967 abortion was illegal – with some discretion for doctors to bend the rules for those who could pay – and resort to the backstreet abortionist was not an attractive option (although it was not until the 1960s that graphic accounts of what it entailed became available in the media).[68] Throughout these decades, despite efforts by eugenicists and some feminists to promote family planning and female-controlled barrier methods of contraception, modern methods of birth control remained controversial. In working-class marriages it was in any case the husband who normally took responsibility for contraception; and condoms had a high failure rate, as did withdrawal.[69] It might seem, then, that the demographic trends of the half-century after 1914 *must* have depended on old-fashioned abstinence from intercourse. Oral history research has, however, recently produced new evidence of the ways in which couples might combine abstinence and restraint with a variety of contraceptive practices, developing in the process intimate and pleasurable relations despite – sometimes even because of – the 'culture of silence and strict moral codes' surrounding sex in these generations.[70]

We do have evidence, though, of a thoroughly unmodern regime of fear, repression and ignorance for the unmarried young, girls especially, which changed slowly and by stages. Sexual offences against girls under the age of consent (16) were often viewed by the courts as evidence that the girl was 'in moral danger' or 'in need of care and protection': that was treated as a form of deviant behaviour for which she might be sent away to a reformatory or 'approved school'.[71] Illegitimate births might be concealed in various ways, often with help from families, but where that was not possible the stigma fell mainly on the mother. Premarital pregnancy was common in some regions and among the poorer working class – but until 1959 a girl who became pregnant and had no one to support her risked being classified as mentally deficient and institutionalised. For the rest, as late as the 1960s, falling pregnant often led to a shotgun marriage or pressure to have the baby adopted. Information about sex was hard to come by, again for girls especially – apart from the alarming material distributed to warn of the dangers of venereal disease.[72] Most mothers told their daughters little about the facts of life. Even menstruation might be treated as a taboo subject.[73] Middle as well as working-class girls grew up 'in a culture in which feminine respectability was tied to notions of sexual innocence'.[74] Sex education was not encouraged in schools until the 1940s. Yet by the 1950s and 1960s, survey evidence shows that the age at first intercourse was falling. Opinion was becoming more tolerant towards premarital sex – on the understanding that it really would lead to marriage. As Frank Sinatra's 1955 chart hit put it:

> Love and marriage, love and marriage,
> Go together like a horse and carriage.
> This I tell you brother,
> You can't have one without the other.

The baby booms of the mid-century were accompanied by a steady fall in the age at first marriage: by 1971, 37 per cent of men and 60 per cent of women aged 20–24 had married.[75]

This was the background to the reduction in the legal age of majority from 21 to 18 in 1969. In general it seems that, in the 1960s and after, parliament took its cue from trends in behaviour and mores. An Act of 1967 allowed local health authorities to make contraceptive advice available to unmarried as well as married women; in 1974 free contraception was provided on the National Health Service. As Claire Langhamer points out, the mid-century cult of romantic love that made premarital sex acceptable also hardened opinion against adultery and the loveless marriage, strengthening the case for divorce law reform.[76] In 1969 irretrievable breakdown of the marital relationship was recognised as grounds for divorce. More welfare support for lone mothers also became available after the Finer Report on One Parent families (1974). Divorce law reformers believed that enabling people to escape bad marriages would strengthen marriage as an institution: not realising how far conventional morality depended on legal and social sanctions, they were unprepared for what happened next. As we have seen, divorce rates rose exponentially in the 1970s and 1980s, marriage rates fell sharply, and childbirth outside marriage became socially acceptable. Parliament again responded to changing norms when the term 'illegitimate' was dropped from official use under the 1987 Family Law Reform Act.

It is hard to resist the conclusion that some sort of sexual revolution did take place in the late twentieth century. For women the consequences were sometimes debatable. 'What an uproar when a *woman's* magazine decides to have a *male* pin-up!', wrote the UK editor of *Cosmopolitan* in 1972, claiming that 'Cosmo girls love men and like looking at their bodies'.[77] The deregulation of pornography was however to become a concern for women of many shades of opinion, from Christian conservatives to radical feminists. The convent-educated broadcaster and journalist Libby Purves, at university in 'the experimental pill generation' in the 1970s, found that 'for a lot of my women friends, the new freewheeling attitude to sex was just another kind of slavery'.

> The phenomenon now known as 'date rape', and which lands young men in court, was then rarely complained of. It was part of almost every girl's experience to wake in the morning with a hangover and a sense of guilty regret, and to blame herself for 'sending out the wrong signals'.[78]

'Women have very little idea how much men hate them', wrote Germaine Greer, describing the guilt and disgust that could be triggered by the experience of casual sex.[79] In the era of the pill that became a more common experience: there was less to inhibit the expectation that girls and women would be sexually available.

On the other hand the contraceptive pill, backed up by access to abortion and increasingly by the practice of sterilisation, did finally give women the means to control their own fertility. The outcome was a rise in the mean age at first childbirth, and a fall in family size back to the levels of the 1930s. The right of choice in sexual relationships was recognised more fully by the end of the century than ever before. It was wives who initiated a majority of the rising numbers of divorce petitions – nearly three-quarters (73 per cent) of them by 1981–5.[80] Rape within marriage was finally recognised as a crime in 1991 (1989 in Scotland). Cultures associated with sexuality did of course

4. The Gateways Club in Chelsea, early 1950s. The club featured in the 1968 movie 'The Killing of Sister George'. Historian Alkarim Jivani was told that mid-century lesbians chose a role, butch or femme. "If you were butch it mean that you dressed in boyish clothes and the femmes were dressed in nice skirts and blouses and hair all very highly lacquered.... It was aping heterosexual relationships... and it wasn't till years later, when people actually came to terms with being gay that they were themselves".[iv]

continue to vary across ethnic communities and social classes; but for the great majority of women this was a period of expanding freedom. A survey financed by the Wellcome Trust found that the median age at first intercourse for girls born between 1965 and 1975 was 17: for those born in the early 1930s it had been 21. By the 1990s it was 'clear that the necessity of marriage as a precondition for sex is becoming very much a thing of the past', although expectations of fidelity within marriage remained strong.[81] As for same-sex relationships, conservative attitudes were slower to recede. A statutory ban on 'promoting homosexuality' as a 'pretended family relationship' in schools was in force between 1988 and 2003. Although no one was ever prosecuted under this legislation, its repeal was strongly resisted in the House of Lords. Yet in the decades since the 1960s, when the Gateways Club in Chelsea was London's only lesbian club, lesbian relationships had become much more visible and socially accepted.[82] The 'right to self-defined sexuality', as claimed by the Women's Liberation Movement from 1974, was no longer a radical demand. Legal recognition eventually came with the Civil Partnerships Act of 2004.

By the end of the century it was teenage pregnancy that chiefly attracted public concern – and a degree of stigma. The rate was much the same as in the 1960s, but most teenage mothers had then been married: now they were mostly unmarried and dependent on state welfare.[83] The decline in pressures to marry was another aspect of the new regime that could be experienced in more than one way. 'Delighted by reports that by the turn of the millennium a third of all households will be single', wrote Helen Fielding's Bridget Jones in her diary. 'At last we are no longer tragic freaks.' On reflection, though, she and her friends were not altogether happy about the way things were going – haunted by 'stereotypical notions of shelves, spinning wheels and sexual scrapheaps' and exasperated by the 'Emotional Fuckwit-age' prevalent among men in the 1990s.[84] From the metropolitan world of Bridget Jones to the council estates of Essex or South Wales, incentives for men to commit to long-term relationships had evidently become much weaker.

Feminisms and Femininity

The history of British feminism is controversial and not easy to get into focus. On the one hand we need to see it in a context of British politics; on the other, to recognise feminism as a transnational phenomenon. The texts in Chapter 5 were chosen mainly to represent feminist ideas. The impact of feminist or women's movements is dealt with mainly in the chronological chapters that follow. The aim is to do justice to both transnational dimensions and the ways in which feminism has manifested itself in Britain.

The familiar cyclical 'three wave' model of the history of modern feminism originated in the United States but has recently been criticised by historians on both sides of the Atlantic.[85] It makes most sense in relation to movements of the later twentieth century. The self-styled Second Wave feminists of the late 1960s and 1970s, and the young women who proclaimed a Third Wave in the 1990s, were conscious of developing contemporary feminist agendas and of a generation gap, particularly on attitudes towards sexuality and femininity, between older and younger women. Both represented an upsurge in activism, and both were shaped by their socio-political contexts. The Women's Liberation Movement (WLM) of the 1970s grew out of the neo-Marxist New Left and the civil rights and colonial and sexual liberation movements of the sixties. The so-called Third Wave, beginning in the 1990s, reflected the post-Marxist individualism of its time and mobilised support increasingly by social networking and use of the internet. But the 'wave' metaphor does have disadvantages. There were continuities as well as differences between generations of feminists, and incremental developments as well as peaks of agitation. As a recent oral history study of the WLM has shown, much of that movement's 'intellectual work' was 'about rediscovery and rethinking'.[86] Karen Offen notes that writing the history of feminism was one of the real achievements of the WLM.[87] Above all, the term 'First Wave' feminism, applied retrospectively, is anachronistic and unhelpful in understanding the extremely diverse strands of feminist thought that pre-dated the 1960s.[88] The extracts in Chapter 5 include theoretical contributions that anticipate some characteristic themes of the 'Second Wave' era, such as Eleanor Rathbone's critique of the male breadwinner family and Virginia Woolf's analysis of modern patriarchy.

The term feminism entered the English language only at the turn of the last century. Its meaning has always been unstable and contested, and the word itself goes in and out of fashion. By no means all supporters of women's movements have identified with it. Even Edwardian suffragists felt that they were fighting for 'the common cause of humanity'.[89] And as Caitriona Beaumont points out, women's influence between the wars was promoted not only by organisations with their roots in the suffrage struggle but also by mass-membership 'mainstream' organisations that were explicitly not feminist. Some were committed to a religious agenda, like the Anglican church's Mothers' Union or the Catholic Women's League. Others – the Women's Institutes (WI) and Townswomen's Guilds – aimed simply to be inclusive and apolitical.[90] But the WI took over 'the Women Voters' Hymn', as the suffrage leader Millicent Fawcett described Hubert Parry's setting of William Blake's 'Jerusalem'.[91] Maggie Andrews argues persuasively that the WI always 'provided a significant space for feminist activity'.[92] Both organisations and individuals with values sympathetic to feminism – Virginia Woolf in *Three Guineas*, for example – may have their reasons for rejecting the label 'feminist'. Again, women who choose to have nothing to do with women's movements may give reasons that are not necessarily to be taken at face value. The sociologist Viola Klein suggested one interpretation of their position in a pioneering deconstruction of the ideology of femininity, first published in 1946. 'In a society whose standards are predominantly masculine, women form an "out-group"', she wrote, in a passage clearly influenced by her own experience as a Jewish refugee from Central Europe and an immigrant in England. Like other marginal groups – 'foreigners, Jews, Negroes, etc.' – women are subject to stereotyping: 'preconceived opinions are applied more or less summarily to the class as a whole'. Stereotypes of this kind are resented, and yet the individual member of a marginal group tends unconsciously to adopt the perspectives of the dominant majority.

> He is highly critical of the deficiencies of his own group, an attitude which very often involves self-contempt and self-hatred. Jewish self-hatred is almost proverbial [...] The general contempt of women shown by women – and particularly by the more cultivated ones – is commonly known. The fact that so many women intensely dislike women's organizations or clubs [...] cannot be accounted for solely on the ground that women 'instinctively' prefer the company of the other sex. It is much more due to the fact that the accumulation of so many of their despised kind is almost unbearable to them. It is as if they would see their own grimace reflected from a multiple distorting mirror.[93]

For those who did identify as feminists, the years after 1914 raised fundamental questions about the place of women in politics. Was their duty in wartime to show patriotic solidarity, or to form international alliances against militarism? The feminist internationalists of World War I, although in a small minority, began a tradition of activism that gained recognition for gender equality in the League of Nations and United Nations, and also in the Treaty of Rome (1956) – with ultimately important results for equality legislation in Britain, as a member from 1973 of the European Community. After World War I, the enfranchisement of British women brought questions about the terms on which they would join the political community. Was the goal integration into existing political institutions or a more effective women's voice in politics? Mere equality before the law or better provision for women's distinctive needs, above all their needs as mothers? These were issues that would rumble on over the years.

This is not to deny that there were genuinely new features in Second Wave feminism. The British WLM revived the separatist and militant tradition of the Edwardian suffragettes and, in the Greenham Common women's

5. British delegates at the Women's League for Peace and Freedom Conference, Zurich, 1919. The women's movement lobbied vigorously after the First World War for peace, disarmament and inclusion in the League of Nations remit of such issues as the prevention of trafficking in women and children. Dame Rachel Crowdy, an Englishwoman known for her war work superintending VADs on the continent, became in that year chief of the social questions section of the League of Nations.[v] Courtesy of LSE Library.

peace camp of 1981–2000, a feminist pacifist tradition that dated back to World War I. But it also borrowed freely from contemporary American feminism, as Juliet Mitchell explained in her early insider's account of the movement.[94] Among these borrowings were key concepts – 'the personal is political', 'consciousness-raising', 'male chauvinism', 'sexism' (the latter term popularised by Kate Millett's book *Sexual Politics*, first published in New York in 1970) – and also the movement's distinctive principles of organisation.

> Opposing any form of domination in theory [...] all Women's Liberation politics act on the basis of developing collective work and preventing the rise of ego-tripping leaders.

Collectives ran Women's Liberation activities, rotating responsibilities within the group. 'The basic unit of organization' was 'the small group of anything from six to two dozen women'. These small, women-only groups became the arena for consciousness-raising, described by Mitchell as:

the process of transforming the hidden, individual fears of women into a shared awareness of the meaning of them as social problems, the release of anger, anxiety, the struggle of proclaiming the painful and transforming it into the political [...] [It] is the reinterpretation of a Chinese revolutionary practice of 'speaking bitterness' – a reinterpretation made by middle-class women in place of Chinese peasants [...] These peasants, subdued by violent coercion and abject poverty, took a step out of thinking their fate was natural by articulating it [...]; it is this acceptance of a situation as 'natural', or a misery as 'personal' that has first to be overcome.[95]

New perspectives on the position of women in a male-dominated culture emerged from these practices, and they were informed by the intellectual repertoire of the mid-twentieth century: Freudian psychoanalysis, French existentialism (notably Simone de Beauvoir and the post-colonial theorist Frantz Fanon), and the neo-Marxist Frankfurt School's analysis of the modern 'culture industry'.

The WLM's rejection of leadership and traditional methods of organisation made it hard for contemporaries to evaluate and has led some historians to underrate its influence.[96] Politically it was always a divided movement. For Marxist and socialist feminists, women's liberation was above all part of the struggle against capitalism. As in America, an alternative radical strand of feminism focused on the struggle against patriarchy and on issues of sexuality. Some issues of the 1970s were far from new, particularly violence against women, which produced some of the most characteristic forms of WLM activism, such as refuges for victims of domestic violence ('battered wives'), Reclaim the Night marches and the campaign group Woman Against Rape. The five-year reign of terror of the serial murderer known as the Yorkshire Ripper heightened tensions, recalling the atmosphere that gave rise to late-Victorian purity movements.[97] 'The Ripper killings are only at the extreme end of the violence women face every day', claimed the feminist magazine *Spare Rib*, introducing an article on 'how Leeds sisters are fighting for the right to live without fear'.[98] A 'revolutionary feminist' group in Leeds now took radicalism a stage further, urging feminists to embrace 'political lesbianism' and reject heterosexual relationships. After 1978, internal divisions put an end to the national WLM conferences which had been held each year since 1970. But there followed more than a decade of initiatives that kept the ethos of the movement alive. They included single-issue campaigns – against violence and rape, in defence of access to abortion, the

Greenham peace protest against nuclear weapons – and activism within local government, where 'municipal feminism' took root as members of WLM groups promoted refuges, rape crisis centres, nurseries and feminist cultural projects.[99] Feminist bookshops, magazines and publishers continued to flourish: *Spare Rib*, which ran from 1972 to 1993, had a peak circulation of around 100,000; Carmel Callil's Virago was only the best known of the 21 feminist publishing houses in existence by the early 1990s.[100] Academic feminism became an established feature of the university scene. A third of the WLM activists interviewed for the 'Sisterhood and After' oral history project went on to academic careers.[101] Women's Studies courses, which British universities introduced first in extra-mural adult education, were adopted as graduate and undergraduate degree programmes.[102] More importantly, theoretical approaches rooted in the politics of the WLM – the perception, for example, that (in the words of the film theorist Laura Mulvey) 'images of women are a political issue and site of struggle', and that psychoanalysis, structuralism and semiotics can help us understand them – came to influence the work of scholars across a range of disciplines.[103]

Taking stock in the mid-1980s, the psychologist Lynne Segal concluded that, above all, 'at least at the ideological level, many men's attitudes have changed'.

> Feminist issues are no longer ridiculed and rejected out of hand as they were in the early seventies. The issues of sexual harassment, childcare, abortion and women's equality generally are on the agenda of most trade unions [and] many local councils [...] Feminist goals have become 'respectable'. They are genuinely supported by at least some men of goodwill, whatever the hostility they arouse from others. Pornography, violence against women and overt sexist behaviour are now taboo for some of the young generation of men who have been influenced by feminism.[104]

It was true that feminists remained divided. Segal lamented the decline of socialist feminism and the growth in the 1980s of essentialist perspectives on gender difference. Concern with gender cultures had apparently displaced the struggle for equality:

> The dominant popular conception of feminism today is one which stresses basic differences between women and men, and asserts the moral and spiritual superiority of female experience, values,

characteristics and culture: women's oppression on this view results from the suppression of this woman-centred vision or separate female 'world' [...] The real problem with the popular 'new feminism' which sees women as essentially virtuous and men as essentially vicious is that it serves the forces of reaction as surely as it serves the forces of progress.[105]

And yet, as Barbara Caine noted a decade later, criticism of white feminists from black women intellectuals in the 1980s had the effect of promoting a less dogmatic approach to differences within the movement.[106] The anti-racist sympathies of most WLM activists encouraged respect for both cultural difference and the insistence of black women on political autonomy; and that, in its turn, made for a more pluralistic ethos. There are, after all, many cultural and intellectual traditions within feminism, and also a number of genuinely difficult issues on which opinions are bound to differ. What *should* feminists think about pornography – a matter of taste, or a form of violence against women? Or about the commodification of femininity in the fashion and beauty industries, which give so many women pleasure? Or the sex industry in which so many women work? The English Collective of Prostitutes has since 1975 made a case for decriminalisation that remains highly controversial.[107] Increasingly, then, it seems appropriate – for historians as well as activists – to think of feminisms in the plural, manifesting themselves in a variety of different ways.

The Great War, 1914–18

More than 6 million men served in the British forces in World War I, of whom over 720,000 are recorded as military casualties and 1.68 million were wounded.[108] Separation, bereavement, care of the disabled – these were experiences of war shared by countless women, women of the 'officer classes' above all, since officers had the highest casualty rates.[109] Uniformed auxiliary branches of the armed services, the Women's Army Auxiliary Corps (WAAC), Women's Royal Naval Service (WRNS) and Women's Royal Air Force (WRAF), created for the first time in 1917–18, employed over 80,000 women in non-combatant roles (mostly clerical, communications, domestic or catering work). About 20,000 became agricultural workers with the Women's Land Army. Others served, mostly as military nurses, with uniformed voluntary organisations set up before the war, such as the First Aid Nursing Yeomanry (FANY) and Voluntary Aid Detachments (VADs). One journalist, reporting on British women serving in uniform in France,

6. Munitions workers in 1917 at the National Shell Filling Factory, Chilwell, Nottinghamshire. This was one of the largest shell factories in the country. The government publicised images of women's industrial war work to encourage employers to take on women workers. © Imperial War Museum (Q 30018), used with permission.

found that there were rigid class distinctions between these unpaid volunteers, who ranked as officers, and the women's auxiliary services: 'At tea with the Fannies I asked them whether they were WAACS – when I knew more I saw it was as though I had asked a Brass Hat whether he belonged to the Salvation Army'.[110] But this was overwhelmingly a men's war. The roles that women played in it, insofar as labour shortages required them to cross gender boundaries, were controversial at the time, and historians debate whether they had any long-term consequences for the position of women in Britain.

A decade of suffrage agitation had preceded the outbreak of war. It was echoed in the 'Women's Right to Serve' demonstration staged in London in July 1915 by the leader of the militant Women's Social and Political Union (WSPU), Emmeline Pankhurst, this time with government backing, to break down resistance to the employment of women as munitions workers. A 'woman processionist' noted:

> There was one thing that troubled us on our long march through the rain and the mud: it was the number of young men of service age in mufti who came out shamelessly to look at us. Only one of them passed a contemptuous remark, reminiscent of former marches. Quickly a young girl carrying a pennon turned on him. 'We're going to do our bit,' she cried, 'are you going to do yours?' [...] It was a strange sight to see Mr. Lloyd George fearlessly fraternizing with Mrs. Pankhurst; it was as if Daniel had invited the lion to his den.[III]

Nicoletta Gullace has argued that the new configuration of opinion in wartime, in which male 'pacifists, "shirkers" and conscientious objectors' became targets of press and public hostility, meant that the cultural construction of citizenship changed, weakening resistance to the enfranchisement of women: 'patriotism replaced manhood as the fundamental qualification for the parliamentary vote'.[112]

Much that was required of women in wartime tended however to reinforce conventional gender roles: managing what became known as the 'home front', knitting or sewing for the troops, and for upper- and middle-class women fund-raising and voluntary social work – relief work with refugees, running canteens or nurseries, monitoring the behaviour of working-class girls and women in factories or on the streets. Before conscription was introduced in March 1916, urging young men to enlist or shaming those who did not, as in the white feather campaign, also counted as a contribution to the war effort. But women as well as men differed widely in their perspectives on the war, as texts in Chapter 6 show: from Mary Henderson's eulogy to the Scottish Women's Hospitals, to the horror and shame in Edith Sitwell's poem 'The Dancers' (1916); and from the patriotic enthusiasm recorded in Vera Brittain's diary in the first months of war to the pacifist disillusionment of her memoir, *Testament of Youth* (1935).

As for the suffrage societies, the war divided them. The National Union of Women's Suffrage Societies (NUWSS) created a Women's Emergency Corps to organise war work. Pacifists and supporters of a negotiated peace broke ranks to found the Women's International League for Peace and Freedom (as it became in 1919). In 1917–18 the Women's Peace Crusade mobilised support among working-class women. But many suffragists saw active service, some in medical units funded by private donations, others as officers in the women's auxiliary forces. Lettice Fisher, founder of the National Council for the Unmarried Mother and Her Child, was among those who worked

to shape welfare policy. Christabel Pankhurst and her mother aligned themselves with popular patriotism, rebranding the WSPU as The Women's Party
in preparation for the first general election in which women would have
the vote. But the view that it was straightforwardly women's war work that
earned them the vote, though much aired at the time, has nowadays few
defenders. After the pre-war suffrage campaign it would have been hard to
resist making concessions to women once Britain adopted universal manhood suffrage – and the war made that necessary to reward men who had
fought for their country.[113] In order to avoid creating an electorate in which
men were in a minority, the 1918 Representation of the People Act enfranchised only women over 30 who were householders, or wives of householders,
or university graduates. This meant that the vote was given to most mothers
of soldiers and some war widows, but not in fact to young single women who
had worked in munitions factories or served in the forces. 'Flappers' had to
wait for the vote for another ten years.

How far did the experience of war create other opportunities? Women
in Glasgow famously went on strike against inflationary rent increases.
The Times reported:

> Almost 800 women and children of the respectable working-class
> type held a demonstration in the streets yesterday carrying banners
> with the words, 'Our husbands, sons and brothers are fighting the
> Prussians of Germany. We are fighting the Prussians of Partick'. A
> deputation waited on the Town Council and [...] protested against
> the threatened eviction of tenants, including the wives of soldiers at
> the front.[114]

The outcome was the 1915 Rent Restriction Act which fixed rents at pre-war
levels. The claim that war conditions brought greater sexual freedom was
apparently borne out by increased illegitimacy rates – yet these were affected,
in communities with high peacetime rates of premarital pregnancy, by conscription and the direction of male labour. But for the war, the mothers
of many 'war babies' would have not have remained unmarried. The war
economy put money in some women's pockets, though sometimes at a high
price: TNT poisoning in the munitions industry, surveillance for wives of
soldiers in receipt of the 'separation allowance' (which was part of the husband's wage and could be withdrawn if the wife was unfaithful). Robert
Roberts maintained that in Salford the status of women rose while the men

were away at war, as women took over men's jobs in industry (see p. 106–7). But in heavy industry, women's war work was above all temporary. 'Dilution' agreements of 1915 ensured, with support from women trade unionists, that returning soldiers would be able to reclaim their jobs. A Restoration of Pre-War Practices Act duly became law in 1919. The 1921 census shows fewer women employed in manufacturing industry than in 1911. Only in clerical and shop work was there a permanent increase in jobs for women. When female munitions workers were laid off, they were not even eligible for unemployment pay if they refused jobs in domestic service. It is easier to document wartime anxieties about gender norms – hostility to the spectacle of women in khaki, groundless moral panics about women's drinking or promiscuity among servicewomen – than it is to find evidence of lasting shifts in gender regimes caused by World War I.

Franchise and After, 1918–39: the Modern Woman?

The writer and *Woman's Own* agony aunt Leonora Eyles claimed that the reign of George V (1910–36) had 'seen more striking changes in the status of women, both in their relation to the state and as individuals, than any other period in history'. Women were now emancipated and conscious of bearing the responsibilities of citizenship. 'It is in women's changed social outlook that the chief pioneering work has been done.'[115] These changes had their critics; and in the workforce especially women remained second-class citizens. But historians tend now to follow Pat Thane in dwelling on the positive features of the interwar years for women.[116] Opportunities for associational life expanded and so did women's presence in the public sphere, as magistrates and members of voluntary organisations as well as in political life. The housewife's lot improved as families got smaller and wages (for those in work, at least) rose.[117] Emancipation took other forms, too: more physical exercise and broader horizons – dancing and sport, keep-fit, bicycling and hiking; movies, radio, women's magazines and the lifestyles they encouraged. The social scientist Barbara Wootton, a young professional woman in the 1920s, recalled the thrill of buying her first car:

> It was an open, air-cooled, two-cylinder Rover, more like a wild animal than a piece of mechanism [...] What it cost I forget but I know that I paid for it by selling the superannuation policy which I had acquired from my two years on the staff at Girton, and borrowing the balance from the bank'.[118]

7. The women's hockey team at the co-educational London School of Economics, 1920–1. University women – and not only at the women's colleges – led the way in popularising women's sport.[vi] Courtesy of LSE Library.

Even in the depressed 1930s, Muriel Spark found her wages as an office worker in an exclusive Edinburgh women's department store:

> enough to live on fairly well. My mother was greatly impressed. I used to treat her to lipsticks and scent (Coty's *L'Aimant*), besides contributing to the household expenses[…] Employees were allowed a discount on any purchases they made. I made as many as I could afford, for I always cared for charming clothes.[119]

In the 1920s and 1930s reports in the popular press of women's activities or achievements and advertisements for new domestic technologies made much of the image of the 'modern woman'. Often she embodied the 'conservative modernity' explored by Alison Light through middle-class women's writing of the period.[120] There was keen interest, as Adrian Bingham notes, in 'women's firsts' of all descriptions, whether as sportswomen, aviators or barristers.[121] A novel very much of its time was Enid Bagnold's *National Velvet* (1935), in which a teenager, the daughter of a woman channel swimmer,

8. Nancy Astor campaigning in the Plymouth by-election of November 1919. The American-born wife of newspaper proprietor Waldorf Astor, she became the first woman to sit in the House of Commons. She was adopted as Conservative candidate when her husband succeeded to his father's peerage, and held the seat until 1945. Courtesy of LSE Library.

wins the Grand National dressed as a boy: filmed in 1944, starring the young Elizabeth Taylor, it became a box-office hit. But the housewife too was a focus of press attention. Since 1908 the *Daily Mail* had sponsored the Ideal Home Exhibition at the Earl's Court Olympia Centre in London. Now the middle-class woman was urged to embrace the new labour-saving devices as the solution to the 'servant problem' – the 'Olympia Electric Home' was the 'real Ideal Home wherein Electricity makes the Household work as easy and more interesting than play and where cleanliness and health reign supreme'.[122] Despite Lord Rothermere's opposition to the 'flapper vote', newspapers encouraged women who had the vote to use it, and canvassed their support for press campaigns – the *Daily Mail*'s Anti-Waste League in the early 1920s, the Empire Free Trade campaign a decade later.[123] The 'modern woman' was identified as a reader, a consumer and a citizen, to be treated with respect.

Women were also taken more seriously by the political parties now that they were voters. Legislation of the 1920s included long-awaited reforms, among them equal access for wives to divorce and equal guardianship rights over children; pensions for widows and orphans; and ambitious housing programmes introduced in turn by the postwar Lloyd George Coalition and by Labour and Conservative governments. All parties appealed directly for women's votes in general election manifestos of the twenties. A commitment to peace and disarmament was part of that appeal: the League of Nations had broad-based support within the women's movement. Stanley Baldwin looked for support from the 'Chancellor of the Exchequer of the Home', but Labour and Liberals also courted her in the 1920s, pledging to resist tariffs and keep food prices down.[124] All parties claimed in principle to support equal rights for men and women. Labour made capital from the fact that the party had supported equal suffrage since 1912: Labour 'was advocating the cause of Equal Citizenship when the Tory and Liberal parties were either utterly hostile or hopelessly divided on the question'.[125] Women for their part joined political parties in droves. By the late 1920s, when party membership peaked, about a million belonged to the Conservative party, about 300,000 to constituency Labour parties (in both cases outnumbering male members) and 100,000 to the Liberal party. They made up around 25 per cent of the British Union of Fascists' estimated membership of 50,000 in 1934, and the same proportion of the membership of the Communist Party of Great Britain when it peaked at about 56,000 in 1945.[126]

How much influence did women's participation have on interwar politics? The Conservatives won three out of six elections in those years with decisive majorities – in 1924, 1931 and 1935. They were helped by the collapse of the Liberal vote but almost certainly also (as in the years after 1950, for which we have opinion poll data) by the women's vote. Labour did not have a good relationship with the women's movement. Labour women were urged to steer clear of non-party women's organisations; yet it proved difficult, as Dora Russell found in the campaign for birth control, to get women's issues on to the party agenda. In local government there were areas – such as London and Manchester – where women were relatively well represented on councils and had more input into Labour programmes, but in national politics the dominant influence was the trade unions, in which men outnumbered women by five to one. Baldwin, on the other hand, pushed the 'flapper vote' through, unveiled a statue of Emmeline Pankhurst at Westminster and made Millicent Fawcett and Christabel Pankhurst Dames. His wife, Lucy, was highly successful in adapting Baldwinian rhetoric to a female audience. Ross McKibbin notes that Conservative values had in any case more to offer working-class women than those of a party shaped by male workplace culture.[127] In the 1930s the Conservatives even elected more women MPs, though Labour fielded more women candidates. Yet as rising unemployment

1

pushed up spending on National Insurance benefits, both parties made cuts that fell disproportionately on married working women. A regulation under the 1931 Anomalies Act, introduced by Margaret Bondfield as Minister of Labour in Ramsay MacDonald's second Labour government:

> laid it down that a married woman who had not after marriage secured a certain number of stamps should not draw benefit unless she proved that she was normally employed in insurable employment, would normally seek to obtain her livelihood by means of insurable employment and could reasonably expect to obtain insurable employment. Women, therefore, who had paid contributions for years, and who had never drawn anything owing to the fact that they had never been out of work, were no longer entitled to benefit if they lost their work on marriage and had no prospect of obtaining work elsewhere.[128]

The following year the Conservative-dominated National Government reduced married women's entitlements to health insurance benefits to a lower rate than those of a single woman. There was cross-party criticism from women MPs, but they were in a tiny minority in interwar parliaments: no more than 15 women were elected at any general election. When the House of Commons was persuaded in 1936 to vote for equal pay in the civil service, Baldwin had no difficulty in getting the decision reversed on a vote of confidence. So much for Conservative claims to be (in Mrs Baldwin's phrase) '*the* "women's Party"'.

By the late 1930s a reconfigured women's movement had emerged. The National Union of Societies for Equal Citizenship (NUSEC), successor to the NUWSS, had remained the dominant organisation in the 1920s, and proved highly effective in lobbying for legislative reforms.[129] Once universal suffrage was achieved, a range of smaller feminist societies with roots in the suffrage movement continued, alongside a varied array of women's organisations – from the Women's Institutes and Townswomen's Guilds, to professional, trade union, religious and social or social-service based organisations, and single-issue campaign groups like the National Spinsters' Pensions Association, formed in 1935 to campaign for pensions for unmarried working women at 55. There was potential here, and far more so than in the past, for articulating women's concerns and mobilising them for public service. And yet the women's movement was at this stage too fragmented to exercise much influence on public policy. As war became increasingly likely and support for the peace movement waned, pacifist influences became a further obstacle to collective action: they affected not only the left-wing Women's Co-operative Guild but also the WI, with its non-political ethos and concern not to offend Quaker members. Opponents of appeasement included women of all political persuasions – Katharine, Duchess of Atholl; Violet Bonham Carter; Ellen Wilkinson; Eleanor Rathbone – yet it is likely that Neville Chamberlain gained support disproportionally from women during the Munich crisis of September 1938. The 1937 Air Raid Precautions Act had brought home the prospect of bombardment of civilian popula-tions; the distribution of gas masks for infants left no doubt about what that might mean.[130] Julie Gottlieb has stressed the influence on Chamberlain of the thousands of letters and telegrams sent to him and his wife before the Munich Conference by women urging a peaceful settlement.[131] Prepara-tions for war in 1938–9 brought the creation of a new uniformed Women's Voluntary Service for Civil Defence (WVS) run by Stella, Marchioness of Reading, as well as the revival of women's auxiliary services: the Auxiliary Territorial Service (ATS) as the WAAC was renamed, WRNS and the Women's Auxiliary Air Force (WAAF). Apart from Lady Denman, Pres-ident of the Women' s Institutes, who headed the Women's Land Army, it was women of the upper classes rather than the women's movement who provided leadership for these services.

War and Reconstruction, 1939–51

Promoted as a 'People's War' in defence of democracy, requiring equal sacrifice from all, World War II really did bring massive disruption of domestic life and involvement on a new scale for women in the war effort. Compulsory air raid precautions affected every household. The evacuation of children, and sometimes mothers, from cities to the countryside, where they were billeted in other women's homes, was largely managed by the WVS with help from the Women's Institutes and monitored by a Women's Group on Public Wel-fare. 'This war has presented women immediately – and much earlier than in the 1914–18 struggle – with acute, far-reaching problems', claimed a report commissioned by Mass Observation, a social research organisation started in 1937 to document the lives of ordinary people.

> Now it is not only their men who 'go' or who are liable to 'go'. Too often their children have already gone, or other people's children have been admitted under difficult circumstances into their homes. Evac-uation and Reception have set up dislocations in family life which

9. Jam making at the Women's Institute in the mid-Wales village of Meifod, 1941 – a contribution to the war-time food supply. Provided with sugar by the Ministry of Agriculture, the WI produced canned fruit and jam for hospital and canteens.

> are psychic as well as physical [...] [The] woman in the street [...] accepts the war as an inevitable event [...] This is the type of woman, unattached to any organisation, at the mercy of rising prices and the hazards of employment – there has been a severe increase of unemployment amongst wage-earning and salaried women since August – who is bearing the brunt of this home-front war, and this is largely the fatalistic spirit in which she bears it. In addition our investigations have shown that the blackout causes her special uneasiness [...] lending an almost night-mare atmosphere to the prospect of future winters of war.

This report, completed in February 1940, dwells also on the multiplication and growth of women's organisations, noting 'how important a factor for the formation of public opinion and the creation of civilian morale they have become'.[132]

The home front came under growing pressure – food was rationed from early 1940, clothing from 1941, shortages got worse and were to continue after 1945 into peacetime. The sheer scale of aerial bombardment and manpower shortages were also new features of this war. In its early years there was more loss of life among civilians than in the armed forces, mostly in the London Blitz that began in September 1940. By 1945, British military casualties amounted to about 264,000, but enemy action had also killed over 60,000 civilians, more than half of them women or children under 16.[133] For the first time servicewomen were deployed in the front line of defence, on anti-aircraft gun-sites. Manpower shortages led to direction of civilian labour: by mid-1943 about 2 million women were employed in munitions factories, often living and working away from home. In December 1941 women were for the first time conscripted – initially single women of 20–30, who could choose between the women's auxiliary services and working in war industry, civil defence or the Land Army. Age limits were later widened and exemptions for wives and mothers pared down. Even those recognised as not 'mobile' because of family responsibilities were expected to do some form of war work. Part-time employment for married women, the familiar pattern of the later twentieth century, was first seen on a large scale – despite some resistance from employers – in the later years of the war.

How far this war had lasting effects on gender roles is, however, hard to say. Both contemporary Mass Observation reports and later oral history projects bring out the sheer variety of women's wartime experiences – and as Penny Summerfield points out, much depended on the subjective reactions of individuals. Disruption of home life or uncongenial war work was accepted stoically by some women – they 'just got on with it'. Others gained self esteem from the sense that they were 'doing their bit' in the services or munitions factories.[134] So did the Barrow-in Furness housewife Nella Last, the best known of Mass Observation's wartime diarists (portrayed by Victoria Wood in her 2006 ITV play *Housewife, 49*). WVS canteen work and her skills as a cook and needlewoman gave Mrs Last confidence to rebel against her husband's domestic tyranny.

> I suddenly thought tonight, 'I know why a lot of women have gone into pants – it's a sign that they are asserting themselves in some way.' I feel pants are more of a sign of the times than I realised. A growing contempt for men in general creeps over me. For a craftsman, whether a sweep or Prime Minister – 'hats off'. But why this 'Lords of Creation' attitude on men's part? I'm beginning to see I'm a really clever woman in my own line [...] I feel that in the world of tomorrow, marriage will be – will have to be – more of a partnership, less of this 'I have spoken' attitude.[135]

A survey published in 1944 found mixed views among factory workers about prospects for women after demobilisation:

> The question 'Do you think women doing men's jobs should be allowed to go on doing them, or not?' was put to a random sample, with the following results:

Opinion	Men (per cent)	Women (per cent)
Women should be allowed to go on doing men's jobs	30	25
Women should not be allowed to go on doing men's jobs	48	43
Depends on postwar conditions	19	28
No opinion	3	4

> It will be seen that [...] there is not much difference between the attitudes of the sexes. [...] On the question of equal pay there was an overwhelming majority of both sexes believing that a woman doing a man's work should get a man's pay. [...] To sum up – the most general opinion seems to be that women will want to go back home, or take up jobs which were usually considered suitable for women before the war, while awaiting marriage.[136]

On the other hand, this survey found that many women did want to continue in part-time work. A postwar study of women's work at the Peek Frean biscuit factory in south London showed how employers' attempts to return to the traditional insistence on a full-time workforce, hiring married women only on a temporary seasonal basis, were defeated by continuing labour shortages.[137] Employers who resisted part-time working, as in the Dundee jute industry, might face chronic problems of recruitment.[138]

Mass Observation research suggested that recruits to the women's auxiliary services had more opportunity than factory workers to escape from the family and 'think for themselves': 'groups of women, compulsorily brought together in barracks, are exchanging ideas with a frankness that would never have been possible in pre-war days'.[139] As for the armed forces, this was the moment when the place of women in modern warfare was finally accepted: the ATS and WAAF were given military status in 1941 and all three women's services were placed on a permanent footing in 1946

THE WOMEN OF WORLD WAR II

10. Memorial in Whitehall to the Women of World War II, completed for the
fiftieth anniversary of the end of the war. It represents the contribution of all
women to the war effort, in an abstract composition featuring the hats, coats,
handbags and overalls of civilians alongside the uniforms of the auxiliary services.
© Jose L. Marin.

(although conscription for women did not continue in peacetime, whereas
National Service for young men lasted until 1960). Yet the restrictions placed
on servicewomen's roles in World War II still reflected public unease with
the erosion of gender boundaries. The celebrated aviator Amy Johnson led
the Women's Air Reserve; in 1941 she met her death working for the Air
Transport Auxiliary, which delivered planes from factories to the air force.
But women in the WAAF were not allowed to train as pilots. Women in
anti-aircraft batteries did not fire guns; an official ban on women in combat
roles lasted until 1977. In practice the Special Operations Executive, which
was responsible for espionage and subversive warfare in enemy-occupied
areas of Europe, showed that it could be evaded. Women sent to work with

underground resistance movements were enrolled in the volunteer force FANY and given the weapons training they needed. A plaque outside St Paul's church, Knightsbridge, unveiled by Princess Alice in 1948, commemorates members of FANY who died on active service during the war, among them 13 secret agents. The story of one of them, Violette Szabo, was later told in the film *Carve Her Name With Pride* (1958). But in wartime movies the focus was not on female heroism but on more reassuring images: the traditional housewife or supportive service wife in *Mrs Miniver* and *In Which We Serve* (1942); the ordinary, feminine woman as factory worker or servicewoman in films of the following year, *Millions Like Us* and *The Gentle Sex*. Glamour surrounded the 'forces' sweethearts' who entertained the troops – above all Vera Lynn, whose evocative 'We'll Meet Again' was released at the beginning of the war in 1939 – but not the women's services. Problems of recruitment plagued the ATS especially, with its unflattering uniform and nickname (the 'Auxiliary Tarts' Service'), despite the enrolment of Winston Churchill's daughter Mary and the 19-year-old Princess Elizabeth (who trained as a driver and mechanic). To the disappointment of veterans, even after the war there was to be no memorial specifically to commemorate British servicewomen.[140]

It seems remarkable with hindsight how little influence women had in wartime policy making.[141] The Churchill coalition included two women as junior ministers, Ellen Wilkinson (Labour) and Florence Horsburgh (Conservative); and when Clementine Churchill took up a cause – such as the welfare of bombed-out Londoners – she was capable of 'giving orders like a *senior* minister'.[142] But the absence of women from the Cabinet attracted comment:

> Is it possible to believe [...] that there is not a woman in the country who is of sufficient capacity to be a member of the War Cabinet? Is it not likely that a woman in the War Cabinet would, in this third year of total war (with its greater demands on the stamina, self-sacrifice and intelligence of women than ever before) make a useful contribution to the thinking and the planning of both immediate and long-term policy for which the War Cabinet is responsible?[143]

The government proved resistant to lobbying from the cross-party Woman Power Committee formed by backbench women MPs in 1940. Complaints at the London Women's Parliament bore witness to the inadequate support for those who had to combine domestic responsibilities with war work. It was eventually conceded in 1943 that compensation paid for injuries in air-raids should be at the same rate for men and women, but the case for equal pay was firmly resisted. An amendment to the 1944 Education Act in favour of equal pay for schoolteachers passed in the House of Commons but was lost after Churchill threatened to resign. When a watered down version of Family Allowances was introduced in 1945, the government's original plan was that they should be paid to the father rather than the mother. This insensitive proposal was reversed only after a public campaign led by Eleanor Rathbone with all but unanimous support from British women's organisations.[144]

Nor was the postwar Attlee government much more woman-friendly. Nurseries and nursery schools set up during the war were closed down. The issue of equal pay was shelved. Some of the older women's organisations were critical too of the Attlee Welfare State: a social insurance system based (as the Beveridge Report of 1942 had recommended) on the male-breadwinner principle, treating married women as dependants, and a National Health Service that excluded provision for contraception.[145] Women – mothers especially – did in practice benefit from welfare reform and the NHS, measures that were broadly in harmony with the agenda of interwar social feminism. But as managers of household budgets they bore the brunt of shortages and inflation. As early as 1946 the British Housewives' League, founded by the London clergyman's wife Irene Lovelock, showed that tolerance for queues and austerity was wearing thin and led a protest movement against bread rationing. Gallup Polls (if we can believe them) pointed to a sharp swing in the women's vote towards the Conservatives in the 1951 general election, when 54 per cent claimed to have voted Conservative (compared with 46 per cent of men).[146]

The 1950s and 1960s

The conservative 1950s are often contrasted with the radical 1960s, and not without good reason as far as women are concerned. The Conservatives' commanding lead in the women's vote lasted throughout the 1950s, whereas in the 1966 general election only 44 per cent of women voted Conservative and 48 per cent voted Labour. Women born in the 1940s and 1950s proved more likely to vote Labour than their male contemporaries (although the older generations of women remained more conservative than men of their age).[147] Key indicators of social change that were rising by the 1960s – rates of divorce and illegitimacy – were stable, even falling at times, in the previous decade.

Yet both decades belong to a postwar era that was shaped by international developments: the Cold War, decolonisation and Britain's turn to Europe, economic growth that remained buoyant until the 1970s. And economic and demographic trends of these years had their origins pre-war Britain. Rising real incomes brought a general rise in consumer spending such as the more prosperous parts of the country had seen in the interwar years. The 'marriage boom' that peaked in 1972 had begun in the late 1930s, and the baby boom of 1955–65 was preceded by a smaller surge in births beginning in 1943.

These were years when women were under pressure to marry and to mother. Domesticity seemed almost to be taking over their lives. Husbands remained the main breadwinners. The decline of domestic service meant that the middle-class housewife spent almost twice as long on housework in 1961 as in 1937 (an average of 450 minutes per day compared with 250 minutes).[148] More wives went out to work, mostly part-time, but this was not always welcomed by husbands. Anxieties about working mothers even found their way into the Liberal party's 'policy for women' in their general election manifesto in 1950:

> Liberals oppose the bringing into industry of married women
> with young children, but would not discourage schemes of industrial
> outwork to help the family's budget by work done at home.[149]

As Helen McCarthy has shown, the work of social scientists who wrote of the modern woman's 'dual role' in home and labour market did nothing to encourage state provision or subsidy of child care: the mother's place was still with her young children in the home.[150]

At the same time the 'housewife' seemed to be gradually losing her political salience, edged out by the ungendered 'customer' or 'consumer'. The founder of the Consumers' Association (1956) which provided advice and campaigned on their behalf was a man, Michael Young. Election manifestos of the 1950s did still feature appeals to the housewife. Labour claimed credit not only for postwar welfare provision and social security but also for full employment, recalling the years of depression when:

> Each man feared that the next pay-day would be the last. The wife
> feared that the housekeeping money would suddenly vanish. Often it
> did. Her husband was handed his cards, he drew the dole, then she
> had to make do with a fraction of her previous money – and despite
> all her sacrifices the children suffered.[151]

lix

Postwar inflation remained an issue, however, and here it was the Conservatives who targeted the woman voter:

> Multiply the Ministries and clamp on the controls [...] that was precisely [Labour's] policy after the war. It led, despite heavy food subsidies, paid for out of taxation, to a 40 per cent rise in the cost of living in six years and to the perpetuation of shortages and queues, ration-books and black markets, snoopers and spivs. All these things will inevitably come back if the Socialists get their way. They seem to think that the British housewife is incapable of deciding for herself; we are sure that it is the customer, and not 'the gentleman in Whitehall', who knows best.[152]

Yet by the 1960s, when Labour had more success in challenging the record of Conservative governments, there was little in party manifestos aimed specifically at women. 'The country needs fresh and virile leadership. Labour is ready' was a rallying cry in 1964. The party's pitch in the 1966 election on 'the family in the new welfare state' was addressed to 'the responsible citizen [...] and his [*sic*] family'.[153]

Many questions remained after the war about the shape Britain would now take and the place of women in it. At the 1951 Festival of Britain, a celebration of social democratic modernity, women figured as consumers of modernistic design, or as competitors in the 'Miss World' spectacle, the latest in commercialised 'beauty queen' contests. Designed by Eric Morley, publicity officer for Mecca Ltd, it became a popular annual event, staged at the Royal Albert Hall, and attracting by the 1960s some competitors 'with wealthy backgrounds and public school educations'.[154] Traditionalists preferred to think in terms of a 'New Elizabethan Age', associating the young Queen with the achievements of her sixteenth-century predecessor.[155] Elizabeth II made clear her own commitment to the modern, family-centred image of the monarchy cultivated by her parents. Yet in various contexts women were associated with tradition rather than modernity. In fashionable society the Princesses Elizabeth and Margaret had led the way in adopting Christian Dior's 1947 'New Look' – full, longer skirts, a silhouette reminiscent of the Edwardian era.[156] The ceremonial presentation of debutantes at Court was revived between 1947 and 1958. Meanwhile in London's East End sociologists reported that most working-class families, influenced by the mothers, were still insisting on the archaic ritual of the 'churching' of women after childbirth:

'It's the Mums. It's not that I actually believe in it, but I'd get an uneasy feeling if I didn't do it. You don't like to break tradition'. […] The idea still lingers on that childbirth has in some way made the mother unclean. Many wives, even while talking about superstition, still believe it is wrong to go out in public until the service is over. […] Out of the forty-five wives in the marriage sample, all except four were churched after the birth of their last child.[157]

Women were not always on the side of social conservatism. Critics of draconian measures taken against street prostitution in 1959 included both policewomen and women peers (first admitted to the House of Lords under the 1958 Life Peerages Act). For feminists in the tradition of Josephine Butler, opposed to the double standard in sexual morality, this was a step in the wrong direction.[158] But women committed to traditional Christian teaching were among the vocal opponents of 'permissive' trends of the sixties. The Mothers' Union denounced the liberalisation of Anglican policy on divorce. The evangelical Anglican Mary Whitehouse campaigned against relaxation of censorship at the BBC.

Postwar culture was in some respects more masculine than ever. Reconstructed cities dominated by tower blocks and urban motorways were planned by, and (apparently) largely for, men. Hannah Gavron described the plight of young mothers in London who could no longer rely on 'the kind of "street life" traditionally associated with working-class life':

This depends on a stable population, familiar with the area and its inhabitants, a street level front door, reasonable safety from traffic, and perhaps most important of all a large number of home-based women, available during the day. The young working-class mother [among respondents to her social survey] […] was confined to her home in a way that previous generations may not have been. The extension of employment amongst older married women, combined with changed urban conditions, has meant a fair degree of isolation for the mother with young children who has to be at home.

If street life gave the mother an opportunity for social intercourse, it also solved the problem of where the children played. But […] to allow young children to play in the streets was [now] considered very dangerous. And the children's play was a constant source of worry to 77 per cent of the mothers involved in trying to keep children under five happy in two rooms, possibly with neighbours underneath who were sensitive to noise.[159]

Memories of war and Cold War fantasies promoted cultures of masculinity. The macho tone of British World War II films of the 1950s was if anything amplified in the early James Bond films, released from 1962. It is there too in the 'Movement' writing of the fifties, and the New Wave movies of the sixties with their focus on young men's experience of working-class life. 'There was an awful lot of sex objectivism', recalls Julie Christie, whose role in the 1965 film *Darling* associated her with the 'swinging sixties'. 'In films [...] women were there to be disliked by the heroes over and over and over again. They were treated so badly.'[160]

A rare exception was an award-winning play by the Salford bus conductor's daughter Shelagh Delaney – *A Taste of Honey*, the story of a mixed-race affair and teenage pregnancy told from the girl's point of view. First produced in 1958 by the Theatre Workshop director Joan Littlewood, it became a West End and Broadway hit and in 1961 an award-winning film. Change did begin to come with the 1960s, not least in political cultures. Radical movements around the world – the civil rights movement in the United States, colonial liberation movements – were now challenging established hierarchies. Closer to home, so did the rise of Celtic nationalism, represented at Westminster in Scotland's case by Winnie Ewing after the Hamilton by-election of 1967. 'Ulster sends a crusader to fight at Westminster' was *The Times* headline when she was joined by Bernadette Devlin (mid-Ulster, 1969), a 21-year-old student representing the Irish civil rights movement's struggle against the '"tyranny" of the Orange Order and the Union Party'.[161]

Until the later 1960s the women's movement looked much the same as it had in the 1930s. The Equal Pay Campaign Committee, now led by Conservative MP Thelma Cazalet-Keir and backed by the Women's Institutes and National Council of Women, succeeded in getting equal pay in the public sector phased in from 1955 to 1961. As Harold Smith has shown, R. A. Butler persuaded the Cabinet that this was the price of avoiding Conservative defeat in the 1955 general election.[162] The Abortion Law Reform Association, founded in 1936, mobilised support from mass-membership women's organisations – the National Council of Women, Women's Co-operative Guild and Townswomen's Guilds – in the campaign that led to the 1967 Abortion Act. Much needed reforms in the law on property rights of divorced wives accompanied relaxation of the divorce laws, although it was not until 1973 that they gained the right to stay in the family home. Feminists of the Married Women's Association (Edith Summerskill and Vera Brittain among them) campaigned for these reforms, again with support from 'mainstream' women's organisations. New organisations of a different sort, foreshadowing the grassroots women's groups of the 1970s – though without their feminist tone – were the National (originally Natural) Childbirth Trust (1958), which provided antenatal classes and became an important social nexus for young mothers, and the pre-school playgroup movement, launched in 1962 to fill the gap left by withdrawal of state support for nursery schools.[163]

The radicalisation of the women's movement in the last years of the decade came about in the context of a surge in industrial unrest and student protest, which happened to coincide in 1968 with the fiftieth anniversary of women's enfranchisement.[164] A strike by sewing machinists at the Ford Dagenham works (dramatised in the 2010 film *Made in Dagenham*) revived the issue of sex discrimination in industry and paved the way for the passage in January 1970 of Barbara Castle's Equal Pay Act. Meanwhile, young university-educated women involved with New Left movements, disillusioned by the way they were treated as women but inspired by what seemed like a revolutionary moment, looked for ways of mobilising support. Women's Liberation groups sprang up in London in 1969, coordinated by a London Women's Liberation Workshop.[165] The trade union college in Oxford, Ruskin College, home of the History Workshop movement, became in February 1970 the venue of the British WLM's first national conference. Angela Carter, in a much-quoted passage, recalled these years as above all formative in focussing her mind on 'the social fictions that regulate our lives – what Blake called the "mind-forged manacles"'.

> Towards the end of [the 1960s] there was a brief period of public philosophical awareness that occurs only very occasionally in human history; when truly, it felt like Year One, that all that was holy was in process of being profaned and we were attempting to grapple with the real relations between human beings. So writers like Marcuse and Adorno were as much part of my personal process of maturing into feminism as experiments with my sexual and emotional life and with various intellectual adventures in anarcho-surrealism [...] I can date to that time and to some of those debates [...] in the summer of 1968, my own questioning of my reality as a woman. How that social fiction of my 'femininity' was created, by means outside my control, and palmed off on me as the real thing.[166]

Here was a radical shift in perspectives on gender, originating in an *avant garde* of activists but not without influence on mainstream culture in the last decades of the century.

Women's Lib to Post-Feminism? 1970 – 2000

The end of the economists' postwar 'Golden Age', marked by the oil price shock of 1973 and rampant inflation, brought social transformations to Britain that could hardly have been predicted in the 1960s. Large-scale deindustrialisation changed both landscapes and social structures. Together with globalisation and the ascendancy of economic neo-liberalism in both Thatcherite Conservatism and post-Cold-War New Labour, it produced increased inequality in incomes and lifestyles. The mid-century trend towards class convergence was reversed, creating a society very different from that imagined by socialist or Marxist feminists in 1970. The new geography of poverty and prosperity, together with the growth of ethnic diversity, makes generalisations about women's place in recent British history far from straightforward.

Yet the contours of a new and more benign gender regime do seem to have emerged in the 1970s and after: a regime of low fertility and new freedoms for the young single woman; unprecedented access to higher education and, for qualified women, well-paid jobs; dual-earner partnerships, increasingly the norm – except in areas of high unemployment and in Muslim communities – across the social classes. Politically sensitive issues remained – among them, financial support for lone mothers and their children (policed from 1993 by the unpopular Child Support Agency), and the rights and responsibilities of absent fathers. But the trend in these decades was in most respects in the direction of gender equality. In the wake of – or sometimes in anticipation of – the 1975 Sex Discrimination Act women gained admission to ancient institutions previously closed to them, from the Stock Exchange (1973) to the Anglican priesthood (1994). In some cases – the professions, the media, Oxbridge colleges – the removal of barriers led to a rapid influx of women. A Hansard Society report (1990) noted that a 'glass ceiling' still blocked women's way to top jobs. On the other hand that metaphor expressed a new expectation, a belief that women *ought* to be equally represented in the elites of a modern democracy; and for those who wanted it the sky *should* be the limit. The pace of change was at some points forced by European Commission (EC) directives – and as Sheila Rowbotham has noted it was a judgment of 1983 in the European Court that eventually gave the Dagenham sewing machinists the right to equal grading with male workers that they had struck for in 1968.[167] Equal opportunities and equal pay in the private sector proved difficult to enforce: gendered pay gaps remained significant both for higher paid employees and for part-time women workers at the bottom of the scale.[168] But the equality and human rights programmes of the EC, and from the late 1990s 'gender mainstreaming' approaches pioneered in UN development agencies, did have positive effects on workplace rights and conditions, particularly for full-time, younger, professional women workers.[169] As for the balance of power in the working-class family, some felt that it had shifted decisively in favour of women. *The Independent* published a letter from a Scotswoman protesting against an early twenty-first century BBC series on the declining quality of white working-class life.

> The story of working-class women is somewhat different. They can now engage with further education, employment, travel and family planning, and have freedom and independence which did not exist for them when apparently life was fair and pride ubiquitous for working-class men. [...] I am a woman, from a white working-class background, who is very grateful not to live as my mother and grandmothers did, subordinate to husbands who controlled the lives of all within their households as they saw fit.[170]

The political domain showed signs of change from the early 1970s. In the evenly balanced October 1974 election the parties once more competed directly for the women's vote, the Conservatives with a list of pledges for 'Women – at home and at work' and Labour with 'A Charter for Women'. One outcome, supported by both parties, was the creation of an Equal Opportunities Commission. Labour's wide-ranging Sex Discrimination Act and increased income support for lone parents under the Wilson–Callaghan governments of 1974–9, reflected the growing influence of women in the Labour movement. Grassroots activism raised awareness of the plight of 'battered wives', starting with Erin Pizzey's Chiswick Women's Aid centre (1971), the first of many refuges set up to provide support and accommodation.[171] With government backing a Domestic Violence and Matrimonial Proceedings Bill (1976) made it possible to get a legal injunction against a violent husband. More women now lobbied effectively, participated in community protest movements, joined trade unions and took part in high profile strikes. The TUC was persuaded to back women's causes – defence of the right to choose abortion, a code on workplace sexual harassment.

But if the political salience of women's issues grew during the seventies, it was also made very clear that they could be approached from more than one perspective. Most socialist and Marxist feminists prioritised workplace rights, but they were not without critics within the WLM. A 'Wages for Housework' campaign, led by Selma James, Marxist champion of the unwaged worker, argued instead that women should be paid for the work they did at home. It attracted both media attention and support from some working-class wives and mothers. As a correspondent to the WLM newsletter *WIRES* wrote in 1978:

> Before I had a child the last thing I wanted was to be a housewife
> [...] But now I have a kid of my own who brings me more pleasure
> than anything in my life has up to now, I find I am dependent on a
> man to support me[...] I have to do his housework as well as my own
> and the child's, not because he is a male chauvinist pig, bless him,
> but because in order to support the three of us he has to work 50–60
> hours a week at a tiring job, and he doesn't have time for shopping or
> cooking. Women who tell me £30 a week wages for housework would
> be bad for my political soul, or that I should stick my kid in a nursery
> and go and get a job, make me bloody angry.[172]

Shortly before the general election that brought her to power, Margaret Thatcher put her personal view on record:

> I do believe *passionately* that many women take the view, and
> quite rightly, that when their children are young their first duty is to
> look after the children and keep the family together. I wasn't a Member of Parliament until after my children were six [...] And I do say
> this to you very seriously indeed: it is every bit as worthy an objective
> and an ambition to stay at home and look after the family as it is to
> go out to work.[173]

Opinions continue to differ on the significance for women of Mrs Thatcher's years in office as Britain's first female Prime Minister (1979–90). Laura Beers, evaluating the sometimes contradictory evidence of opinion polls, suggests that she retained majority support among all but the youngest and most unionised women voters, although the traditional 'gender gap' in voting narrowed over the years.[174] The savagely deflationary policies and spending cuts of her first ministry were presented as the 'commonsense economics' of the housewife. For Thatcher herself they also represented the 'values and virtues of middle England' as opposed to the financial laxity of the '"wet" Tory establishment'. Of one minister dismissed in 1981, Christopher Soames (son-in-law to Winston Churchill), she wrote:

> I got the distinct impression that he felt the natural order of things was being violated and that he was, in effect, being dismissed by his housemaid.[175]

Many women participated or were caught up in the strikes and riots of the early 1980s, as unemployment soared; but the spotlight could also be trained on victims of the trade unions. Thatcher wrote of a visit from representatives of the 'Miners' Wives back to Work Campaign' in 1984:

> I was moved by the courage of these women, whose families were subject to abuse and intimidation [...] They explained to me how small shops in the coalfields were being blackmailed into supplying food and goods to striking miners and withholding them from work-ing miners. [...] Of course, the vital thing for these women was that the N[ational] C[oal] B[oard] should do everything it could to pro-tect miners who led the return to work [...] I said that we would not let them down, and I think I kept my word. The whole country was in their debt.[176]

It was, characteristically, not a feminist point of view – and Thatcher was notorious for not promoting women within her governments – but it was a *woman's* point of view, articulated by a powerful woman who had no doubt of her credentials as prime minister. Shirley Williams, Thatcher's contemporary and a leading politician of the centre left (Labour, then Social Democrat and Liberal Democrat), said of her in a 1992 radio interview on *Woman's Hour*:

> Her major impact was not in supporting women's causes. One can even say that women went backwards during her time. Her major contribution was that she laid to rest for ever the argument that women are incapable of being leaders. There are few people this century who have been tougher than Mrs Thatcher. When I look back and think for a minute when women as possible prime ministers were first discussed, I remember that one of the arguments that was always made was that they would probably come to power at the time that women have the menopause and they would be incapable of making

any decisions. Mrs Thatcher, presumably at one stage or another, went through the menopause. There was not a single indication that she did and one never saw anything in her behaviour that would suggest the slightest ups and downs. Since that time, no one has ever said that women can't be tough enough to be politicians.[177]

That said, it was left to the Labour party in the last years of the century to bring about a long overdue increase in the numbers of women MPs. Before 1997 women had never held as many as 10 per cent of seats in the House of Commons, but by 2010 the proportion of women MPs had risen to one in four. The key decision, prompted by pressure groups within the party – the Labour Women's Network and Emily's List – and taken at the party conference of 1993, was to require that parliamentary candidates should be selected from all-women shortlists in 50 per cent of all vacant Labour-held and marginal seats.[178] Positive discrimination was controversial: all-women shortlists were successfully challenged in an industrial tribunal in 1996 and ceased to operate until an Act was passed in 2002 to make them legal. But meanwhile more women were selected from open shortlists. After the landslide election of 1997, women amounted to a quarter of the parliamentary Labour party – 101 of them to the Conservatives' 19 women MPs. Even more striking was the high proportion of women returned to seats in the Welsh and Scottish parliaments after devolution in 1999 – 40 per cent and 37.2 per cent respectively. That result was no doubt influenced by the use of proportional representation rather than the standard British first-past-the-post electoral system, but it also reflected a new gender-awareness in Celtic nationalism. Talk of a 'democratic deficit', caused by Margaret Thatcher's imposition of unpopular policies – closure of coal mines and a regressive 'poll tax' – on regions where Conservatives had little support, had helped to raise the issue of fair representation of the sexes. More positively, according to the New Left academic Tom Nairn, a proposal of the 1990s that 50 per cent of the Scottish parliament's members should be women had become a 'nationalist banner [...] an emblem of the kind of country and the style of nationalism that people really want'. It would redeem modern Scotland from the 'past shame' of misogynistic religious tradition.

> The democratic side to Calvinist Election was always dragged down by a fearful, Hyde-like social culture for which, as Satan's chosen entry to the kingdom, the female soul was a potential enchantress or witch [...] The 50 per cent proposal [...] also strikes at Westminster's

pitiable record over the same issue: a supposedly more liberal society which manages just six per cent representation for women.[179]

How far did increased representation of women at Westminster make a difference in practice? In the short term that seemed doubtful. When the 1997 New Labour government failed to reverse Conservative cuts to the benefits of single mothers, 'Blair's Babes' (a phrase coined incautiously by Labour minister Mo Mowlam) came in for criticism. 'New Labour women or Maggie's? You the jury decide', was an *Observer* headline, above a celebratory photograph of women MPs with Tony Blair, taken only six months earlier.

> They tripped out of Church House on a bright May day and lined up in Westminster for the defining picture of the New Era. Blair's babes exploded with colour and promise as they were captured surrounding the leader. Only wary observers noted the similarities between their pose and the shots of *Playboy* bunnies gazing at Hugh Hefner.[180]

Criticism of Labour policy on lone parents was perhaps misplaced. It was the Blair government that took the decisive step of providing high-quality, subsidised child care, making it possible for more single mothers to go out to work. Together with the introduction of a statutory minimum wage and benefits targeted at the poorest families, this strategy was to produce a significant reduction in child poverty.[181] But it is interesting that the 1997 cohort of women MPs do seem to have made a less distinctive contribution to House of Commons debates than their predecessors. Earlier women MPs tended – even though most saw themselves not as feminists but as party politicians and representatives of their constituents – to speak in the Commons mainly on gendered issues. Between the wars, for example, 'Woman's special sphere seemed to be the family, welfare and international peace'.[182] For the years after 1945, analysis of digitised Commons debates shows that female speakers used a markedly different vocabulary. From 1997 these gendered differences were reduced, and women MPs also spoke less frequently.[183] A study commissioned by the Fawcett Society did however produce evidence that increased numbers made it possible to exert influence in other ways: 'feminizing the agenda' within the political parties, and promoting all-party parliamentary groups on topics of special concern to women.[184]

What can we say about the impact of women's movements on late twentieth-century public policy? The Fawcett Society, heir to the traditions of the constitutional women's suffrage movement, represents continuities in twentieth-century British feminism, and techniques of lobbying with a long track record. The WLM was a more exotic manifestation of feminism, shaped by the ethos of the 1960s and 1970s, and historians continue to debate its impact. Some of its demands were in fact quite practical (see Chapter 5) and they were met – at least in part – fairly quickly. On some issues of sexuality and the principle, at least, of workplace equality a case can be made that young feminists of the seventies were pushing at an open door, helped above all by pressure from Europe, where the principle of equal pay (Article 119 of the Treaty of Rome) was seen as a safeguard against unfair competition.[185] On equality issues, and in the formidable 'Women in Media' group, there was more collaboration between the older feminist societies and the WLM – 'Trads and Libs' as Mary Stott of *The Guardian* women's page called them – than was publicised at the time. Case studies have shown convincingly, on the other hand, that campaigns rooted in the WLM achieved results in defending rights of access to abortion and in changing judicial thinking on rape within marriage.[186] But in both cases success depended on shifting opinion and winning support in the mainstream media. Changing the culture, always at the heart of the WLM project, is a process not easily evaluated.[187]

Talk of 'post-feminism' in the 1980s and after can be seen as a backlash against what had been achieved, or simply as the latest version of an anti-feminist critique that was present as one strand in the media and public discourse throughout the century. To some extent it reflected changing fashions. The vogue for 'glamour' – perhaps most conspicuously seen in the popularity of the 'people's princess', Diana, Princess of Wales – was at odds with the ethos of the WLM. So was the 1990's vision of 'girl power' represented by the Spice Girls, with their faith in Thatcherite individualism and the American Dream. For some, these were signs that feminism was played out – or that the young had deserted it. For others, the foregrounding of femininity and girl culture was instead the hallmark of a Third Wave feminism, with renewed appeal to the young (and a place in the youth music scene).[188] Debates were to open up at the end of the century on matters of substance as well as style.[189] A 'new gender settlement, a new social contract between women and men' was proclaimed by women in the New Labour camp.[190] The minimum wage and family policies of the Blair government did win feminist approval.[191] But socialist feminists were deeply suspicious of the notion that 'gender mainstreaming' and better representation of professional women within policy making elites would prove to be an effective post-modern way of defending women's interests.[192] Inequalities among women, as among men, continued to widen in the new century. And renewed concern with gender inequalities remained a dominant theme in feminist manifestos from Natasha Walter's *The New Feminism* (1999) to the non-partisan Women's Equality Party (WEP), launched in 2015 with a familiar claim in its mission statement:

> Equality for women isn't a women's issue. When women fulfil their potential, everyone benefits.[193]

That is not a principle that can be taken for granted, a matter of general agreement. But the six-point programme of today's WEP does encourage reflection on the scale of change in gender regimes and expectations that took place in the twentieth century. Equal representation, equal pay and opportunity, equal parenting and care-giving, equal education, equal media treatment – the sheer ambition of the first five demands on its website is striking. So is the absence from the programme of some issues of concern to twentieth-century feminist movements – welfare provision, sexuality and reproductive rights. The expansion of state welfare support for mothers and families, like the demand for equal citizenship, had been on the agenda of reformers from the beginning of the century: by the millennium, although benefits were liable to be pared back in times of austerity, the major battles had been won. Other 'transformations', to use Paul Addison's term, belong to the 1970s and after.[194] Three related areas of change stand out: radical changes in sexual mores and in gender roles within the family; the opening of employment opportunities at all levels to women, whether married or single; and increased access to higher education and professional training. The assumption that there is a new consensus on these matters, that there can be 'no turning back', underpins the WEP's uncompromising agenda. It is echoed by the claim made on the Fawcett Society's website, 'Together we can end sexism and misogyny for good'.[195] A case can certainly be made, based on the general direction of late twentieth-century socio-economic and cultural changes, that the outcomes of sexual and gender revolutions of that era are here to stay. But the sixth demand in the WEP programme – an end to violence against women, a goal of the women's movement for well over a century – suggests that there is after all nothing inevitable about progress. Some aspects of dysfunctional gender relations and cultures are still not well understood.[196] Bets on the future may be risky. But historians can at least hope to contribute to a better informed future by working towards an inclusive, source-based version of British history.

Notes

1. Bingham, A., 'The Digitization of Newspaper Archives. Opportunities and Challenges for Historians', *TCBH*, 21:2, 2010; Sutcliffe-Braithwaite, F., 'Observing the Eighties', *TCBH*, 25:3, 2014.

2. Abrams, L., *Myth and Materiality in a Woman's World. Shetland 1800–2000* (Manchester University Press, 2005).

3. Priestley, J. B., *English Journey* (London: W. Heinemann in association with V. Gollancz, 1934; repr. London: Mandarin, 1994), pp. 397–8, 401–3.

4. Gallie, D., 'The Labour Force', in Halsey, A. H. & Webb, J. (eds), *Twentieth-Century British Social Trends* (London: Macmillan, 2000), p. 288.

5. Lawrence, J., 'Class, "Affluence" and the Study of Everyday Life in Britain, c. 1930–64', *CSH*, 10:2, 2013, pp. 273–300; Sutcliffe-Braithwaite, F., 'Discourses of "Class" in Britain in "New Times"', *CBH*, 31:2, 2017, pp. 294–317.

6. Heath, A., Martin, J. & Elgenius, G., 'Who Do We Think We Are? The Decline of Traditional Social Identities', *British Social Attitudes*, 23, 2007, p. 4.

7. 'Trends in Births Outside Marriage', *Population Trends*, 81, 1995, p. 17.

8. Smith, S., *Novel on Yellow Paper* (London: 1936; repr. Virago, 1980), pp. 146, 208–9.

9. Mitford, N., 'The English Aristocracy', *Encounter*, v:3 (Sept. 1955), pp. 5–12.

10. Christie, A., *An Autobiography* (London: Collins, 1977), p. 122.

11. Roberts, R., *The Classic Slum. Salford Life in the First Quarter of the Century.* (Harmondsworth: Penguin Books, 1973), pp. 42–4.

12. Davies, M.L., *Life as We Have Known It, by Co-operative Working Women* (London: L. and V. Woolf, 1931; repr Virago, 1977), p. xxiii.

13. Introduction to Spring Rice, M., *Working-Class Wives* (London: Routledge, 1939), p. xvi. Before the coming of the National Health Service, women who were not in employment and covered by National Insurance were eligible for free medical care only in pregnancy and after childbirth.

14. Summers, A., 'Public Functions, Private Premises. Female Professional Identity and the Domestic Service Paradigm in Britain, c. 1850–1930', in Melman, B. (ed.), *Borderlines: Gender and Identities in War and Peace, 1870–1930* (London: Routledge, 1998).

15. Diary of Mrs Trowbridge, 16 October 1941, in Dorothy Sheridan (ed.), *Wartime Women. A Mass-Observation Anthology* (London: Heinemann, 1990), p. 151.

16. Blandford, L., 'The Making of a Lady', in MacDonald Fraser, G., *The World of the Public School* (London: Weidenfeld and Nicolson, 1977), p. 204.

17. Peach, C., Rogers, A., Chance, J. & Daley, P., 'Immigration and Ethnicity', in Halsey, A. H. & Webb, J. (eds), *Twentieth-Century British Social Trends* (London: Macmillan, 2000), pp. 146–7, 154.

18. McDowell, L., *Working Lives. Gender, Migration and Employment in Britain, 1945–2007* (Chichester: Wiley-Blackwell, 2013), p. 68.

19. Coleman, D., 'Population and Family', in Halsey, A. H. & Webb, J. (eds), *Twentieth-Century British Social Trends* (London: Macmillan, 2000), p. 58.

20. *Ibid.*, p. 54.

21. *Ibid.*, p. 61.

22. Cited in Rathbone, E., *The Disinherited Family* (London: Edward Arnold & Co., 1924), pp. 159–60.

23. Gallie, 'Labour Force', p. 297.

24. Lewis, J., 'Marriage', in Zweiniger-Bargielowska, I., *Women in Twentieth-Century Britain* (London: Pearson, 2001), p. 73.

25. Coleman, 'Population', p. 80.

26. Gallie, 'Labour Force', p. 292.

27. Meynell, A., *Public Servant, Private Woman. An Autobiography* (London: Gollancz, 1988), pp. 88–9.

28. Marsden, D., 'Mill Girls', in Jackson, B., *Working-Class Community* (London: Routledge and Kegan Paul, 1968), pp. 80–4.

29. Horlick, N., *Can You Have It All?* (London: Macmillan, 1997), p. 96.

30. McDowell, L., 'Changing Cultures of Work: Employment, Gender, and Lifestyle' in Morley, D. & Robins, K. (eds), *British Cultural Studies* (Oxford University Press, 2001), p. 35.

31. Callan, H. & Ardener, S. (eds), *The Incorporated Wife* (London: Croom Helm, 1984).

32. Logan, A., 'In Search of Equal Citizenship: The Campaign for Women Magistrates in England and Wales, 1910–1939', *WHR*, 16:4, 2007, p. 503.

33. Webster, W., *Imagining Home; Gender, 'Race' and National Identity, 1945–64* (London: UCL Press, 1998).

34. Hoggart, R., *The Uses of Literacy* (Harmondsworth: Penguin, 1959), p. 38.

35. Bowlby, J., *Childcare and the Growth of Love* (London: Penguin, 1953), pp. 11–12; *Forty-Four Juvenile Thieves: Their Characters and Home-Life* (London: Bailliere Tindall, 1947).

36. Thatcher, M., *The Downing Street Years* (London: HarperCollins, 1995 edn), 628–31.

37. McCloskey, D., 'Paid Work', in Zweiniger-Bargielowska, *Women*, pp. 169–70.

38. Zweiniger-Bargielowska, I., 'Housewifery', in *Ibid.*, p. 161.

39. Schreiner, O., *Woman and Labour* (London: T. Fisher Unwin, 1911).

40. de Vries, J., *The Industrious Revolution. Consumer Behaviour and the Household Economy, 1650 to the Present* (Cambridge University Press, 2008).

41. McDowell, *Working Lives*, p. 57.

42. Dyhouse, C., *Students: A Gendered History* (Abingdon: Routledge, 2006), pp. 84–5, 137–54.

43. Royal Commission on Oxford and Cambridge Report, 1922, p. 173, quoted in Rita McWilliams-Tullberg, *Women at Cambridge. A Men's University – Though of a Mixed Type* (London: Gollancz, 1975), p. 199.

44. Dyhouse, *Students*, p. 18.

45. Routh, G., *Occupation and Pay in Great Britain, 1906–79* (Basingstoke, Macmillan 1980), p. 17.

46. Newsom, J., *The Education of Girls* (London: Faber and Faber, 1948), p. 109.

47. Dyhouse, *Students*, p. 116.

48. McCrum, N. G., 'The Academic Deficit at Oxford and Cambridge', *Oxford Review of Education*, 20, 1994, p. 19; 'The Legacy', *Oxford Magazine*, 134, 1996.

49. Arnot, M., David, M. & Weiner, G., *Closing the Gender Gap. Postwar Education and Social Change* (Cambridge: Polity, 1999), p. 25.

50. Arnot, M., 'A cloud over coeducation' in Walker, S. & Barton, L. (eds), *Gender, Class and Education* (Lewes: Falmer, 1983), p. 81.

51. Peel, M., *The New Meritocracy. A History of UK Independent Schools* (London: Elliott & Thompson, 2015), Chapter 12.

52. Bone, A., *Girls and Girls Only Schools. A Review of the Evidence* (Manchester: Equal Opportunities Commission, 1983).

53. Benn, C. & Simon, B., *Half Way There: Report on the British Comprehensive School Reform* (2nd edn, Harmondsworth: Penguin, 1972), pp. 417–19.

54. Mahony, P., *Schools for the Boys? Coeducation Reassessed* (London: Hutchinson, 1985), pp. 34–185; Peel, *New Meritocracy*, p. 185.

55. See McCrum, 'Academic Deficit'.

56. Dyhouse, C., 'Education', in Zweiniger-Bargielowska, *Women in Twentieth-Century Britain*, p. 130.

57. Gillborn, D. & Mirza, H. S., *Educational Inequality. Mapping Race, Class & Gender* (London Office for Standards in Education, 2000), pp. 22–3.

58. Lewis, J., 'The Failure to Expand Childcare Provision and to Develop a Comprehensive Childcare Policy in Britain during the 1960s', *TCBH*, 24:2, 2013; Davis, A., *Pre-school Childcare in England, 1939–2010. Theory, Practice and Experience* (Manchester University Press, 2015), pp. 118–27.

59. Young, M. & Wilmott, P., *Family and Kinship in East London* (London: Routledge & Kegan Paul, 1957), p. 147.

60. Russell, W., *Educating Rita* (London: Methuen Drama, 2007), p. 19. The play was first performed in 1980 and in 1983 released as an award-winning movie with Michael Caine and Julie Walters.

61. Sharpe, S., '*Just Like a Girl'. How Girls Learn to be Women. From the Seventies to the Nineties* (London: Penguin Books, 1994), p. 249.

62. Royden, M., 'Modern Love', in Gollancz, V. (ed.), *The Making of Women. Oxford Essays in Feminism* (London: Allen & Unwin, 1917), pp. 38–9, 43. Cf. 1 *Corinthians* 6:19: 'Do you not know that your bodies are the temples of the Holy Spirit?'

63. Jennings, R., *Tomboys and Bachelor Girls* (Manchester University Press, 2007), p. 6.

64. 'If only youth knew'. 'If only age could, Kitty'. Waugh, E., *Vile Bodies* (London: Chapman & Hall, 1930; repr. Harmondsworth: Penguin, 1938), p. 130.

65. Tweedie, J., *Eating Children: Young Dreams and Early Nightmares* (London: Viking, 1993), p. 131.

66. Szreter, S., 'Victorian Britain, 1831–1963: Towards a Social History of Sexuality', *Journal of Victorian Culture*, 1, 1996, pp. 136–49.

67. Coleman, 'Population', pp. 51, 55.

68. In, for example, Nell Dunn's account of Battersea slum life *Up the Junction* (London: 1963), adapted as a television play in 1965 and a film in 1968.

69. For inter-war estimates of failure rates of various methods of birth control see Cook, H., *The Long Sexual Revolution. English Women, Sex, and Contraception, 1800–1975* (Oxford University Press, 2004), Table 5.1, p. 140.

70. Szreter S. & Fisher, K., *Sex Before the Sexual Revolution. Intimate Life in England, 1918–1963* (Cambridge University Press, 2010), pp. 386–7.

71. For a review of this issue see Bingham, A., Delap, L., Jackson, L. & Settle, L., 'Historical Child Sexual Abuse in England and Wales: The Role of Historians', *History of Education*, 45, 2016, p. 422.

72. For survey evidence from the social researcher and organiser for the National Association of Girls' Clubs Pearl Jephcott, see her *Rising Twenty* (London: Faber and Faber, 1948).

73. See McCrindle, J. & Rowbotham, S. (eds), *Dutiful Daughters. Women Talk About Their Lives* (London: Allen Lane, 1977), pp. 218–19.

74. Szreter & Fisher, *Sex Before the Sexual Revolution*, p. 385.

75. Coleman, 'Population', p. 58.

76. See Langhamer, C., *The English in Love. The Intimate Story of an Emotional Revolution* (Oxford University Press, 2013).

77. Hopkirk, J., 'Our Cosmo World', *Cosmopolitan*, 2 April, 1972, p. 10.

78. Purves, L., *Holy Smoke. Religion and Roots: A Personal Memoir* (London: Hodder & Stoughton, 1998), pp. 145–6.

79. Greer, G., *The Female Eunuch* (London: Paladin, 1971), p. 249.

80. Coleman, 'Population', p. 62.

81. Wellings, K., Field, J., Johnson, A. M. & Wadsworth, J. (eds), *Sexual Behaviour in Britain. The National Study of Sexual Attitudes and Lifestyles* (Harmondsworth: Penguin, 1994), pp. 84, 244, 248–52.

82. On the Gateways Club see Jivani, A., *It's Not Unusual: A History of Lesbian and Gay Britain in the Twentieth Century* (London: Michael O'Mara Books, 1997), pp. 133–5.

83. Of births to women under 20, 18.8% were 'illegitimate' in 1960 compared with 88% in 1996, Coleman, 'Population', pp. 52–3.

84. Fielding, H., *Bridget Jones's Diary. The First Columns* (London: *The Independent*, 2005), pp. 12–13. First published in *The Independent* from 1995.

85. For example, Offen, K., *European Feminisms, 1750–1950* (Stanford University Press, 2000), pp. 25–6; Gillis, S. & Munford, R., 'Genealogies and Generations: The Politics and Praxis of Third Wave Feminism', *WHR*, 13, 2004, pp. 176–7; Browne, S. F., *The Women's Liberation Movement in Scotland* (Manchester University Press, 2014), pp. 182–5.

86. Available at https://www.bl.uk/sisterhood/themes/who-we-were-who-we-are. *Sisterhood and After: the Women's Liberation Oral History Project* (www.bl.uk/sisterhood) is a collaboration between the British Library and the University of Sussex. Sixty WLM activists were interviewed between 2010 and 2013 for the project.

87. Offen, K., 'Writing the history of feminism (old and new): impacts and impatience', in Schulz, K. (ed.), *The Women's Liberation Movement: Impacts and Outcomes* (New York: Berghahn Books, 2017).

88. For alternative accounts of the phases or waves of British feminism, see Harrison, B. H., *Finding a Role. The United Kingdom 1970–1990* (Oxford University Press, 2010), pp. 43–4; Pugh, M., *Women and the Women's Movement in Britain since 1914* (3rd edn, Basingstoke: Palgrave Macmillan, 2015), p. 326, note 5.

89. The heading on the front page of the suffrage journal *Common Cause* when Maude Royden was its editor; Fletcher, S., *Maude Royden* (Oxford: Blackwell, 1989), p. 84.

90. Beaumont, C., *Housewives and Citizens: Domesticity and the Women's Movement in England, 1928–64* (Manchester University Press, 2013).

91. Rubinstein, D., *A Different World for Women. The Life of Millicent Garrett Fawcett* (Hemel Hempstead: Harvester, 1991), p. 242.

92. Andrews, M., *The Acceptable Face of Feminism. The Women's Institute as a Social Movement* (London: Lawrence & Wishart, 2016 edn), p. 11.

93. Klein, V., *The Feminine Character. History of an Ideology.* (3rd edn, London: Routledge, 1989), pp. 4, 173–4.

94. Mitchell, J., *Woman's Estate* (Harmondsworth: Penguin, 1971).

95. *Ibid.*, pp. 56–66.

96. For example, Addison, P., *No Turning Back. The Peaceful Revolutions of Post-War Britain* (Oxford University Press, 2010), p. 219; Harrison, *Finding a Role*, pp. 237–8.

97. See Walkowitz, J., *City of Dreadful Delight. Narratives of Sexual Danger in Late-Victorian London* (London: Virago, 1992), pp. 229–45.

98. Fairweather, E., 'Leeds: Curfew on Men', *Spare Rib*, 83, June 1979.

99. Bruley, S., 'Women's Liberation at the Grass Roots: A View from Some English Towns', *WHR*, 25:5, 2016; Browne, *The Women's Liberation Movement in Scotland*.

100. Delap, L., 'Feminist Bookshops, Reading Cultures and the Women's Liberation Movement in Great Britain, c.1974–2000', *HWJ*, 81, 2016, pp. 171–96; Cameron, D. & Scanlon, J. (eds), *The Trouble and Strife Reader* (London: Bloomsbury Academic, 2010), pp. 4, 216.

101. Jolly, M., 'After the protest. Biographical consequences of movement activism in an oral history of women's liberation in Britain', in Schulz, *Women's Liberation Movement*, pp. 298–314.

102. Bird, E., 'Women's Studies and the Women's Movement in Britain: Origins and Evolution, 1970–2000', *WHR*, 12:2, 2003, pp. 283–8.

103. 'Memories of 1970s Independent Cinema' in Mulvey, L. & Clayton, S. (eds), *Other Cinemas* (London: 2007); and see her 'Visual Pleasure and Narrative Cinema', *Screen* 1973, repr. in Mulvey, L., *Visual and Other Pleasures* (Basingstoke: Macmillan, 1989).

104. Segal, L., *Is the Future Female?* (London: Virago, 1987), pp. 38–9.

105. *Ibid.*, pp. 213, 246.

106. Caine, B., *English Feminism, 1780–1980* (Oxford University Press, 1997), pp. 267–71.

107. Walkowicz, J. R., 'The Politics of Prostitution and Sexual Labour', *HWJ*, 82:1, 2016, pp. 188–98.

108. Winter, J. M., *The Great War and the British People* (London: Macmillan, 1985), pp. 72–3.

109. *Ibid.*, 'The Slaughter of Social Elites', pp. 92–102.

110. Tennyson Jesse, F., *The Sword of Deborah. First-hand Impressions of the British Women's Army in France* (London: Heinemann, 1919), pp. 18–19.

111. *The Times*, 19 July, 1915.

112. Gullace, N., *'The Blood of Our Sons': Men, Women, and the Representation of British Citizenship During the Great War* (New York: Palgrave Macmillan, 2002), pp. 9–10.

113. See for example, Pugh, M., *The March of the Women: A Revisionist Analysis of the Campaign for Women's Suffrage* (Oxford University Press, 2000).

114. *The Times*, 8 October, 1915.

115. 'Changed Status of Women', *The Times*, 3 May 1935.

116. Thane, P., 'What difference did the vote make?', in Vickery, A. (ed.), *Women, Privilege and Power* (Stanford University Press, 2001), pp. 253–87.

117. Crafts, N., 'Living standards', in Crafts, N., Gazeley, I. & Newell, A. (eds), *Work and Pay in 20th Century Britain* (Oxford University Press, 2007): Table 1.1, p. 20 gives an increase of 35 per cent in real wages between 1913 and 1938. Depressed regions that did not see wage increases include the coalfields of South Wales; see Bruley, S., *The Men and Women of 1926: A Gender History of the General Strike and Miners' Lockout in South Wales* (Cardiff: University of Wales Press, 2010).

118. Wootton, B., *In A World I Never Made. Autobiographical Reflections* (London: Allen & Unwin, 1967), p. 64.

119. Spark, M., *Curriculum Vitae. An Autobiography* (London: Carcanet Press, 1992), p. 110.

120. Light, A., *Forever England. Femininity, Literature and Conservatism between the Wars* (London: Routledge, 1991).

121. Bingham, A., 'Enfranchisement, Feminism and the Modern Woman: Debates in the Popular Press, 1918–1939', in Gottlieb, J. V. & Toye, R., *The Aftermath of Suffrage. Women, Gender and Politics in Britain, 1918–1945* (Basingstoke: Palgrave Macmillan, 2013).

122. *Daily Mail*, 3 March 1925.

123. Bingham, A., '"Stop the Flapper Vote Folly": Rothermere, the *Daily Mail* and the Equalisation of the Franchise 1927–28', *Twentieth Century British History*, 13, 2002, pp. 17–37.

124. Craig, F. W. S., *British General Election Manifestos, 1900–1974* (London: Macmillan, 1975), pp. 32, 54.

125. *Ibid.*, 30, 54, 85.

126. Thane, ' What difference did the vote make?', pp. 264–5; Gottlieb, J., *Feminine Fascism: Women in Britain's Fascist Movement, 1923–1945* (London: I.B.Tauris, 2000), pp. 45, 50; Morgan, K. *et al.*, *Communists and British Society, 1920–1991* (London: Rivers Oram, 2003), pp. 14–15.

127. McKibbin, R., *Parties and People. England 1914–1951* (Oxford University Press, 2010), pp. 97–100.

128. Reiss, E., 'Changes in the Law', in Ray Strachey (ed.), *Our Freedom and Its Results* (London: L. and V. Woolf, 1936), pp. 105–6. This volume gives a broadly optimistic account of the consequences of women's enfranchisement.

129. Law, C., *Suffrage and Power: The Women's Movement, 1918–28* (London: I.B.Tauris, 1997).

130. Grayzel, S. R., *At Home and Under Fire. Air Raids and Culture in Great Britain from the Great War to the Blitz* (Cambridge University Press, 2012).

131. Gottlieb, J. V. *'Guilty Women', Foreign Policy and Appeasement in Inter-War Britain* (Basingstoke: Palgrave Macmillan, 2015), pp. 197–8.

132. Schofield, S., File Report 26, 'Women's Organisations in Wartime' (copy held at the Imperial War Museum). Available at www.massobservation:amdigital,co.uk/ Documents/Details.

133. Dear, I. C. B. & Foot, M. R. D., *Oxford Companion to the Second World War* (Oxford, 1995), p. 1136.

134. Summerfield, P., *Reconstructing Women's Wartime Lives. Discourse And Subjectivity in Oral Histories of the Second World War* (Manchester University Press, 1998).

135. Diary entry for 1 August 1943, Broad, R. & Fleming, S. (eds), *Nella Last's War. A Mother's Diary, 1939–45* (London: Sphere, 1983), p. 255.

136. Mass Observation, *The Journey Home* (London: 1944), pp. 64–6.

137. Jephcott, P., Seear, N. & Smith, J. H., *Married Women Working* (London: Allen & Unwin, 1962).

138. Morelli, C. & Tomlinson, J., 'Women and Work After the Second World War: A Case Study of the Jute Industry c.1945–54', *TCBH*, 19:1, 2000, pp. 61–82.

139. Mass Observation, *Journey Home*, p. 62.

140. Peniston-Bird, C. M., 'The People's War in Personal Testimony and Bronze. Sorority and the Memorial to the Women of World War II', in Noakes, L. & Pattinson, J., *British Cultural Memory and the Second World War* (London: Bloomsbury, 2014).

141. See Jones, H., *Women in British Public Life, 1914–50. Gender, Power and Social Policy* (London: Longman, 2000), pp. 179–206, 244–5.

142. Purnell, S., *First Lady. The Life and Wars of Clementine Churchill* (London: Aurum Press, 2015), p. 202.

143. Harrisson, T., 'Appeals to Women', *Political Quarterly*, 13:3, 1942, p. 279.

144. Pedersen, S., *Eleanor Rathbone and the Politics of Conscience* (London: Yale University Press, 2004), pp. 364–6.

145. For criticism of the Beveridge Report for 'denying to the married woman, rich or poor, housewife or paid worker, an independent personal status', see Abbott, E. & Bompas, K., *The Woman Citizen and Social Security* (London: Mrs Bompas, 1943), p. 3.

146. Zweiniger-Bargielowska, I., & Francis, M., *The Conservatives and British Society, 1880–1990* (Cardiff: University of Wales Press, 1996), p. 198. Cf. McKibbin, *Parties and People*, p. 173, note 91.

147. Norris, P., 'Gender: a gender-generation gap?', in Evans, G. & Norris, P. (eds), *Critical Elections. British Parties and Voters in Long-Term Perspective* (London: Sage, 1999), pp. 156–7.

148. Bowden, S. & Offer, A., 'Household Appliances and the Use of Time; the United States and Britain Since the 1920s', *Economic History Review*, 47, 1994, p. 734.

149. Craig, F. W., *British General Election Manifestos, 1900–1974* (London: Macmillan, 1975), pp. 128–9.

150. McCarthy, H., 'Social Science and Married Women's Employment', *P & P*, 26:1, 2016, pp. 269–305.

151. Craig, *British General Election Manifestos*, Labour Party manifesto, 1950, p. 126.

152. *Ibid.*, Conservative Party manifesto, 1955, p. 166.

153. *Ibid.*, Labour Party manifestos, 1964, 1966, pp. 229, 276.

154. Morley, E., *The 'Miss World' Story* (Maidstone: Angley Books, 1967), pp. 216–17.

155. Conekin, B., Mort, F. & Waters, C. (eds), *Moments of Modernity. Reconstructing Britain, 1945–64* (London: Rivers Oram Press, 1999), pp. 1–3, 228–46.

156. Wilson, E. & Taylor, L., *Through the Looking Glass: A History of Dress from 1860 to the Present* (London: BBC Books, 1989), pp. 149–52.

157. Young, M. & Wilmott, P., *Family and Kinship in East London* (London: Routledge & Kegan Paul, 1957), pp. 39–40.

158. Jackson, L., *Women Police: Gender, Welfare and Surveillance in the Twentieth Century* (Manchester University Press, 2006), pp. 179–81; Laite, J. A., 'The Association for Moral

and Social Hygiene: Abolitionism and Prostitution Law in Britain (1915–59)', *WHR*, 17, 2008, p. 219.

159. Gavron, H., *The Captive Wife: Conflicts of Housebound Mothers* (London: Routledge & Kegan Paul, 1966), pp. 132–3.

160. Christie, J., 'Everybody's darling', in Maitland, S. (ed.), *Very Heaven: Looking Back at the 1960s* (London: Virago, 1988), p. 171.

161. *The Times*, 19 April 1969.

162. Smith, H., 'The Politics of Conservative Reform: The Equal Pay for Equal Work Issue, 1945–55', *HJ*, 25, 1992.

163. See Davis, A., *Modern Motherhood. Women and Family in England, 1945–2000* (Manchester University Press, 2012).

164. Thane, P., 'Women and the 1970s: Towards liberation?' in Black, L., Pemberton, H. & Thane, P. (eds), *Reassessing 1970s Britain* (Manchester University Press, 2013), p. 171.

165. Setch, E., 'The Faces of Metropolitan Feminism: The London Women's Liberation Workshop, 1969–79', *TCBH*, 13:2, 2002, pp. 171–90.

166. Carter, A., 'Notes from the Front Line', in Michelene Wandor (ed.), *On Gender and Writing* (London: Pandora, 1983), p. 70.

167. Rowbotham, S., *A Century of Women. The History of Women in Britain and the United States* (London: Viking, 1997), p. 493.

168. Connolly, S. & Gregory, M., 'Women and Work since 1970' in Crafts, N., Gazeley, I. & Newell, A. (eds), *Work and Pay in 20th Century Britain* (Oxford University Press, 2007), pp. 160–5.

169. Wolf, A., *The XX Factor. How Women are Creating a New Society* (London: Profile Books Ltd, 2013), p. 140.

170. Letter from Godsman, D., *The Independent*, 10 March, 2008.

171. Pizzey, E., *Scream Quietly or the Neighbours will Hear* (Harmondsworth: Penguin, 1974).

172. Quoted in Phillips, A., *Divided Loyalties: Dilemmas of Sex and Class* (London: Virago, 1987), p. 117.

173. Scottish Press Conference, 26 April 1979, MTFW 104045, quoted in Beers, L., 'Thatcher and the Women's Vote', Jackson, B. & Saunders, R. (eds), *Making Thatcher's Britain* (Cambridge University Press, 2012), p. 119.

174. *Ibid.*, pp. 113–31.

175. Thatcher, *The Downing Street Years*, p. 151.

176. *Ibid.*, pp. 364–5.

177. Murray, J., *The Woman's Hour* (London: BBC Books, 1996), p. 199.

178. See Criddle, B., 'MPs and Candidates' in Butler, D. & Kavanagh, D., *The British General Election of 1997* (Basingstoke: Macmillan Press, 1997), pp. 189–91.

179. Nairn, T., 'Gender Goes to the Top of the Agenda', *The Scotsman*, 28 Dec 1994. See L. McAllister, 'Gender, Nation and Party: An Uneasy Alliance for Welsh Nationalism', *WHR*, 10, 2001 for the more hotly contested negotiations on women's representation in Plaid Cymru, which had never elected a woman MP or Member of the European Parliament before 1999.

180. Nick Cohen in the *Observer*, 23 November 1997.

181. Lister, R., 'The Third Way's social investment state', in Lewis, J. & Surinder, R. (eds), *Welfare State Change. Towards a Third Way* (Oxford University Press, 2004); Shaw, E., *Losing Labour's Soul? New Labour and the Blair Government, 1997–2007* (London: Routledge, 2007), pp. 49–50.

182. Harrison, B., 'Women in a Men's House. The Women MPs, 1919–1945', *HJ*, 29:3 1986, p. 636.

183. Blaxill, L. & Beelen, K., 'A Feminized Language of Democracy? the Representation of Women at Westminster Since 1945', *TCBH*, 27:3, 2016, pp. 412–19.

184. Sones, B., Moran, M.C. & Lovenduski, J., *Women in Parliament: The New Suffragettes* (London: Politico's, 2005), pp. 154–95.

185. McCarthy, H., 'Gender equality' in Thane, P. (ed.), *Equalities in Britain since 1945* (London: Continuum, 2010), pp. 112–13.

186. McBride Stetson, D., 'Women's movements in defence of legal abortion in Great Britain', in Stetson (ed.), *Abortion Politics, Women's Movements and the Democratic State: A Comparative Theory of State Feminism* (Oxford University Press, 2003); Williamson, A., 'The Law and Politics of Marital Rape in England, 1945–94', *WHR*, 26:3, 2016, pp. 382–413.

187. See Schulz, *The WLM: Impacts and Outcomes*, for transnational case studies on that theme.

188. Gillis & Munford, 'Genealogies and Generations', pp. 168–74.

189. McRobbie, A., *The Aftermath of Feminism. Gender, Culture and Social Change* (London: SAGE, 2009).

190. Walby, S. & Short, C., *New Agendas for Women* (Basingstoke: Macmillan, 1999).

191. King, O., 'Why we still need feminism', in Walters, N. (ed.), *On the Move. Feminism for a New Generation* (London: Virago, 1999), pp. 48–61.

192. McRobbie, *Aftermath of Feminism*, pp. 152–6.

193. Available at www.womensequality.org.uk

194. Addison, *No Turning Back*, pp. 259–410.

195. Available at www.fawcettsociety.org.uk.

196. See, for example, successive editions of Susie Orbach's *Fat Is A Feminist Issue* (London, 1978; latest edn, Arrow Books, 2016).

  i. Note to Figure 2: Purnell, S., *First Lady. The Life and Wars of Clementine Churchill* (London: 2015); Harrison, B., 'Churchill, Clementine Ogilvy Spencer, [*née* Clementine Ogilvy Hozier], Baroness Spencer-Churchill (1885–1977)', *Oxford Dictionary of National Biography*. Available at https://ezproxy-prd.bodleian.ox.ac.uk:4563/10.1093/ref:odnb/30929.

  ii. Note to Figure 3.iii: Callander, J., 'Garrod, Dorothy Annie Elizabeth (1892–1968)', *ODNB*. Available at https://ezproxy-prd.bodleian.ox.ac.uk:4563/10.1093/ref:odnb/37443.

  iii. Note to Figure 3.iv: In the *Observer* and *Daily Telegraph*, quoted in Ferry, G., *Dorothy Hodgkin. A Life.* (London: Bloomsbury Reader, 2014), p. 359.

  iv. Note to Figure 4: Jivani, A., *It's Not Unusual; a History of Lesbian and Gay Britain in the Twentieth Century* (London: Michael O'Mara Books, 1997), pp. 133–4.

  v. Note to Figure 5: See Miller, C., 'Geneva – the Key to Equality. Interwar Feminists and the League of Nations', *WHR*, 3:2, 1994, pp. 219–45.

  vi. Note to Figure 7: See McCrone, K., *Sport and the Physical Emancipation of Englishwomen* (London: 1988) and 'Emancipation or Recreation? The Development of Women's Sport at the University of London', *International Journal of the History of Sport*, 7, 1990.

Chapter 1

Class, Region and Ethnicity

1. i   The economist Mabel Atkinson (1876–1958) explains why middle and working-class women have different perspectives on the 'right to work'.

Mabel Atkinson, *The Economic Foundations of the Women's Movement* (1914).

At the present time there are two main sections in the modern women's movement – the movement of the middle class women who are revolting against their exclusion from human activity and insisting, firstly, on their right to education, which is now practically conceded on all sides; secondly, on their right to earn a livelihood for themselves, which is rapidly being won; and thirdly, on their right to share in the control of Government .... These women are primarily rebelling against the sex-exclusiveness of men, and regard independence and the right to work as the most valuable privileges to be striven for.

On the other hand, there are the women of the working classes, who have been faced with a totally different problem, and who naturally react in a different way. Parasitism has never been forced on them. Even when the working class woman does not earn her own living in the world of industry – though practically all the unmarried girls of the working classes do so – her activities at home are so unending, and she subconsciously feels so important and so valuable, that she has never conceived of herself as useless and shut out from human interests, as was the parasitic middle class woman. What the woman of the proletariat feels as her grievance is that her work is too long and too monotonous, the burden laid upon her too heavy ....Therefore, among the working women there is less sex consciousness .... The working woman feels her solidarity with the men of her class rather than their antagonism to her. The reforms that she demands are not independence and the right to work, but rather protection against the unending burden of toil which has been laid upon her. A speaker at a working women's congress said once, 'It is not work we want, but more love, more leisure to enjoy life, and more beauty.'

(Reprinted in S. Alexander (ed.), *Women's Fabian Tracts*: London: Routledge, 1988, pp. 270–1).

1. ii   Novelist Naomi Mitchison (1897–1999), a long-standing Labour supporter, recalls how the need for domestic servants was taken for granted in the early twentieth century.

Naomi Mitchison, 'The class structure as it seemed to us', *You May Well Ask. A Memoir, 1920–1940* (1979).

Before World War I and with a hangover into the Twenties at least, middle- or professional-class housing depended on having servants to cook, clean and generally take charge. Most houses, especially the older ones, had this as their norm. Now this pattern of having servants is probably the strangest part of our lives for those two generations on who may well find the idea not only embarrassing but definitely shocking. Too bad. For us, in what I suppose I should call the upper middle class, having servants was part of the normal pattern of life. We took it for granted.

For me the servant basis meant that I could have parties, without having to think about the washing up, in the ground-floor dining room and the very pretty L-shaped drawing room on the first floor of 17 Cheyne Walk [in Chelsea] …. Above this was our bedroom with a lovely view across the trees and the river, off it a dressing room usually serving as a child's room, and a bathroom. On the floor above was the nursery …. Behind it a double and crowded maids' room. I am sure another bathroom was squeezed in but after a couple of years we added a storey … , for by then we had two children and another on the way, as well as cook, housemaid, parlour maid and nurse …

The Twenties and Thirties were a curious transitional period for women who were for a few decades free of the household chores which had been thought for so long to be women's work. Quite a number of women took advantage of this new freedom to write, paint, do scientific or historical research, become doctors, lawyers and so on. I was one. Clearly without domestic help I could not have had a family and been a successful writer ….

I am fairly sure that my household staff were on the whole happy and felt they were doing a worthwhile job, skilled enough to be satisfying, not very arduous and more secure than many an industrial job at that time. I have discussed this since with intelligent women who were in domestic service, though today with more education they might have been in offices or shops. What mattered to them was that their mistress should be 'a lady'. What qualities did that imply? Being considerate, not putting on airs, willingness to help, patience, humour, but also some degree of apparent worth and leadership.

(London: Victor Gollancz, 1979, pp. 19, 27–8).

I. iii   A less optimistic view of the servant's lot was taken in the 1920s by the psychologist Violet Firth (1890–1946).

Violet Firth, *The Psychology of the Servant Problem* (1925).

No one can deny that girls from working-class homes show the strongest possible disinclination to take up domestic service, especially that which includes 'living in' in private houses; there is less disinclination for service in hotels and boarding-houses, and still less for daily work; but even at its best domestic service has an evil reputation among those who are in the best position to know its conditions, i.e. the servant class themselves.

The employer class, on the other hand, cannot understand this reluctance, thinks it absurd and prejudiced …. The material conditions of domestic service are, nowadays, better than those of many trades that draw girls away from the kitchen; the girl engaged in housework has good food, good housing, and far more spare cash than the girl who keeps herself out of her earnings. What factory hand or shop assistant could afford to live at the same standard as the domestic servant and still have thirty odd pounds a year pocket money? …

The problem is a psychological one, not a material one …. To be a servant is very painful to one's self-respect, and no amount of money will compensate that injury to anyone who has independence of spirit; education fosters independence of spirit. and therefore reduces the number of those willing to be humiliated. A mistress does not demand of her servant work only, she also demands a certain manner, a manner which shall clearly indicate her superiority and the inferiority of the woman who takes her wages …. The girl who accepts this position is despised by the girl who has found a trade in which she can sell her labour without selling her independence, hence the contempt in which servants are held by their own class.

(London: The C. W. Daniel Co., 1925, pp. 18–22).

1. iv   Oral history testimony shows why domestic service nevertheless had attractions for Irish and Welsh women migrating to English cities.

Catherine Ridgeway, in M. Lennon, M. McAdam & J. O'Brien (eds), *Across the Water. Irish Women's Lives in Britain* (1988).

I went back to Dublin with the family in 1922 and I got work as a kitchen maid. But I was getting fed up with living in the Row. There was a factory at the back and they demolished two big huts which scattered a whole load of rats into our houses, and in the meantime we'd developed bugs as well .... Then my aunt encouraged me to go to London, so I came in 1928 ...

I thought London was a great place .... I got a job as a chambermaid in a commercial hotel off Tottenham Court Road ... and then moved on to two or three other places, all chambermaid jobs. There were lots of Irish and Welsh girls in that type of work. I had to have somewhere I could live-in. I think that was the object of a lot of girls. It was another reason for so many nurses coming from Ireland, because it was just as difficult then to rent a flat or a room as it is today. So we all took jobs where you were assured of your bed and board.

Well, as a chambermaid, you'd be up in the morning about seven and you'd have to go around first with tea trays and then with jugs of hot water as there were no washbasins in small hotels at that time .... You might have ... a couple of hours off in the afternoon. But you'd be back again in the evening to lay out nightdresses and pyjamas and see that everything in the room was all right .... It would be about 9 o'clock at night before you'd finish. You'd have a half-day a week off and a half-day on Sunday, and the wages were ten shillings a week ...

Then I moved into a block of service flats .... The conditions were better but you had long hours just the same. Now, I got my break by leaving the block of flats .... I got into the Oxford and Cambridge Club in Pall Mall. The linen keeper's job was to issue the clean linen out to the chambermaids and send it out to the laundry. You checked it when it came in and did any repairs .... You assisted the housekeeper and when she was off-duty, took her place. I got £1 a week ....

During that period I didn't mix much with Irish people. Mostly English. I think my aunt and uncle put me off. They said, 'Don't get involved in Irish clubs or anything like that', because there was still the political background .... you always had at the back of your mind that if anything crops up and you are involved, you might be deported or something like this. And I never wanted to leave London. I went home regularly, but I saw England as my home.

(London: Virago, 1988, pp. 48–50).

i. v The formalities of etiquette in the leisured classes are set out in this manual, first published in 1926 and last reprinted in 1958. Laura Troubridge (1866–1946), a member of the well-connected Gurney family, was a popular novelist married to Sir Thomas H. Cochrane Troubridge (Bart).

Lady Troubridge, *The Book of Etiquette* (1931 edn).

Calls and Calling

Calling has become a very important part of social life, and if its rules are neglected ... the result is not only to lessen the number of one's friends, but to show an ignorance of the rules which govern society ....

The matter of paying the first call is often a delicate one .... The following rules will help those ... who are anxious to follow the correct usage and thus avoid blunders that may result in broken friendships.

The newcomer to a country neighbourhood must wait for older residents to call upon her. If she has friends who can vouch for her and who will write to one of her neighbours saying, 'Mrs Smith has come to live near you. She is an old friend of mine and such a charming woman', or something to that effect, it is all to the good for the newcomer.

A bride waits to be called upon after her return from the honeymoon.

When two ladies meet at the house of a friend it is for the lady of highest rank or superior social position to make the first advance. She should say, 'I should so much like to come and see you,' and should call shortly after, or this advance may be met with, 'That would be delightful – but won't you come to tea? I should be so sorry to be out when you came'; or the more important or older lady might say, 'Do come and see me. I am always in to tea' or 'after five,' or 'on Thursdays,' as the case may be ...

A mutual friend of two ladies may say, 'I do so wish you knew Mrs. So-and-So – shall I ask her to call?' In these ways the social circle is enlarged.

Presentation at Court

Presentation to the King and Queen at a Court at Buckingham Palace marks the formal and official entry of the young girl into society, and again as a bride after her marriage. Those entitled to be presented at Court are the wives and daughters of the members of the aristocracy, the wives and daughters of those holding high official appointments in the Government, the wives and daughters of Members of Parliament, the county gentry, the town gentry, the wives and daughters of the naval and military officers, of the legal, clerical, medical and other professions, the wives and daughters of merchants, bankers, and of members of the Stock Exchange, and the wives and daughters of men engaged in commerce on a large scale.

The Courts are held in the evening. A presentation can only be made by a lady who has herself been presented ....

Dress for a Court

At the present time a train not more than two yards long and a veil surmounted by three feathers are the essentials of Court dress. A bouquet and fan, or both, are matters of personal choice.

(Kingswood, Surrey: The World's Work, 1931, pp. 80, 83–4, 152, 159).

1. vi   In the third volume of Grassic Gibbon's trilogy (*Grey Granite*) the heroine, Chris Guthrie, is reduced to helping run a boarding house in one of Scotland's industrial cities. A minister's widow, she retains her distinction as 'gentry'.

Lewis Grassic Gibbon, *A Scots Quair* (1932–4; 1998 edn).

Ma said, coming down to Chris in the kitchen after collecting the lodgers' fees, she went round each room of a Sabbath morning before the breakfast time or the kirk: *The Murgatroyd creature's fair in a stew, her dividends are all going down she says and she hardly knows how she'll Pay her Way. She's a bittie of a shareholder in Gowans and Gloag's and there's not a cent from the firm this year. Aren't they brutes to mistreat a respectable woman?*

Chris asked if that meant that she'd have to leave, and Ma shook her head. Oh no, not her, she'd a bit of a pension as well as an income, a three hundred pounds a year from a trust. Chris stared: *Then what's coming over her?* and Ma sighed that Chris didn't understand and hadn't a proper sympathy, like, with financial straits of wealthy folk – like herself and their wee Miss Murgatroyd ...

And Ma sat down ... smoothing out the pounds and the ten bob notes .... *Four, five, two halves, a one and ten silver, that's our little bit English pussy-cat. Sitting up there and reading a book – can you guess what the book is about now, lass? ... Well, then, it's a Manual of Birth Control.*

What think you of that and our Ellen Johns ... ? ... And it's all to the good of the trade, anyhow. Chris asked *How?* and Ma said *Why, she'll be able to sin as she likes and go free, with no need to marry .... So we'll be able to keep her our lodger .... Twelve, thirteen, ten, Ake Ogilvie – ay, faith, he's made of the old-time stuff ... a bonny man, well-shouldered and canty, it's a pity you're gentry.*

Chris had heard this before now hardly smiled, if it was gentry to know her own mind, the things that she liked and the things that she didn't, well then, she was gentry down to the core. And Ma ... cried out *Hoots now, now don't go away and take offence. I'm just a coarse old wife and must have my bit joke ...* and went on with her counting ...

(Reprinted: London: Penguin, 1998, pp. 407–8).

1. vii   Travelling through England during the inter-war depression, J. B. Priestley (1894–1984) was struck by the regional effects of economic change. Teesside represents the England of the industrial revolution, by contrast with the new consumer society of the South.

J. B. Priestley, *English Journey* (1934).

To East Durham and the Tees

I met some of [the miners'] wives, sitting round a fire in a sewing circle. They were worn but neat and smiling women, mostly on the small side. Their frank talk about their men's wages was not pleasant to listen to. They were glad to see me and were neither resentful nor whining, but nevertheless they made me feel like a fat rich man .... The younger women among those miners' wives were emphatic on one subject. *Their* sons were not going into the pits. No more coal-mining in the family for them. And when a North-country woman begins a statement with '*My lad*' in that tone of voice, you may depend upon it that unless her lad is peculiarly obstinate he will not do what she says he must not do. In these parts the women have far more influence than they would appear to have at first .... It is generally assumed among them that although men have the muscle and perhaps, for contriving, arguing, book-learning purposes, the brains, women have the *sense* the *gumption* .... It is not because a pitman's life is hard and dangerous. These women, the wives and daughters of pitmen ... know all about that and are ready to take the chances their mothers took. But they see no reason why their lads should work in the pits for wages that look more like pocket-money than real pay.

7

To the End

The new post-war England [belongs] far more to the age itself than to this particular island. America, I supposed, was its real birthplace. This is the England of arterial and by-pass roads, of filling stations and factories that look like exhibition buildings, of giant cinemas and dance-halls and cafes, bungalows with tiny garages, cocktail bars, Woolworths, motor-coaches, wireless, hiking, factory girls looking like actresses, greyhound racing and dirt tracks, swimming pools, and everything given away for cigarette coupons .... It is, of course, essentially democratic .... In this England, for the first time in history, Jack and Jill are nearly as good as their master and mistress .... Jack, like his master, is rapidly transported to some place of rather mechanical amusement. Jill beautifies herself exactly as her mistress does.

(Reprinted: London: Mandarin, 1994, pp. 332–4, 401–2).

1. viii   Elizabeth Andrews, Labour Party organiser in Wales, highlights the region's poverty. In mining areas where there were no jobs for women, there were high rates of maternal mortality as well as TB.

'Wales and her Poverty', *Labour Woman*, July 1939.

For the last few months the Report of the Inquiry into Anti-Tuberculosis Services in Wales and Monmouth has had a great deal of publicity from Press and platforms.

We know that there are several factors that account for this disease, but we also know, as Socialists, that poverty is one of the chief causes ...

The women are blamed by some, and are told they do not know how to cook, but the average woman's reply is: 'Give us something to cook, and we will show you that we can do it.'

Low Wages, Unemployment Insurance Benefit and Means Test Allowances allow very little for food, when rent has been paid. So we maintain that poverty is the main factor. Nutrition and environment depend on wages.

Tuberculosis attacks the young particularly .... Our adolescents are not having the quantity and quality of food that nature needs for body building. Right food is the essential basis for the health of our future citizens. Young mothers die from TB because of the strain of motherhood under poverty.

(Reprinted in U. Masson (ed.), Elizabeth Andrews, *A Woman's
Work is Never Done: and political articles*: Dinas Powys: Honno,
2006, pp. 110–11).

1. ix   Government concern to boost rates of saving lay behind this
war-time survey, which revealed interesting regional variations in the
distribution of income within families.

'Family Income', in Charles Madge, *War-time Patterns of Saving and
Spending* (1943).

We have treated family income as a single whole .... But in practice, it is
usually divided into two parts – 'Housekeeping Money' and 'Pocket-Money'.
The husband either gives his wife her housekeeping allowance and retains
the rest of his earnings for his own private use; or else he may, less commonly,
give her the whole contents of his wage-packet, receiving back an allowance
of pocket-money ...

Of all the main earners in Glasgow, 14% were giving all their weekly
earnings to the housewife .... In Bristol 11% of the main earners gave *all* their
earnings; in Bradford, 15%; in York, 7%; in Slough, 5%. For Leeds the figure was 24%, but in this are included families where full information about
spending showed that give and take between husband and wife was so great
that income was virtually pooled. Only in Blackburn was the situation different: there we found 49% of the main earners giving all their earnings
to the housewife. I believe that if we had tested other Lancashire cotton
towns we would have found that they, like Blackburn, were exceptional in
this respect. In other parts of industrial Britain, our evidence suggests that it
is the husband who is the dominant economic figure. The contrast between
Lancashire and the West Riding is all the more interesting because they are
both textile areas, where women, including married women, are, and have
long been, mobilized for industry in a special degree .... It is certainly my
impression that women are the dominant personalities of Lancashire, and
men of Yorkshire; but why this should be remains a problem in anthropology.
(N.I.E.S.R. Occasional Papers, 14, Cambridge,
Cambridge University Press, pp. 52–3).

1. x   The Polish sociologist Ferdynand Zweig was among the first to
explore the meaning of class to working-class women, in interviews
carried out mainly in London and the North of England.

Ferdynand Zweig, 'Class Consciousness', from *Women's Life and Labour* (1952).

Perhaps I ought to say from the outset that a working-class girl has very
vague ideas on the whole subject [of class]. It would be better to describe

them as feelings and attitudes rather than ideas in the strict sense. She has rarely thought about it, and in many cases it is all new to her ...

She would often think of the whole matter as invidious, and somehow linked with the hateful snobbery of class distinctions .... She will tell you at once: 'I am as good as anybody else. The only difference is money'. If you ask: 'Do you regard yourself as working-class?' the answer in the majority of cases would be: 'I suppose so', but with a touch of regret that such a question was asked ...

The element of aspiration is much stronger than the factual element. The first thing a woman would say when the subject is discussed would be: 'There should be no class distinctions' ...

This element of aspiration is much stronger among young girls than older women for understandable reasons .... Young girls expect or hope that they will be able to cross the borderline of their class by marriage. Marriage, not work or study, is the main door of escape from class membership, and the status of a woman is primarily determined by the status of her husband .... However, it is different with older women who have acquired a definite status by marriage and know where they stand by now. The middle-aged spinster approaches in many respects the position of a man. Her status is largely her own doing, if not determined by the status of her parents.

Men's class consciousness contains the idea of class solidarity: the working class has interests of its own which need defending in opposition to other classes .... That is rarely encountered among women .... Their range of vision is much narrower; they do not think in those broad terms; they see their family, their friends, their locality but rarely beyond that. Only rarely do you find working-class women with definite awareness of class solidarity, and then it is mainly those better educated ('blue-stockings'), or with no family responsibilities or married to trade unionists and to politically minded men ...

Women see themselves primarily as consumers, not as workers. A job plays a much smaller part in women's life than in men's life, even if they go out to work, but all of them are primarily concerned in making both ends meets ...

Working-class women divide themselves not so much by the jobs their husbands do – and still less by the jobs they themselves do – but rather by ways of life .... The main line of division is respectability, and the sense of respectability, i.e. conformity to accepted standards, is much stronger among women than men. A labourer's wife, if she is respectable and leads a clean and reasonable life, doing her bit and coping sensibly with adversities, is much more respected and classed higher in the social hierarchy than a craftsman's wife who leads the irresponsible life of a waster.

To 'know the value of money' is the main virtue, and many working-class women have actually the mentality of middle-class males …

The working-class girl can be first discerned by the way she speaks, not so much by the way she dresses …. All the same it is not too difficult to distinguish between a working-class and a middle-class girl by appearance, perhaps not so much by their looks as by the characteristic expression of the face …. In fact, the sense of inferiority of working-class women is so strong that this in itself can be the distinguishing mark of the class but it hardly finds its conscious expression in discussion, which is all the time centred on aspirations.

(London: Gollancz, 1952, pp. 121–5).

I. xi   Questionnaires completed by readers (mainly working and lower-middle class) of a popular Sunday newspaper the *People* formed the basis of this survey carried out by the freelance social anthropologist Geoffrey Gorer.

Geoffrey Gorer, *Exploring English Character* (1955).

Nine out of ten English people feel no hesitation in assigning themselves to a social class …

It would seem that … women at home take their class position from their parents, and, after marriage, from their husbands: a married woman from a small town near Southampton describes herself as 'Low class by up-bringing (since marriage I should say middle class)'; and a 20-year-old girl from Studley in Warwickshire, with some university education writes 'Middle class, i.e. I come from a decent family and have had a good (average) education. I have never worked in a factory not that I should mind doing so I am not snobbish.'

If a woman's social class depends on that of the man who is the head of the household, then what is the status of the spinster living alone or of the widow? It would seem to be indeterminate, and it is precisely from these groups that most of our claimants to middle class status derive …. Far more women than men claim middle class status: 33 per cent of the women compared with 21 per cent of the men in the main sample …. But, at least in the main sample, women have consistently more secondary and university level education than men …. It seems at least possible that about one woman in ten receives some vocational training in school for such jobs as secretaries, while their brothers are serving an apprenticeship in the works; and that, during this training, and in their subsequent pre-marriage employment in offices, they acquire an, as it were, professional middle class status which they may not always relinquish at marriage, even though their husbands call themselves working class, and which they cling to in spinsterhood and widowhood.

(London: Cresset Press, 1955, pp. 34, 37–8).

I. xii   Margaret Stacey's sociological study of an Oxfordshire town analyses attitudes to neighbours among working and middle-class housewives.

Margaret Stacey, *Tradition and Change. A Study of Banbury* (1960).

It is often said that the poorest people are the most neighbourly and this is widely believed both by those who are poor and those who are not. 'I suppose it is because they live on top of each other' remarked one house-wife on a post-war housing estate …

The wife of the weekly-wage-earner, who buys in goods as they are needed and who has neither large stocks nor resources, is more dependent than the middle-class housewife. The wage-earner's wife may need to bor-row if there is some unusual demand and it is from the neighbours that she borrows. A mutual dependence develops …. Since it is the poor and the bad manager who borrow most frequently, to be independent of your neigh-bours in this sense is a mark of prestige. Mrs Morgan in Tracey Avenue said: 'My mother taught me not to rely on other people.' …

The working-class concept of neighbouring in fact changes with sta-tus …. Within the working class in Banbury there are three status groups: the 'rough', the 'ordinary', and the 'respectable'. The self-styled 'ordinary working-class people' … follow closest the traditional concept of neighbour-ing. The 'roughs' … and the 'respectables' … deviate most from it.

The 'roughs', often the poorest families, would like to lean heavily upon their neighbours but they are discouraged. Their personal appearance and the state of their houses add to their unattractiveness as companions. The 'respectables', on the other hand, are not expelled, they withdraw; they are 'stand-offish'. They are bent on improving their own social positions and intimate neighbouring is part of the life of the social class they wish to leave behind.

The middle class are far less dependent on their neighbours for borrowing, for they have greater resources. Further, they depend less on their neighbours as a group from which to pick their friends. They have friends in other parts of the town and more frequently belong to associations. Even the young mother tied to the house may talk to friends by telephone and she can 'phone the shops or the doctor in a crisis .... Generally, borrowing and lending is in non-essentials: an exchange of cuttings for the garden, keeping an eye on the house when its occupants are on holiday, perhaps baby-sitting.

(Oxford: Oxford University Press, 1960, pp. 104–6).

1. xiii   The feminist social scientist Gail Lewis, daughter of a Jamaican father and an English mother, remembers her childhood in North London. (For more recent thoughts on the subject see her 'Birthing Racial Difference; conversations with my mother and others', in *Studies in the Maternal*, 1, 2009; www.mamsie.bbk.ac.uk.)

Gail Lewis, 'From Deepest Kilburn' in Liz Heron (ed.), *Truth, Dare or Promise. Girls Growing Up in the 50s* (1985).

The first home I remember was a basement flat at number 61 Granville Road, Kilburn. We lived there until 1960 and so my memories of the 1950s are split between that house and that of my Mum's mum who lived in Harrow on a late-twenties council estate .... The Granville Road ... house, a big late-Victorian terrace, was let as a tenement ... to black people, mostly Jamaicans .... My Mum was the only white person who lived in the whole house, a point not unnoticed by me since I often asked her how come she lived there with us when everyone else was black – or brown as I would have said then. As she would later remind me, children can say very painful things ...

We had two rooms and a kitchen, with our own outside toilet .... We had no bathroom at all in the whole house but there were public baths and a laundry at the end of the road so we would have our weekly bath there, and in the week have a full wash-down in the sink. We children were always told to emphasise the 'full' of the wash lest people think we were dirty, and given that most white people thought all black people were dirty it was a counter to any racialist-type thoughts that people might be harbouring. This may seem pretty elaborate when you consider that this was the situation for most people in the street and that the white working class had a tradition of 'proving' their cleanliness too. But it's illustrative of the way in which 'race' and prejudice serve to fracture the working class and make for an inability to share common experiences. In this case there was a kind of cleanliness chart, and we black people and Mum were aiming to be at the top ...

Our house was in fact firebombed during the 1958 Notting Hill riots ... luckily there were people at home and they put out the fire right away. But it did serve to make everyone acutely aware of the potential danger we were in. We children were kept under lock and key and I was sent up to my Nan's for a few days until it cooled down a bit ...

The difference between the Jamaican and English aspects of my life at that time often revolved round food. Saturdays really exemplified it. Saturday-morning breakfast would usually be fried dumpling and egg or saltfish fritters, sometimes sardine. If it was at my Nan's it would be cornflakes or porridge, the Scottish way, with salt – my Grandad was from Edinburgh. Then for Saturday dinnertime (lunch) my Mum would let me go and have pie, mash and liquor at the pie and mash shop. She would give me a shilling and I would go off and eat this very English working-class food sitting on a wooden bench at a marble table. I was the only black person in the shop .... Dinner in the evening would be either saltfish and ackee ... home-made oxtail or pea soup, or maybe pigs' trotters and rice ...

In my case most of the family or household events were racially mixed occasions. The kind of 1960s integrationist dream, where we can all dance together, all eat 'ethnic', be beatifically patronising (as only the English know how) and become the 'experts' on black people. Nevertheless, they were important ... times and served to distinguish between those white relatives who would have nothing to do with us and those in whose houses we were welcomed. That division still exists today ...

(London: Virago, pp. 213–16, 221–6).

1. xiv   The isolation experienced by immigrant women from the Indian subcontinent is analysed by the writer and political activist Amrit Wilson.

Amrit Wilson, *Finding a Voice. Asian Women in Britain* (1978).

Rezia Begum is forty one. She lives in a street near Russell Square. There is no bell on the door, To get in I and the friend who is taking me hammer and hammer on the door, shout over and over again in Bengali "It's us, it's us, let us in". These precautions are essential because of the danger of racial attacks. Finally Rezia throws the keys down from an upstairs window .... We go up several flights of stairs to the room where Rezia lives with her husband and son. It isn't large: two wide beds almost fill it. There is almost no other furniture. Clothes hang on a line at one side of the room. In one corner is a gas ring, in another a table with some school books on it. The room is tidy, a few pictures decorate the walls.

Rezia spends almost all her time in this room. She rarely goes out and has never been beyond the street she lives in on her own. She speaks no English and knows hardly anyone. In her first year in Britain no one visited her. Her husband is a restaurant worker. He is out all day from 11 am to midnight ...

The isolation and emptiness of Rezia's life is typical of what many Asian women in Britain face. Those who have come from a joint family in India, Pakistan or Bangladesh to live alone with their husbands in Britain suffer most ...

Isolation is seen from the outside as a result of women not speaking English, or of being forced to stay at home for cultural reasons. But it is much more than this. It is a state of mind, one of shock and withdrawal. Weakened by the separation from their families ... these Asian women find themselves in a strange unknown society. The realisation that this is a racist society, a society which wishes them dead for the colour of their skin, accentuates their loneliness, and their isolation in turn makes it harder for them to fight against racism ...

What young mothers suffer from almost more than anything else is having constant responsibility for their children. In Bangladesh children under the age of five or six are looked after by the whole family. All the children in the joint family are looked after together. They are taken to the pond for a bath perhaps by one daughter-in-law, and she baths them all. Then they all come in and sit down to eat. Perhaps the youngest daughter in law has cooked the meal. Another woman feeds them. As for playing, children play out of doors with natural objects .... Maybe there is a favourite aunt, she tells them ... stories. But at night when they get sleepy they always go to their mother and sleep in her embrace. But other women ... have such strong relationships with the child that it is not uncommon for them to be called Big Mother or Small Mother. Here, in Britain, the attitude of women is quite different; they may say why should another woman look after my baby or even touch my baby ...

Often Asian women coming from joint families in the Indian subcontinent to join their husbands in Britain do succeed in making the necessary emotional adjustment, but for many of them it takes months if not years; for some coping with the total emotional dependence on the husband alone is just not possible.

(London: Virago, 1978, pp. 16–17, 20–1, 25–7).

I. xv The position of women in the class structure, much debated amongst feminists in the 1970s and after, is here discussed by the sociologist Ann Oakley.

Ann Oakley, *Subject Women* (1981).

In 1911 … mortality among the babies of unskilled men was twice that among the babies of upper-class men …. In 1977 there was a similar gap: the perinatal mortality rate of social class V (classified on the basis of father's occupation) families was 22 per 1000 live births and in social class I it was 11 …. These social class differences in perinatal mortality fit into a general pattern of social inequalities in health and illness …

In Marxist theory social classes are defined by their relation to the means of production …. Women have been seen as having only one kind of attachment to the class structure, and that is through the mediation of the male head of the family …. There is no escaping the fact that the Marxist approach to women's situation under capitalism is fatally weakened by androcentrism. Are women, then, a class on their own? Like relations between different ethnic groups, those between men and women are characterized by a permanent caste-like status: neither one's 'race' nor one's sex are categories that can be disowned …

Yet … if women are a separate class from the point of view of the gender structure, then there must be some similarity … in the way all women relate to all men …. However, it is a somewhat crucial aspect of women's position that the relations of different women in different social groups to men are rather different …

Another difficulty with the argument that women are a class is that it disputes the centrality of their own relations to the means of production. Unless two different concepts of class are distinguished – that of 'gender' class and that of 'economic' class – the problem is insoluble.

(Oxford: Martin Robertson, 1981, pp. 285–6, 289–90).

1. xvi   Two social scientists review women's perceptions of class in the 1980s.

Pamela Abbott & Roger Sapsford, *Women and Social Class* (1987).

As a crude indicator of the perceived relationship between classes, respondents were asked to choose between two 'attitude items' one of which likened life to a ladder while the other suggested that stability was more desirable; this may be seen as tapping views about the possibility and desirability of social mobility. Seventy per cent seemed to think that mobility was both possible and desirable .... Fewer than 30 per cent thought that conflict between bosses and workers was characteristic of modern Britain ...

A considerable amount of agreement about the nature of the class structure in modern Britain appears to emerge. Over two-thirds of the women in the sample see British society as composed of three or more classes, with a relative absence of class conflict and with social mobility both possible and desirable. Those who diverge from this consensual image are mainly in manual occupations and are likely to define themselves as working-class, but they are a minority even of their group. It seems, then, that the boundaries of class are clearly perceived as far as self-assignment is concerned – women assign themselves 'correctly' to classes on the whole ... ; on the other hand, more consensus than conflict is perceived in the relationship between classes.

(London: Tavistock, 1987, pp. 122–3).

1. xvii   In a classic feminist biography the social historian Carolyn Steedman reflects on memories of her mother, a proud working-class woman.

Carolyn Steedman, *Landscape for a Good Woman* (1986).

We'd known all our childhood that she was a good mother: she'd told us so: we'd never gone hungry; she went out to work for us; we had warm beds to lie in at night ...

Upstairs, a long time ago, she had cried, standing on the bare floorboards in the front bedroom just after we moved to this house in Streatham Hill in 1951, my baby sister in her carry-cot. We both watched the dumpy retreating figure of the health visitor through the curtainless windows. The woman had said: 'This house isn't fit for a baby'. And then she stopped crying, my mother, got by, the phrase that picks up after all difficulty (it says: it's like this; it shouldn't be like this; it's unfair; I'll manage): 'Hard lines, eh, Kay?' (Kay was the name I was called at home ...).

And I? I will do everything and anything until the end of my days to stop anyone ever talking to me like that woman talked to my mother .... I read a woman's book, meet such a woman at a party (a woman now, like me) and think quite deliberately as we talk: we are divided: a hundred years ago I'd have been cleaning your shoes. I know this and you don't.

(London: Virago, 1986, pp. 1–2).

1. xviii   An encounter between women described by the black Scottish poet and novelist Jackie Kay, who grew up as an adopted child in Glasgow.

'In my country', from *Other Lovers. Poems by Jackie Kay* (1993).

> walking by the waters
> down where an honest river
> shakes hands with the sea,
> a woman passed round me
> in a slow watchful circle,
> as if I were a superstition;
>
> or the worst dregs of her imagination,
> so when she finally spoke
> her words spliced into bars
> of an old wheel. A segment of air.
> *Where do you come from?*
> 'Here,' I said. 'Here. These parts.'

(Newcastle upon Tyne: Bloodaxe, p. 24).

Chapter 2

Family and Work

2. i   Clementina Black (1853–1922), social feminist writer and activist, defends working-class wives who choose to go out to work, reporting on research carried out by the Women's Industrial Council.

Clementina Black, *Married Women's Work* (1915).

It is a general opinion and especially, perhaps, among persons of the middle class, that the working for money of married women is to be deplored. That such work is sometimes made necessary by poverty will be conceded, and wives who earn because they must are pitied; while wives who work not for their own or their children's bread, but rather for butter to it, are regarded as at least somewhat blameworthy.

The underlying implication seems to be that a wife and mother who thus works must be withdrawing from the care of her home and her children time and attention of which they are really in need. Pictures rise before the mind of rooms unswept, beds unmade and dishes unwashed, of children hungry, ragged, unkempt and running wild. But when one has personally visited the homes of a good many such women, and when there have passed through one's hands several hundreds of reports … the real facts begin to arrange themselves …

The great mass of married women of the working class now present themselves to me in four groups:-

(A) Those who, although the family income is inadequate, do not earn.
(B) Those who, because the family income is inadequate – whether from lowness of pay, irregularity of work or failure in some way, such as sickness, idleness, drink or desertion on the part of the husband – do earn.
(C) Those who, the family income being reasonably adequate, do not earn.
(D) Those who, although the family income is adequate for the supply of necessities, yet earn.

In Class A ... are to be found the largest number of women whose homes and children are conspicuously neglected .... It is from Class A, rather than from Class B – in which wives do earn – that the gossipers at doorways and the frequenters of public houses are recruited .... Of course it includes also – as do all the groups – many steady, industrious women who are the very prop and mainstay of their households ...

To Class D belong those reprehensible women who could if they chose afford to live upon their husband's earnings but yet devote many of their hours to paid work. As a rule they are highly skilled and well remunerated; many of them pay for domestic help; the great majority buy educational advantages for their children; very often they are able to pay for health-giving holiday outings. Such women are nearly always conspicuously competent and are marked by an independence of mind which I believe to be derived from the consciousness of their power of self-support .... I may add that they themselves have no consciousness of sin, on the contrary, they are proud of their work and unwilling to relinquish it.

(Reprinted: London: Virago, 1983, pp. 1–7).

2. ii   The daughter of a wealthy business man who served as a minister in Lloyd George's wartime coalition, Margaret Rhondda (1883–1958) inherited her father's title. One of the very few women company directors of the time, by 1919 she was on the boards of 33 companies.

Viscountess Rhondda, *This Was My World* (1933).

When my father was taken into the Ministry [in 1916]. I got on to a good many ... Boards of which he, formerly, had been a member .... It seemed to me that ... there was one all-important guiding principle to bear in mind .... So long as [the other Directors] still thought of me as Woman, until they had got used to me and just thought of me as myself, they must be made to remember as little as possible that there was a woman in the room. Three things were likely to remind them of her presence – (a) direct realisation, (b) the question of smoking, (c) the question of swearing.

So far as direct realisation was concerned, I met it, so far as it could be met, by speaking (except when I had something really urgent or important to say) as little as ever I could ...

The second point, smoking, was really easy enough. These men were in the habit of smoking (some of them heavily), and many of them belonged to a world in which, to some degree, the old drawing-room taboo against women smoking or sitting amidst clouds of tobacco still held; they just had to be made to realise that with me it did not hold in the least. Otherwise there was the danger that they might try to be polite, cut down their smoking, and soon come to find me a perpetual and intolerable nuisance. So far as that was concerned, I began, on every Board, by smoking directly I came into the room, and smoked always, at first consciously but very soon unconsciously, considerably more at Board meetings than I was normally in the habit of doing.

Lastly there was the question of swearing. These men used probably – at least some of them did – a considerable amount of bad language. Well, here there was, so far as I could see, nothing to be done. They might, some of them must, miss being able to use all licence in their speech, but they would feel far more self conscious and uncomfortable if they swore in front of me than if they were merely forced to refrain from it. One could not prevent them from giving it up. They did so most strictly. To this day if a man so much as says 'damn' in my presence (and in all the years I have sat on Boards that is the worst swear-word I have ever heard) he turns and apologises. I on my side refrained from ever using the word myself. I dislike swearing and do it rarely, but my language is distinctly more pure at Board meetings than it is if I happen to feel cross in my own drawing room.

I enjoyed all these new Board meetings; the feeling of tackling interesting problems, concentrating on them, getting things done, was exhilarating. Reporting them back to my father and discussing them with him was fun.

(London: Macmillan, 1933, pp. 263–7).

2. iii   For working-class girls in areas of heavy industry domestic service remained the most common source of employment. Conditions could be hard.

'Lavinia Swainbank, house-maid', from John Burnett, *Useful Toil. Autobiographies of Working People from the 1820s to the 1920s* (1974).

The year 1922 was not an easy time to be starting out on one's career. For those were the days of depression on the Tyne, when the shipyards were idle and the pits closed down and every day the queue of sad-eyed men signing on for the dole grew longer ...

Thus at sixteen, I entered into a career of drudgery where long hours, low wages and very often inadequate food were accepted standards …. The next six years of my life were to be spent graduating from 'tweeny' in a Lakeland hotel, to second housemaid in gentlemen's service …

The type of room I discovered through trial that one always expected in 'gentlemen's service' has an iron bedstead with lumpy mattress, specially manufactured for the use of maids I suspect, a painted chest of drawers, with spotty mirror, lino-covered floor and a strip of matting at the bedside. Oh yes! The alarm clock. Here I was to familiarize myself with The Timetable …

6.30 A.M.   Rise
            Clean grate and lay fire in Dining Room. Sweep carpet and dust.
            Clean grate and lay fire in Library. Sweep and dust.
            Clean grate and lay fire in Billiard Room. Sweep and dust.
            Polish Staircase.
            Clean grate and lay fire in Drawing Room. Polish floor.
            Clean grate and lay fire in Morning Room.
            Sweep and dust vestibule.
            Sweep and dust Blue Staircase.
8 A.M.   Breakfast in Servants' Hall
9 A.M.   Start Bedrooms. Help with bed-making and slops and fill ewers and carafes.
            Clean grates and lay fires. Fill up coal boxes and wood baskets.
            Sweep and dust bedrooms.
            Clean bathrooms
            Change into afternoon uniform.
1 P.M.   Lunch in Servants' Hall.
            Afternoons, clean silver, brass, water cans, trim lamps.
4 P.M.   Tea in Servants' Hall.
5 P.M.   Light fires in bedrooms.
6 P.M.   Cans of hot water to bedrooms.
7.30 P.M.   Turn down beds, make up fires, and empty slops. Fill up coal and wood containers.
            Leave morning trays set in housemaid's pantry.

Here I served twelve months. The anaemia that was to bug my life had made me so weak that awful giddiness overtook me, causing me … to fall down stairs carrying the early-morning tea-set …. I was unfortunate enough to break the cup, saucer and teapot. My mistress called in her own doctor to make sure I had not got into 'trouble'. Anyhow, I … found, to my dismay, that 7s 6d had been deducted from my wage for breakages.

(London: Allen Lane, 1974, pp. 221–4).

2. iv New industries between the wars often used the assembly-line process but elsewhere traditional methods of production persisted. Some believed that women liked mindless routine jobs.

J. B. Priestley, *English Journey* (1934).

Leicester has been a hosiery town these last three hundred years …. The biggest concern in the hosiery and knitted goods trade is the *Wolsey* company, which has factories all over the town. I went over three of them …. Everywhere, except among the vats of dye where men do the work, there were enormous rooms filled with women and girls, who worked with small machines at long tables …. There is still far more hand labour than machine work …. In these factories … you saw long rows of sewing machines worked by electric power but guided by hand. In some rooms there was hardly a revolving wheel to be seen …. But the most relentless of the machines … made cardboard boxes and stuck labels on them. Here the girls had to feed the machines at a very brisk pace with pasted labels and the like …. I saw a girl printing – or rather transferring – the firm's name on pairs of socks. She had a pile of socks on one side, a pile of little transfer papers on the other, and a sort of iron in her hand, and the speed at which she put a transfer on a sock and ironed the name in and then removed the used transfer was enough, merely watching her, to make you dizzy. The manager and I stopped to look on. She was a pleasant-looking girl, and quite bright. She explained that she was on piece-work, had to do so many pairs of socks, hundreds and hundreds a day, and was generally able to make between two and three pounds a week. The manager had been telling me that, in his experience, girls preferred purely routine and monotonous jobs because once they had learned the fairly simple necessary movements they could then work all day and think about something else while they were working … their minds could be far away, wondering how Elsie was getting on with Joe or brooding over the film stars, male and female, whose photographs we saw pinned up here and there …

(Reprinted: London: Mandarin, 1994, pp. 128–30).

2. v   Before World War II there was no part-time working in industry.
Mothers who went out to work saw little of their children, as a woman
from the Staffordshire Potteries remembers.

J. Sarsby, *Missuses and Mouldrunners. An Oral History of Women Pottery
Workers at Work and at Home* (1988).

Mrs Farrier's children were growing up ... in the 1920s and 30s ...:

> *I don't know whether me mother did me – I often sit here and think, I sit
> here hours and think – I often wonder if she did me a good turn or a bad turn
> with having me children, minding them. You miss such a lot of them grow-
> ing up. You miss all the niceness of your children, when you're away at work.*
>
> *[What did you do then? Did you used to work right up to the seventh
> month or eighth month, or something?]*
>
> *Oh aye, I used to be some time about the eighth month. I used to give
> over about four weeks beforehand, then I'd be back when they were a month
> old. Me mother used to have them right away, see. And when I've left 'em,
> I've gone [to] work crying. That's what I think about now.*
>
> *[She] used to tell you little stories, what they did about bringing their
> first books home and the words they were learning and that. Now, me
> mother knew all that, but I'd got to hear it second-hand, when I come home
> from [work] ...*
>
> *And I'd say to every woman now, I would, stay at home and look after
> your kids .... That's what I think nowadays, now all that's past me, because
> you do miss all the niceness of them.*

This the sadness of a woman who spent only one month with each of
her children and who worked a 47 hour week, because of her husband's
difficulties in getting work.

(Milton Keynes: Open University Press, 1988, p. 70).

2. vi   In this classic study of long-term unemployment in the 1930s, its
impact on women is discussed in terms that reflect traditional middle-class
disapproval of industrial work for women.

Pilgrim Trust, *Men Without Work* (1938).

UNEMPLOYMENT AMONG WOMEN

We may now distinguish the three types of problem as it affects women,
encountered in the course of the sample. The first is that of women who do

not normally engage in industry. This is the case, for example, in the Rhondda and in South-west Durham. Here there is no problem of the unemployment of women, but only of the effect on women of the unemployment of men.

Secondly we have, as in Blackburn and Leicester, the situation where it is normal for women to enter the factory at 14 expecting to remain in industry all their lives, carrying when married the double burden of industry and the home. The Blackburn and Leicester woman is a strong, independent, and often very capable type, but her interests are not primarily in the home. She is driven by the pressure of work. She has no leisure …

Our third type of problem is illustrated by Liverpool, where the girl of 14 tends to look upon industrial employment as what has been called a 'meanwhile' occupation, marriage being the ultimate objective. This attitude to employment is apt to cause irresponsibility both in the girl herself and in some employers, who take advantage of this fact to exploit the woman worker, either by turning her out of employment at 16 or 18 years of age, or by the organization of more and more industries on a seasonal and part-time basis. The brunt of this unsatisfactory state of things is borne by the woman who does not marry young and may be left a spinster, or who has to be the main support of her family without the experience and discipline of a good occupation …

As a rule the working-class girl has to find time for some household responsibilities in addition to going out to work, and the married worker must always do so. The woman who is out of work, therefore, is not, on the whole, left stranded by unemployment as is the unemployed man; she has plenty to do, and looks perhaps as healthy or healthier, as happy or happier, than she did when she was working …

Where is it held that it is normal for the woman to work as well as her husband, … there is the advantage that where the husband is thrown out of work … his wife may continue in work and thereby a catastrophic drop in the family income may … be prevented …

On the other hand, … where a woman can devote her whole time to the maintenance of the home, a more genuinely civilized standard is kept up …. In Blackburn … the proportion of homes in which household management was recorded as indifferent or bad was decidedly high …. In the Rhondda and Crook we were impressed, not only by the excellent management of the homes, but by the high cultural level of the family. The woman held a significant place, not only in the family, but also in the political and social life of that community …. In the Rhondda or in South-West Durham the miner's wife does not ordinarily work in a factory, [and] young girls after leaving school do not normally go out to work (except for domestic service, which is in itself a training for home-making), but stay in the family and by taking a considerable share in the running of the family get an experience that the girl who goes into a factory at 14 misses.

(Cambridge: University Press, 1938, pp. 231–2).

2. vii Margaret Cole (1893–1980), writer, political activist and wife of the economist G. D. H. Cole, practised what she preached by combining marriage with literary and public work of her own.

Margaret Cole, *Marriage Past and Present* (1938).

I do not think that anybody can reasonably doubt ... that a girl of average attainments ... will *in the long run*, be more comfortably situated, economically, if she has found a man to support her. Not necessarily in the short run; plenty of young women make an economic sacrifice when they marry .... But the point is that the sacrifice is only immediate and temporary; ... because, in the great majority of women's occupations, the prospects are so meagre. No one will deny that in a few cases ... women on their own can manage to earn a decent competence with provision for their old age. But a good many even of those women ... would be *economically* better off if they had married a man of ability comparable to their own and shared his earnings – particularly as they might still have been able to pick up a bit themselves on the side; and for the vast majority the agitation to make pensions payable to spinsters at fifty-five has much more truth in it. The average woman worker has a rotten hard life, and a pretty poor chance at the end of it of maintaining herself in her old age on anything like a decent scale. This is the fact.

While the pay of men and women in this country continues to be as unequal as it is ... so long will women ... have a strong economic motive for entering upon the career of marriage, since to work simply for pay promises a strait life and a penurious old age ...

[But is marriage], in fact, a job which deserves the dignity of a whole-time occupation? .... I do not believe home-keeping, whether you have a largish house and servants, or a small house and none, or only occasional assistance, is really a full-time job, except, perhaps, for a little while when the children are quite young .... I suggest that advertisements of shops, of cinema programmes, etc., when taken in conjunction with a certain amount of literary evidence, indicate quite clearly that the number of English women who are idle, or partly idle, or who obscure the fact that they are idle by running around filling in their time with occupations which are of no use to any one ... is very large indeed. I believe this to be a heritage of the peculiar views of the Victorian upper class, of the idea that the more utterly useless a woman was, like a diamond, the more she became precious or desirable.

(London: J. M. Dent, 1938, pp. 193–200).

2. viii   A judgment of 1943, in a case involving a couple who had separated, illustrates the weakness of the wife's financial position when a marriage broke down.

Scott, L. J. : This appeal raises the question whether, where money is handed by a husband to his wife for housekeeping purposes, the balance becomes the wife's private property so that she can keep it for herself. The county court judge decided that the husband was entitled to the balance.

In my view there is no justification at all for the contention that, where a husband hands to his wife an allowance for housekeeping purposes, the husband is to be taken as a matter of law as presenting the savings out of that money to the wife for her sole use. The position in law will no doubt depend upon the evidence of what has passed between the parties. Here ... no arrangement was made by which the husband made a gift of the money to her. The result in such circumstances is that any savings remained the property of the husband. It appears that the wife had paid the money, so saved, into an account in her name with a co-operative society and that these savings, together with interest, dividends or bonuses allowed by the society eventually amounted to the sum of £103 10s. It was, however, clear that the source of this money was the husband's weekly allowance and that was sufficient in the absence of any evidence to the contrary that this money was still the property of the husband.

The judgment appealed from was perfectly correct and the appeal must be dismissed with costs.

[1943] 2 AC 579 Blackwell v. Blackwell.

2. ix   Husbands' dislike of their wives going out to work was a common refrain in mid-twentieth century surveys.

Ferdynand Zweig, *Women's Life and Labour* (1952).

A married weaver, who earns £5–£6 a week on automatic looms, told me: 'Whenever I hear on the wireless news about the export drive in the cotton industry, I say to myself: "That's me".' You can hear frequently: ... 'I don't need to ask my husband for permission to spend a shilling as others do. I spend my own money in my own way' ...

I never realised that independence could be such a joy until I came into contact with women in industry .... Why is it that so many husbands, in spite of the fact that they derive great benefits from the work of their wives, dislike their wives' work outside and speak so contemptuously about it, although they do not openly discourage it? .... It is true that the husband has to put up with many inconveniences; he has to wash up and help her to clean or to mind the babies when he is at home and he does not find a hot cup of tea waiting for him when he comes home, but that is not the whole story. The fact is that the whole relationship of husband and wife changes basically .... She is no longer dependent on him economically .... The less reliable the husband ... the better she feels for having a job ...

But even a good husband feels that his wife has developed a double loyalty. Her whole mind is not on the home .... He is not the full boss as he used to be, in spite of the fact that he pays ... 'wages to the Missus' .... And who knows what is going on in the factory, whether she does not speak about their married life to her new friends and what she actually feels about the boss who takes such an interest in her. 'My husband loathes my job but he accepts it,' I was told by a personnel officer, and that is true of a great many husbands.

The position is much worse if she earns more than he does, as sometimes happens with women supervisors and very efficient machinists on piecework.

(London: Gollancz, 1952, pp. 18–19).

2. x   In this anthropological study of Featherstone ('Ashton'), a mining village in West Yorkshire, the division of labour between husband and wife takes a traditional form.

N. Dennis, F. Henriques and C. Slaughter, *Coal is Our Life* (1956).

A man's centres of activity are *outside* his home .... With the exception of a small minority of men who spend a good deal of time pottering about with household improvements or are passionately interested in some hobby, or are very newly married, the husbands of Ashton for preference come home for a meal after finishing work and as soon as they can feel clean and rested they look for the company of their mates, i.e. their friends of the same sex.

The wife's position is very different. In a very consciously accepted division of labour, she must keep in good order the household provided for by the money handed to her each Friday by her husband. While he is at work she should complete her day's work – washing, ironing, cleaning or whatever it may be – and she must have ready for him a good meal …. The wife's ability to complete these tasks by the time of her husband's return from work is very commonly under discussion. The miner feels that he does an extremely difficult day's work; he makes it plain that he thinks it a 'poor do' if his wife cannot carry out her side of the contract. The wife is invariably found to support this view strongly. Housewives boast of their attention to the needs of their husbands, and of how they have never been late with a meal, never confronted a returning worker with a cold meal, never had to ask his help in household duties. If a miner returns from work on a wet day, and finds the washing crowded round the fire-place to dry, he will show a greater or lesser degree of anger … but every woman knows that to present her returning husband with such a scene is not encouraging good marital relations.

This … is only an example of the insistence on the efficient carrying out of each part of the division of labour in the family …. It is not suggested that the miner-husband is a tyrant in this respect. He is likely to construct for his wife, in his spare time, the kind of gadget which makes it unnecessary for the washing to obstruct the fire, or to help in saving for a gas cooker or an electric washing machine … [But] with the given resources she is expected to do the job. [A] typical example of this rule is the customary practice … in refusing a meal – the method is to 'throw it to t' back o' fire' …. One man (aged 27) when presented with 'fish and chips' from the nearby shop on returning from work, threw them into the fire. His wife's job was to find time to cook a proper meal for a working-man, not 'a kid's supper on the street corner', as he put it.

(London: Eyre and Spottiswoode, 1956, pp. 180–2).

2. xi   Richard Titmuss, Professor of Social Administration at the London School of Economics, comments on the implications of demographic change.

Richard Titmuss, 'The position of women', *Essays on "The Welfare State"*(1958).

The typical working-class mother of the 1890s, married in her teens or early twenties and experiencing ten pregnancies, spent about fifteen years in a state of pregnancy and in nursing a child for the first year of its life. She was tied, for this period of time, to the wheel of childbearing. Today, for the typical mother, the time so spent would be about four years ...

What do these changes signify in terms of 'the forward view' – the vision that mothers now have and have had about their functions in the family and in the wider society? At the beginning of this century, the expectation of life of a woman aged twenty was forty-six years. Approximately one-third of this life expectancy was to be devoted to the physiological and emotional experiences of childbearing and maternal care in infancy. Today, the expectation of life of a woman aged twenty is fifty-five years. Of this longer expectation only about 7 per cent of the years to be lived will be concerned with childbearing and maternal care in infancy ...

By the time the typical mother of today has virtually completed the cycle of motherhood she still has practically half her total life expectancy to live ...

For about forty years before 1911 marriage rates among women were declining. [They have] been increasing ever since, and in a striking fashion since the mid-1930s. An increase of nearly one-third between 1911 and 1954 in the proportion of women aged twenty to forty married represents, as the Registrar-General has said, 'a truly remarkable rise'. Never before, in the history of English vital statistics, has there been such a high proportion of married women in the female population under the age of forty and, even more so, under the age of thirty. Since 1911 the proportion at age fifteen to nineteen has risen nearly fourfold; at age twenty to twenty-four it has more than doubled ...

More marriage has been accompanied by a great increase in the years of married life experienced by married couples. Declining death rates have not only lengthened marriage ... but they have brought about a striking fall in the proportion of marriages broken by widowhood and widowerhood under the age of sixty. It is highly probable that the proportion of broken marriages under the age of sixty, marriages broken by death, desertion and divorce, is, in total, smaller today than at any time this century ...

Between 1946 and May 1955 the number of married women in gainful employment rose by two-and-a-quarter million to three-and-three-quarter million or 48 per cent of all women at work. The biggest source of recruitment in recent years has been married women over thirty years of age ...

(London: Allen and Unwin, 1958, pp. 91–3, 99–103).

2. xii   A collaboration between the Swedish social scientist Alva Myrdal and Viola Klein (1908–73), a pupil of Karl Mannheim at the LSE, produced this reassessment of women's social roles.

Alva Myrdal and Viola Klein, *Women's Two Roles: Home and Work* (1956).

Whether married women should be employed outside their homes has become the most topical issue concerning women in recent years and the controversy is carried on with much spirit and profound conviction on both sides ...

At this juncture in our social history women are guided by two apparently conflicting aims. On the one hand they want, like everybody else, to develop their personalities to the full and to take an active part in adult social and economic life within the limits of their individual interests and abilities. On the other hand most women want a home and a family of their own ...

In the old days, women knew where they stood and their lives were spent in the care of their families. Their world was bounded by the walls of their homes. From there, a resolute minority thrust out into the world of business and public affairs and succeeded in being admitted, largely to the extent that they were willing to turn their backs on home and family.

Those pioneering days are now over. With them has gone the need for women to make a fatal decision between irreconcilable alternatives .... The technical and social developments of the last few decades have given women the opportunity to combine and to integrate their two interests in Home and Work .... No longer need women forgo the pleasures of one sphere in order to enjoy the satisfactions of the other. The best of both worlds has come within their grasp, if only they reach out for it.

To make this a reality for more than the chosen few, something in the nature of a mental revolt will be needed. There is no doubt that society can be organized in such a way as to give practical scope for both family life and the gainful employment of women. But more clear thinking ... and a courageous facing of facts, will be required before these two roles will be fused into one harmonious whole.

                    (London: Routledge and Kegan Paul, 1956, pp. xv–xvii).

2. xiii   Revisiting Banbury in the 1970s, Margaret Stacey found that married women's work had not changed their status within the family.

M. Stacey *et al.*, *Power, Persistence and Change. A second study of Banbury* (**1975**).

Banbury women in 1950 saw themselves as part of a family unit, their lives followed a pattern dictated by the family cycle. For them work was regarded as filling in time before marriage, or as an unfortunate necessity in a bad or broken marriage.

The marked increase in married women working might reasonably be thought, and usually is thought, to indicate a notable change in the status of women and in the social arrangements of the families and thus perhaps in the institution of the family itself .... No such effects can yet be recorded ...

Despite ... changes in their pattern of employment, wives still see themselves primarily as part of the family unit. Overwhelmingly, the reasons that were given for wives working related to the benefit of the family: to provide extra material goods, a holiday, a new three-piece suite, better clothes for the children .... Conversely, the reasons given for a wife not going out to work related to the effect it was felt that her employment would have on the family .... Home-making and child-rearing remain the 'central life interest' of the majority of women in Banbury.

(London: Routledge and Kegan Paul, 1975, pp. 105–8).

2. xiv   Ann Oakley's Ph.D thesis was a pioneering feminist sociological study of housework, on which this book is based.

Ann Oakley, *Housewife* (1974).

As the Registrar General neatly and condescendingly puts it, married women 'engaged in unpaid home duties are ... treated as "others economically inactive"'.

Within this definition lie three aspects of the economics of housework. Firstly, the housewife does not herself produce commodities of direct value to the economy. Her primary economic function is vicarious: by servicing others, she enables them to engage in productive economic activity. Secondly, instead of a productive role, the housewife acts as the main consumer in the family ... 'Shopping' is one of the housewife's main work activities .... The government 'appeals' to the housewife to report rising prices, to buy 'wisely' and so on and so forth. In the 1972 British Government price-freeze, the onus was put entirely on 'the housewife' to report illicit price rises ...

The third aspect of the Registrar General's definition is that the housewife's work is not regarded as work because she receives no wage or salary for it .... The housewife is not paid, is not insured, cannot claim sickness benefit, etc: therefore the housewife does not work ...

This central contradiction – housework is work, housework is not work – appears as a constant theme in the analysis of the housewife's situation. On the one hand she is a privileged person: she is exempt from the need, binding on other adult members of society, to prove her worth in economic terms. 'Both my husband and I,' said one reader of a newspaper article on housewives and their work, 'think the housewife is one of the privileged classes.' ...

But while the assertion, 'I am a housewife', acts as a validation of the right to withdraw from economic activity, the admission, 'I am just a housewife,' disclaims any right to feel pride in this status. From privilege stems deprivation.

Housework is low-status work.

(London: Allen Lane, 1974, pp. 2–4).

2. xv **Writer and journalist Jeremy Seabrook laments the demise in the 1970s of the working-class matriarch (represented by Ma Joad in John Steinbeck's *The Grapes of Wrath* or Ena Sharples in the TV soap opera *Coronation Street*).**

Jeremy Seabrook, *What Went Wrong? Working People and the Ideals of the Labour Movement* (1978).

Mum, the formidable and eternal Mum, virago, domestic lawgiver, comforter and martyr, is dying. Ma Joad, Ena Sharples, the East End Mum, the watcher on the doorstep, the layer out of the dead, is herself fading away. You can watch her die. Like everything else it is a public spectacle: on the television adverts the children instruct her as to how she should best provide for them; what she should buy, which supermarkets she should use, with what tasty items of manufactured food she may win their hearts; and vacillating, confused, she complies. Her functions have been usurped. She is becoming extinct.

The role she had, the domestic supremacy, was in part a consolation for her inability to express herself outside her marriage and family; and in this respect may always have been a makeshift, a substitute for forbidden personal satisfactions. But her human and domestic skills were real – the counterpart of those her husband applied to his work ...

Her daughter cannot grow into the role now, even if she wants to .... Even if a woman chooses to adopt a traditional Mum role, if she stays at home, determined to look after the children, she cannot do it without constant reference to all the instruction and advice that assail her from out-side, the benevolent carers on television and in the newspapers .... Only the world of manufacture and expert knowledge possesses the indispensable adjuncts to proper parenthood, without which no child can be expected to grow safely to maturity; and she is compelled to obey.

(London: Victor Gollancz, 1978, pp. 122–5).

2. xvi Feminist author, journalist and campaigner Beatrix Campbell, following in the footsteps of George Orwell, reflects in the early 1980s recession on the decline of the male breadwinner family. UK unemployment rates peaked at 13 per cent in 1983, not far short of the estimated rate when Orwell was researching *The Road to Wigan Pier* (1937).

Beatrix Campbell, *Wigan Pier Revisited: Poverty and Politics in the Eighties* (1984).

Mothers on the Rock and Roll

The massive increase of employment among married women in peacetime has changed the culture we all inhabit and the legal rights of women. Of course, that hasn't happened without resistance: married women's re-entry into the labour market was usually conditional – it was designed not to disturb women's primary responsibility for domestic work. So although women's relationship to wages and work changed, men's didn't. Not sur-prisingly, part-time women were usually left to management's mercies and when recession struck they were usually the first to go. But the fact remains, something is afoot in English society which has prevented the promotion of a back-to-the-kitchen-sink strategy to meet mass unemployment .... No party would now dare to go to the voters promising a prohibition on wom-en's right to work and to a wage. So, times have changed.

But the phenomenon of women breadwinners is in no way equivalent to the experience of the male breadwinners – the new breadwinners are poorer, the legacy of a wage system based on women's economic depend-ence. The failure to equalise men and women's earnings leaves households headed by women poorer than they would be if the breadwinner were a man. In Sheffield I met an assistant in a hospital clinic. She takes home £201 a month. She keeps her boyfriend, who has been unemployed for four years. A couple of times a month she has a drink with the women at work, which is the only time she goes out. She pays £12.50 a week for a one-room flat ....

She has no winter coat or boots and she eats meat once a week, 'and by the end of the month it'll be beans on toast or a can of soup between us. *The women here are paid pin-money, but we are breadwinners*' ...

[A] school-dinner lady in Wigan told me a typical tale:

> *We had a terrible time when my husband was made redundant five years ago. He was in a rotten mood for months. Even now ... I've got to be ever so careful – because he feels it's my money we live on .... I saved up for us to have a holiday, I booked a caravan and paid the coach fares and then on the morning we were due to go he said, 'I'm not going without a penny in my pocket, I can't, I can't'. Up to the eleventh hour he wouldn't go.*

Men's economic dependency seems to face many women with a contradiction over housework – they need the men to change, and yet they feel the need to protect men in crisis. Only rarely did they talk of their men willingly taking over the housework and servicing their breadwinner wives.

(London: Virago, 1984, pp. 59–61).

2. xvii A turn of the century survey found that new areas of work had also opened up for working-class women in London's East End.

'Working for the National Family', from G. Dench, K. Gavron & M. Young, *The New East End. Kinship, Race and Conflict* (2006).

Among working women respondents ... there was no longer much sense of working in a male world .... Women had taken many of their own traditional female activities – once carried out informally as part of family and community life – into the public domain. This may even have increased the occupational segregation of men and women. Older women ... had, or had had, jobs in light industry as machinists, clothing workers, factory cleaners. Some worked in sales, again next to men. Only a few had undertaken specifically 'female' work, usually in domestic service – a job market that went into steep decline after the war.

By contrast many of the women under 35 worked as nursery assistants, in local government departments, or as office workers in service industries. Quite a large number had professional jobs in teaching, medicine and a variety of personal services. None was a machinist, or wanted to be, and those young women who talked about their career aspirations invariably listed teaching and the caring professions as their ideal. They wanted to work 'with people' – and often specifically with children .... Traditional domestic jobs have also seen a recovery, but largely within state social services, rather than the private sector.

The motor of this shift may well have been the expansion of the post-war welfare state, which gave a new national family dimension to citizenship .... It is this which, by pulling much of women's time and labour into the public sector, has made women's work more visible and created a direct voice for them in the state.

(London: Profile Books Ltd, 2006, p. 125).

Chapter 3

Education

3. i   Kathleen Betterton recalls the competition for scholarships (in her case, to the boarding school, Christ's Hospital, Hertford) which could open the way to university for a few children from respectable working-class families.

'Kathleen Betterton', in John Burnett (ed.), *Destiny Obscure.*
Autobiographies of Childhood, Education and Family from the 1820s to the
1920s **(1982).**

Of all the groups in our family album there is one that is a favourite. Taken on a summer's day in 1917, it shows the Infants' class of Queensmill Road School [in Fulham] carefully posed for the camera .... We are all in our party best, scrubbed, brushed and shining. A few of the girls wore white frilled pinafores but these, as we know already with precocious snobbery, are the poorest ones since white pinafores, like white button-up knickers, are already out of date, even among working-class children like ourselves .... Collectively we look prim, almost priggish .... School in those days seemed almost uniformly pleasant. Discipline was strict .... Yet classes must have been in spite of their size fairly informal, and we were most of us on quite intimate terms with Teacher. We would bring her bunches of flowers from the back garden and we would burble about our family affairs .... We brought along our choicest treasures to show her – dolls, foreign coins, picture postcards, seaweed from the seaside ...

Until the age of eight we were graded as Infants. Thereafter we passed into the "Big Girls" and life became more serious. We had entered upon the race for survival. Ahead lay the scholarship stakes; for the winners, free schooling till sixteen or over with the hope of a good job at the end of it; for the 'also-rans', a makeshift education ending at fourteen, and unskilled work that might end in unemployment and the dole.

We thus confronted destiny in the form of the Junior Scholarship at the age of eleven, and our future was decided by our ability to multiply awkward decimals and to write a 'composition' in tolerably accurate spelling and grammar. The chanciness of the system was clearly shown in my own family where my much cleverer brother, later a journalist and writer, was awarded only a place at a Central school, while I, with far less brilliance, climbed steadily up the scholarship ladder till I reached Oxford.

(London: Routledge, reprinted 1994, pp. 207–9).

3. ii **Nancy Astor (1879–1964), Conservative MP for Plymouth, was a vigorous advocate of women's causes. The 'marriage bar' imposed by most LEAs between the wars was primarily a response to unemployment. It became illegal under the 1944 Education Act.**

Hansard, HC Deb, 22 June 1921, cc 1395–6

MARRIED WOMEN TEACHERS.

Viscountess Astor asked the President of the Board of Education whether, although it is stated in the Sex Disqualification (Removal) Act, 1919, that a person shall not be disqualified by sex or marriage from the exercise of any public function or from carrying on any civic profession or vocation, women teachers on marriage are being dismissed by local education authorities, and are thus being prevented from serving the number of years necessary to qualify for a pension under the School Teachers' Superannuation Act, 1918; .... What steps is he prepared to take in order to prevent married women teachers from being debarred by local education authorities from qualifying for pensions?

Mr. H. Lewis: I am aware that some local education authorities are unwilling to employ married women as teachers, and consequently a married woman must serve in the area of some other authority which is willing to employ married women, if she is to qualify for a pension under the School Teachers (Superannuation) Act, 1918. Section 1 (3) of that Act makes a discrimination in favour of married women by making it easier for them to qualify for a pension, but I have no power to compel local authorities to employ married women.

3. iii **The case for gender equality in education was losing ground in the 1920s. Chaired by the Vice Chancellor of Sheffield University W. H. Hadow, the Board of Education's Consultative Committee included the Mistress of Girton Bertha Phillpotts, Roedean headmistress Emmeline Tanner and the Labour educationist R. H. Tawney.**

Report of the Consultative Committee on the Differentiation of the Curriculum for Boys and Girls' Respectively in Secondary Schools, 1922

Many teachers who had had opportunities of teaching both boys and girls had observed that boys in general were more self-assertive, more original and more constructive than girls, who, though they were more persevering and more industrious than boys, were also more passive and imitative. The boy as a rule was inclined to seek self-expression in investigation and construction, and the girl in artistic and emotional channels. Boys seemed to be more experimental and to have the logical faculty more fully developed .... Girls in general seemed to be less able than boys to apprehend and apply general principles and to have less perception of intellectual truth and delight in it for its own sake ...

The examiners of the Oxford and Cambridge Schools Examinations Board corroborated these views. In general the girls' work was, in their view, more even and more neatly presented than that of the boys; but it showed less originality, and the best boys' work was higher than the best girls' work. The girls' answers were often more fluent, but tended to irrelevancy. The difference between the work of the two sexes became most noticeable at later ages ...

The majority of the earlier pioneers of women's education appear to have thought that the claim that women should have as good an education as men, and that they should be free to enter occupations solely on their merits, implied that they should have the same education as men. It is not so clear to-day, however, as it seemed to them, that that conclusion neces-sarily follows. In the first place, the fact that the majority of girls will marry and have the care of a family, if not of such exclusive importance as was generally supposed in the first half of the last century, is yet of very great significance. In the second place, though it be admitted that an increasing number of women will follow the same occupations and have the same civic interests as men, and need both for that and for other reasons a good gen-eral education, it is conceivable that the best medium of such an education will not be the same in each case. Finally it must be remembered that the character of the problem has changed in the last fifteen or twenty years. The education of girls up to almost the end of the last century developed partly under the influence of a more general movement for the emancipation of women. That movement has now perhaps achieved sufficient success to be no longer so potent a source of inspiration. Not less important, the great extension of Secondary Education in the last decade has brought into the Secondary Schools a number of girls from families with a somewhat differ-ent outlook, and with interests diverging in several respects from those of the rather select class of girls who received Secondary Education a generation ago ...

Recommendations for Differentiation between Boys' and Girls' Schools in certain respects.

.... That in Girls' schools the pressure of external examinations, which is in our opinion partly responsible for much over-teaching and for the unduly passive attitude of many pupils, should be reduced wherever possible ...

.... That in ... day schools ... steps should be taken to reduce the amount of preparation required from girls, which, in some instances, is at present excessive in view of the relatively heavy domestic duties often performed by them in their homes.

(London: HMSO, 1922, pp. 94, 132, 139–40).

3. iv Margaret Rhondda points to shortcomings in the education of upper-middle class women. She had herself attended Notting Hill High School (GPDST), the girls' public boarding school St Leonards, St Andrews and for two terms Somerville College, Oxford.

Viscountess Rhondda, *Leisured Women* (1928).

Women are to-day taking a certain, though still very small, share in forming public opinion outside the home – they are taking a larger share in helping to form opinion on public affairs inside the home; and they are beginning to take the largest share in deciding the actual family arrangements inside the home. But ... this change has come about not through any noticeable alteration in the training, lives, or habits of thought of the vast majority of women of the leisured classes, which remain in many ways very much what they were in 1870 .... This change has been produced partly by the agitation of a minority of intellectual, educated, and hard-working women; partly by acceptance of the *fait accompli* which is always so marked a characteristic of British public opinion; partly by the recognition of good work done by individual outstanding women in various fields of labour. Because Madame Curie discovered radium, because Miss Royden can preach a more eloquent sermon than the average bishop, because Dame Louisa Aldrich Blake was one of the best surgeons of her day, the ordinary man is more inclined to take the opinion of the ordinary woman more seriously than he was sixty years ago.

But the average "leisured" woman has not altered very greatly. She is perceptibly better educated, so far as actual book-learning is concerned, than she was sixty years ago. Even at the worst of the private schools that is true.

She plays games, and sometimes plays them well. But apart from these two points – important, certainly, so far as they go – she has changed but little .... She is encouraged not to have overmuch self-confidence, she is induced to regard herself as something slightly inferior. It is not an unknown thing to hear the headmistress of one of our great public schools for girls speak of her school as "only a girls' school"; and this attitude is the common one amongst the headmistresses of the private schools to which the majority of girls of well-to-do parents, who leave the home and the local high school, are still sent. The schoolgirl is still encouraged to regard herself as something which cannot take care of itself by itself, as something to be guarded and protected ...

It is true that the public schools are better in these respects – a great deal better – than the private schools, and that to-day the best of the high schools are, in some ways at least, better than many of the public schools .... But ... it is ... the girls educated at private schools who set the tone for the behaviour of women of the leisured classes ...

There is a 'Smart Set' or its equivalent in every suburb and in every provincial town in England, a set which spends its time playing bridge in the afternoons, motoring round to see its friends, plays a little tennis, dances a good deal, keeps the most fashionable kind of dog it can afford, spends a large proportion of its time – and more of its husband's or father's money than he can easily spare – at its dressmaker, spends all it can squeeze on jewellery. This public reads a large number of novels. It only glances at the papers; its interest in home politics is, for the most part, confined to thinking how wicked the working-man is to want the money and material comforts which it regards itself as all-important; its interest in foreign politics is non-existent. This public is a much larger one than it was sixty years ago and it is a much more serious menace to society.

(London: Hogarth Press, 1928, pp. 20–4, 29–30).

3.v This Cambridgeshire woman interviewed in the 1970s was one of many girls unable to take up grammar school places before the 1944 Act because their parents could not afford to support them.

Marjorie Reeves, from Mary Chamberlain, *Fenwomen* (1975).

Fourteen I was, when I left school. I won a scholarship to Ely High School, but couldn't go because mother couldn't afford it. Straight away I went to work for a man in the village, for two shillings a day. Weeding and picking flowers, potato-picking down the Burnt Fen, in the autumn .... We worked like slaves. All day. You were on all the time, apart from a break for your sandwiches, and really glad to do it …. There weren't nothing else, only service, you see. And I loathed the idea of going to work for someone …

My sister had been to Homerton [Teacher Training] College [in Cambridge], she worked as a maid, and said it was quite nice pay there. So I had a friend in the village and this friend of mine – I was fourteen – and me, after I'd finished potato-picking, we went there. I was there two months ….

There was an Art Mistress, Miss Mortimer. I always remember her. She wanted someone up in the Art Room, to help get the stuff out for the students, … paint and things. And I remember standing there, I modelled for them too, profile, and I had to make paste for them …. That was my job in the morning, and that was lovely compared with waiting on students. I had to do that in the afternoons, at tea and lunch. Standing against the wall, waiting to see if they wanted anything else. I used to loathe it there. Absolutely loathed it. I'm not being big-headed but I used to think, 'I ought to be one of you. Why couldn't I have been one of you?' …

After I left Homerton, I went back to the land. Seasonal work. I'd cycle to Barrowfield, where I got sixpence an hour …

But you know, if I'd been able to go to the High School – I would have loved to have gone – I'd like to have been a model, mannequins they called them in them days. I was ever so thin. Or something artistic, with colours and clothes … . Or I would have liked to have painted, or written a book. Now this Miss Mortimer – I'm not boasting – she used to have me arrange the pictures round the benches in the room and she used to say, 'You're very artistic, Sharman.' She used to call me by my surname, and she said, 'You blend your colours together. You know what colour is.' Stan, my husband, he says to me now, why don't I go to evening classes in art, at Meacham. I often visualise a picture, what I feel, what I would paint. I could try, I know, but somehow I don't know, I can't …

I always feel frustrated, always do, as if there's something I haven't done in life, with my head. That's why I get depressed …

(London: Virago, 1978, pp. 93–6).

3. vi Dame Margaret Miles (1911–1994), headmistress of an early London girls' comprehensive, Mayfield School, looks back on the struggle to get a university education and a job between the wars.

Margaret Miles, … *And Gladly Teach: The Adventure of Teaching* (1966).

At eleven I went ... to Ipswich High School where I got a free place through a scholarship for the children of war victims ...

It had always been assumed at home that I would go to the university .... My parents moved to Surrey and ... I moved to Croydon High School for my third year in the sixth [form]. At Croydon the tradition was for girls to go to Oxford ...

[But] actually it would have been difficult financially for me to have gone to Oxford. There were no 'life size' grants in those days and county and state scholarships were grants towards the cost and were not intended to cover expenses, which were considered the responsibility of parents. Many schools gave small scholarships and grants of something like £20 to £30 and of course there were the open scholarships (also small for girls), as now.

Most schools and some local authorities had loan funds and many young graduates started their teaching career with a load of debt .... Another method of paying one's way was through the Board of Education four-year grant for those who were going to teach. This was known as the "pledge" because those who accepted it, and I was one, had to undertake to teach at the end of their course ...

Though I hated the idea of tying myself to teaching through the pledge, this is what I had to do. It took me to Bedford College for three years and then for one year to the London University Institute of Education ...

At this time I very much wanted to read sociology and not history, and I did actually attend lectures in the sociology department for a time, but my task masters at the Institute disapproved because they said it was not a teaching subject. So I changed back to history ...

Teaching had always been thought of as an honourable profession in my family. It was approved because it was a safer and more suitable profession for girls than others were then thought to be: and also in the Welsh and Nonconformist milieu from which I came it was respected for what it was. But in the thirties there were more teachers than jobs and many were unemployed .... Older headmistress colleagues have told me how they used then to have hundreds of applications for every advertised post.

I was interviewed for a few posts, but by the end of the year neither I nor most of my contemporaries had got jobs. I was lucky then to be told of a possible vacancy at Westcliff High School where the head had been formerly on the staff of Ipswich High School ...

[After six months teaching English in a Swiss finishing school] in February I returned to England to be interviewed for the job at Westcliff High School, which I mercifully got.

(Reading: Educational Explorers, 1966, pp. 19–24, 35–6).

3. vii   In schools of the 1930s the assumption was that Jewish children would assimilate to Christian traditions. There was no attempt to disguise class discrimination.

Ena Abrahams, in Jewish Women in London Group, *Generations of Memories. Voices of Jewish Women* **(1989).**

When I was six ... I went to Fairclough Street School. There, they were nearly all Jewish children ...

My parents spoke English to one another, smattered with Yiddish, and Yiddish to my grandmother .... At school the norm was towards anglicisation. It was done by covert means, because you were never encouraged to talk about your own country or background, and inevitably, there grew within you a feeling that you came from a sub-standard culture ...

And this is true when I went to grammar school as well. You took part in all the rituals of the time, the communal rituals like Empire Day, and Christmas. I think parents didn't want to make you any different, so they allowed you, whatever their thoughts, to take part in the Christmas festivities and all the rest.

I don't think it created conflict between parents and children so much as conflict in the children .... There were things that were mysteries, and things that you didn't talk about ...

When I got a scholarship, you were given a list of schools that you could apply to and for most of them you had to take a separate entrance exam. My mother wanted me to go to the City of London. So I sat the entrance and I passed; and then we were called to the school again. The headmistress spoke to my mother about our circumstances, what my father did – my father was unemployed at the time. She said to my mother that she didn't think I could *benefit* from that type of school, because my background would be so different from the other girls that it would be impossible for me actually to *integrate* into the school. I remember we came away from that school and we crossed one of the bridges of the river. I remember my mother crying all the way across the bridge. I remember it clearly, holding my hand and crying .... The headmistress said to my mother that if we went to Dame

Alice Owen's School, they had more girls of my … *class*, is what she was really saying, and they might take me, you know, graciously. Graciously. And they did.

I remember going to the school dressed in a very nice, plain, dark-red dress that my mother had made for me. I had silk socks with clocks up the side, black patent shoes and white gloves for the interview …

I often think there's a parallel when I see clothes that people of Caribbean origin wear here today; the accent on fashion. The Jews did *exactly the same thing*. If you live in poor surroundings, if your life chances are not very great, I think that one way in which you can actually develop any sort of feeling of self-image is likely to be through your clothes, through externals. Things that make you feel a bit up.

(London: Women's Press, 1989, pp. 85–9).

3. viii   Social anthropologist Judith Okely describes the anti-intellectual ethos of her private boarding school in the 1950s.

Judith M. Okely, 'Privileged, Schooled and Finished: Boarding Education for Girls', in *Own or Other Culture* (1996).

It is not surprising that the dilemma between a career and marriage scarcely arose in a middle-class and relatively undistinguished boarding school such as mine. Ideally, marriage was the ultimate vocation …. If there was academic intent, this was not borne out by the girls' performance, since the majority left after taking a few GCE 'O' levels. Out of a class containing up to 35 girls, six or less remained to take sometimes a single 'A' level …. The pattern after school tended to be a year at a private domestic science or finishing school, preferably in Switzerland, and progress to an exclusive secretarial college. The ideal was to be a debutante, before making a 'good marriage'. Another respectable vocation was nursing, and then only at select London hospitals. Teachers' training was *déclassé*. Whereas work as a private secretary or nurse offered contact with a man of the right social class, teaching did not. Few, if any, of the girls entered into occupations comparable to their brothers'.

Scholarly achievements and higher education were, nevertheless, reserved for a few girls, possibly marked as vocational spinsters. These had also to conform to the school's ideas of good conduct. Academic proficiency did not guarantee encouragement.

With 13 'O' levels and while studying for four 'A' levels, I was summoned to the senior mistress. She declared I would be 'selfish to go to University, *even*

Aberystwyth', thereby depriving a worthier person of a place. She suggested a career which would make use of my 'A' levels in French and Art – by training as a designer of corsets and lingerie for a famous company in Switzerland.

(London: Routledge, 1996, pp. 150–51).

3. ix   The increasingly common phenomenon of the graduate wife and the problems she faced were the subject of this study by Judith Hubback, a Newnham graduate who later found her vocation as a Jungian psychologist.

Judith Hubback, *Wives Who Went to College* (1957).

It is sometimes remarked, perhaps rather cynically, that the university is the best possible marriage market for an intelligent girl, because there she will meet such a high concentration of her mental equals; and of course, the university years are those during which it is perfectly natural for a girl to fall in love …

The marriage rate among graduates, and, by extension, among educated women generally, is now not far from the rate for the rest of the population. It used to be considerably lower than the general rate. The early pioneers for the higher education of women thought of themselves mainly in terms of future salary-earners and as competing with men in the professions, which were (thanks to them) gradually opened to women. They sometimes seem, to one of my generation, to have overstressed the incompatibility between the intellectual and biological sides of women's lives. Or, as we owe them so much, should we perhaps say instead that they were more willing to sacrifice the biological aspects of womanhood than we are? …

Fewer of the graduate wives concerned in this survey remain childless than do the general run of wives …. Relatively twice as many of the analysed graduate women as of all women have families of three and four children. And the graduates also show rather more two-children families than does the general population …

The educated wife of today has to steer a careful course: she must avoid both the rocks of aggressive insistence on her status and also the mud-flats of self-deprecation. She must be both feminine and masculine, but not lean too far one way or the other. She must try to combine in herself some at least of the attitudes which were once believed to be found only in men, with a liberal allowance of the qualities that marriage and motherhood engender. In a predominantly masculine world she must restate feminine values and she must insist on the importance of human relationships. Unless her husband agrees with her wholeheartedly, these combinations and new orientations will be very difficult to achieve. With his love, his trust and his help she will do great things.

(London: Heinemann, 1957, pp. 25–6, 29, 159).

3. x   Naomi Mitchison's daughter Lois (educated at Badminton School and Oxford) provoked a lengthy correspondence on the *Guardian* women's page with this article questioning the value of higher education for a generation of girls largely destined to be housewives.

Lois Mitchison, 'The price of educating women', *Guardian*, 8 January 1960.

If higher education really is a frill for a girl who gets married immediately she leaves her university, society, as well as her family is spending unnecessarily …

I have been told that an educated girl makes a better companion to her husband, a better mother, and a better housekeeper …

I have also been told by an Oxford woman graduate that she thought her university training had definitely hindered her in working in her house and looking after her two small children. She says that at Somerville she was taught to concentrate on a particular problem, excluding all irrelevancies from her mind. What she has to do as a wife and mother, she says, is never to concentrate so that she excludes the irrelevant. Otherwise she finds that while she is concentrating on the pudding for lunch, her 2-year-old has poured her milk over her brother, and the baker's van has passed without her catching it.

A far more obviously disastrous consequence of a university education in some women is that they become discontented and guilty about their work in their home. Here in Oxford I have met women at parties who introduced themselves blightingly as 'just a wife', and apparently saw themselves as exiles from a glamorous outside world …

One of the difficulties, I think, is that some schools and colleges lay the foundations of later guilt by assuming that careers and celibacy are the highest aims for women, or even the normal aims. I suppose that in the generation that grew up after the 1914–18 war particularly a professional woman was not very likely to get married. There were not enough men to go round, and educated girls were not socially acceptable everywhere.

To-day there are more young men than young women, and no woman under 25 is likely to have to remain single …

What I wonder is whether schools have accepted this changed social situation? It is surely a mistake to make girls feel guilty about abandoning their career for marriage if that is what the majority of them are going to do anyway.

3. xi   The Crowther Report, produced by the Central Advisory Committee on Education, took for granted the gendered pattern of careers, which explained why fewer girls than boys studied three 'A' levels or went to university. It argued that there were positive advantages in their freedom to follow a more varied Sixth Form curriculum.

15 to 18, vol. 1 (1959).

By 'Sixth Forms with a Difference' we mean ... courses which are not linked with university entrance requirements .... Schools have in consequence a much freer hand to plan the course to suit the individual requirements of the pupils – there is time to give good measure to ... art or music; or to subjects with a new vocational interest and value such as dressmaking and commercial subjects.

A PROVISION FOR GIRLS ...

This chapter is largely about girls' schools. The reason for this is clear. There were until very recently few careers open to a boy who ... ended his full-time education at 18 instead of at 16 .... But girls have long had available to them a large number of openings in careers which accept entrants at 18 ... , and which entail further education, but not to a university standard ...

PREPARATION FOR TEACHING

The outstanding example of a career which has normally demanded some Sixth Form education, but not necessarily the standard pattern of two or three Advanced level subjects is teaching in primary and non-selective schools .... In actual numbers the teachers' training colleges are nearly twice as important an outlet for girls as are the universities. For boys the universities are nearly five times as important numerically as the training colleges. The minimum academic qualification for admission to a training college is five passes at Ordinary level in the G.C.E., a qualification which can be obtained without entering a Sixth Form. The minimum age qualification is 18, so that a girl can have one or two years in the Sixth Form without the necessity of working for a formal examination ...

NURSING AND COMMERCE

... Nursing makes no preliminary academic demands which cannot be satisfied below the Sixth Form level, and indeed it recruits many girls who have never been to a grammar school, but it does impose a minimum age of entry of 18, and this fits in well with a two-year Sixth Form course .... The kind of general course, incorporating an element of specialisation, which [is] ... coming into vogue for potential teachers, is the best preparation also for ... future nurses ...

The majority of girls who take up [business and secretarial] work leave school at 16 or before, but a good many schools have commercial courses in the Sixth Form and there is no doubt that a longer general education is a great asset to girls who have the ability and the ambition to occupy a position which corresponds roughly to a technician's, as distinct from a skilled craftsman's, among careers for boys. Many are realising this. It is the general education that counts in the end; it is the vocational skills that attract at the start. Shorthand, typewriting and, in some schools, accounts are the core round which secretarial courses are developed ...

(London: HMSO, pp. 302–7).

3. xii   **The economist Lord Robbins believed Britain needed more graduates, women as well as men. The Robbins report points out the relatively low take-up of university education by women, and the new opportunities opening up for married women to return to professional work after a career break.**

Robbins Report on Higher Education (1963).

In the case of women, only 7.3 percent of the age group entered all full-time higher education in 1962, compared with 9.8 per cent in the case of men; if part-time education is included, the comparison is between just under 8 per cent for women and over 22 per cent for men. The difference is substantial .... But the important point is that the difference between the sexes ... has its origin long before the age of entry to higher education. Although nearly as many girls as boys pass the General Certificate of Education at Ordinary level, many fewer stay on beyond this stage to take Advanced level. Of those who do stay on and obtain passes in the Advanced level ... , the proportion going into full-time higher education is as high for girls as for boys. But here again there is a difference in pattern. In 1962/3, a quarter of the students in British universities were women: in [Teacher]

Training Colleges in England and Wales two thirds of the students were women ...

The percentage of women among those entering full-time courses of degree level in Great Britain (28) is rather higher than in the federal German Republic or the Netherlands but lower than in Sweden (35), France (40) or the Soviet Union (42). The larger number of girls entering Training College in Britain redress the balance, so that amongst entrants to all full-time courses in percentage of women is 40 – the same percentage as in the United States. But British part-time and correspondence courses recruit very few women students: if all levels and methods of study are taken together, the percentage of women entrants in Britain is only 25 overall, compared with 40 in the United States and 45 in the Soviet Union ...

Before the war over three-quarters of the women in employment were unmarried; now more than half of them are married. Many more married women go out to work .... At the same time the age of marriage has fallen and the expectation of working life has lengthened. As a result a new career pattern has emerged: a short period of work before marriage, and a second period of work starting perhaps fifteen years later, and continuing for twenty years or more .... The prospect of early marriage leads girls capable of work in the professions to leave school before they have entered the sixth form and, even after sixth form studies, too many girls go straight into employment instead of into higher education. When their family responsibilities have lessened many of them will desire opportunities for higher education. And many if not most married women who have already enjoyed higher education will need refresher courses before they can return effectively to professional employment.

(London: HMSO, pp. 17, 40, 167–8).

3.xiii   To the Marxist-feminist Juliet Mitchell it seemed that unequal educational opportunities were the key to labour-market discrimination against women. At that time a university lecturer in English literature, she later became Professor of Psychoanalysis and Gender Studies at Cambridge.

Juliet Mitchell, 'Women: the Longest Revolution', *New Left Review*, 1966.

The whole pyramid of discrimination rests on a solid extra-economic foundation – education. The demand for equal work, in Britain, should above all take the form of a demand for an *equal educational system*, since this is at present the main single filter selecting women for inferior work-roles.

At present, there is something like equal education for both sexes up to fifteen. Thereafter three times more boys than girls continue their education. Only one in three 'A'-level entrants, one in four university students is a girl. There is no evidence whatever of progress. The proportion of girl university students is the same as it was in the 1920s. Until these injustices are ended, there is no chance of equal work for women. It goes without saying that the content of the educational system, which actually instils limitation of aspiration in girls, needs to be changed as much as methods of selection. Education is probably the key area for immediate economic advance at present.

3. xiv   A study of 700 children in Nottingham revealed significant class differences in the way mothers brought up their children.

John & Elizabeth Newson, *Four Years Old in an Urban Community* (1968).

Perhaps the most salient way in which total patterns of upbringing differ from one class to another can be seen in the *kind* of control which mothers attempt to exert over their children .... The characteristic attitude of middle-class mothers ... [shows] a preference for managing children as far as possible through the use of reasoning .... The mother will try to give the child an explanation rather than a bald command, and will be (theoretically at least) prepared to countenance argument and to meet it with calmness and further explanation .... Working-class mothers, on the other hand, are less likely to embark upon any course which looks like involving them in lengthy verbal explanations of the why and wherefores of their actions ...
   Driver's mate's wife:

> *I don't believe in all these books which tell you 'Don't smack'. If you're going to talk the child out of it, you're going to spend half your day standing there talking to them. I think it does them good to have a smack if they've done something wrong, you know, I think it lasts longer than simply talking to them ...*

A greater proportion of working-class mothers specified 'no talking at the table' .... The difference in mothers' behaviour reflects in fact a difference in attitude to the importance of conversation: those who forbid talking take the view that a child should 'shurrup and gerrit down' – 'you can do your talking afterwards' – whereas the middle-class woman likes to think of mealtimes as social events and the dining-table as a focus for intelligent discussion of the day's happenings, and only discourages talking if in practice it deteriorates to mere noise.

(London: George Allen & Unwin, 1968, pp. 433–4, 441).

3. xv   In 1973 a government-commissioned survey by HM Inspectors investigated differences in the curriculum for boys and girls and their implications for equality of opportunity.

Department of Education and Science, Education Survey 21, ' *Curricular Differences for Boys and Girls*' (1975).

Of the 302 mixed [secondary] schools visited in the English sample, 98 per cent separate boys and girls for some subjects below the age of 16. In the early years, such separation is of two kinds: that which divides the sexes for a particular subject and that which, in effect, provides different subjects for boys and girls. Physical education and games belong in the first category; the second includes home economics and needlework for girls, and wood and metal work for boys ...

Some of the patterns of curriculum developed in the first three years of secondary schooling produce, either purposely or by accident, restrictions on what appears to be a free choice of options for the fourth-year stage. One example of this is a school which separates home economics and nee-dlework (girls) from woodwork and metalwork (boys) in years 1–3. In the fourth form, technical drawing is introduced as a supposedly free choice for both boys and girls. The craft department, in line with contemporary prac-tice and thinking, is unwilling to teach technical drawing in isolation, and insists that it must be linked with metalwork. Only those pupils who have previously taken metalwork are allowed to study technical drawing. This kind of pre-emptive pattern can apply equally to the sciences, to commerce and to languages. Of all mixed schools in England, 27 per cent reveal such pre-emptive patterns in the curriculum of the first three years ...

[In the fourth and fifth years] the predominance of boys in physics and chemistry and of girls in biology, suggesting as it does that a higher percentage of boys is likely to take two or more sciences, raises important questions about the content of scientific studies followed .... For girls tak-ing one science, the choice is almost invariably biology which, unsupported by other sciences, has limited value as a qualification for continued edu-cation .... Again, the preponderance of girls taking French and German suggests that if girls are potentially at a disadvantage where the sciences are concerned, boys may equally miss opportunities in the field of foreign languages ...

Girls are more likely to choose a science and boys a language in a single-sex school than they are in a mixed school, though in a mixed school a higher percentage of pupils may be offered these subjects ...

[A]t advanced level, three times as many boys as girls choose to take mathematics and further mathematics. Between two and three times as many girls as boys choose to study English literature. Economics, usually begun in the sixth form, is taken by nearly three times as many boys as girls.

The comparison of the percentages of boys and girls respectively choosing physics, chemistry or biology indicates that trends established in earlier years have continued .... In languages, the difference in percentage take-up is increased: the ratio is now three to one in favour of girls studying French. A similar extension of the trend is observable in German ...

In general ... any correlation between the sex of the pupil and the popularity of a subject is markedly greater in mixed schools than in single-sex schools.

(London: HMSO, pp. 7, 12, 15–16).

3. xvi   The mid-twentieth-century trend towards coeducation was criticized by some feminists, who believed female pupils and teachers fared better in single-sex schools. Sexual harassment of women teachers in a boys' school was the subject of this article.

Anne Whitbread, 'Female Teachers are Women First: sexual harassment at work', in D. Spender and E. Sarah (eds), *Learning to Lose. Sexism and Education* (1980).

New members of staff and students on teaching practice were the principal targets of sexual abuse .... The general tactic employed by the boys was to 'make a grab' while milling around in a group on the stairs or in the corridor, and then to run, leaving the victim unsure of the identity of the offender and frightened to make a false accusation. Equally humiliating were the obscenities shouted from a distance or the appraising remarks exchanged within hearing.

Amongst most of our male colleagues the subject of sexual harassment was either a joke or an embarrassment. After all, more than a few of them considered it perfectly within their rights to pat or pinch female staff at will .... Even those men who were genuinely sympathetic could do little more than offer strong arm support as a deterrent. This seemed unlikely to attack the real root of the problem which we saw as the image of women generally in the eyes of the boys. It became obvious that if this kind of abuse was a strictly female problem it needed the women to come together to work out a proper solution ...

It was very reassuring for the student teachers and younger staff to hear that the older staff had also suffered similarly in their early days and to realise that it was not a personal failure on their part. Unanimously we decided it was a problem that must be taken seriously and that we should never allow the slightest untoward touch to go unnoticed, even under the cover of a group, but without undue histrionics we would roundly address all present as to our feelings about the matter .... In the case of a serious abuse to a new or student member of staff, we made the decision to refer the offender to a senior female member of staff. One of the perennial problems faced by women teachers in a boys' school mainly staffed by men is the belief among the boys that women are 'soft' and can't control classes without a man to help them and back up their disciplinary measures ...

We reported the discussion and decisions of our first meeting back to the Staff Council .... Our strategy was supported, verbally at least, and a general discussion of sexism within the school began. To be fair, it is temptingly easy for a man to achieve instant camaraderie with a class of boys on the level of sex when it might be hard to unite with them on issues of race or class. It is easier for the boys too. Similarly, it is more difficult for a man to overcome the boys' expectations that he will, ultimately, use physical force to control them, even though in succumbing to this demand he will make it doubly hard for a woman to teach after him using different methods of control. (The two popular forms of abuse in the school are 'woman' and 'poof'.) The hidden curriculum is all-important here and it is difficult to change attitudes reinforced since birth.

(London: Women's Press, 1980, pp. 91–3).

3. xvii The engineer N. G. McCrum, Fellow of Hertford College (one of the first five Oxford colleges to go mixed), discusses the gap between proportions of women and of men getting First Class Oxbridge degrees in the 1980s and after. The explanation was in part that admission was now less competitive for women than in the days when they were confined to a few single-sex colleges; and possibly also that the ethos of mixed colleges

inhibited them. But some subjects did appear to be less 'even-handed' than others in their selection, teaching or examining practices.

N. G. McCrum, 'The Gender Gap at Oxford', *Oxford Magazine* 143 (1997), pp. 6–9.

The position today can be summarised as follows. Taking the probability of a male Class 1 to be 100, the probability of a female Class 1 in Engineering, Economics and Management is 111: EEM is the most female-friendly subject at Oxford. There are four other subjects – Biochemistry, Geology, Physiology, and Geography – which may be placed with EEM in the Premiership. These subjects have respectable female Class 1 probabilities, in the range 111 down to 81.

The second group, Division 1, comprises Law, Literae Humaniores [Classics], Experimental Psychology, Mathematics, and Human Sciences, five subjects with a range in Class 1 female probability from 73 down to 66. This division is the second largest, accounting for about one fifth of Oxford's graduates.

Division 2 is the largest, two fifths of Oxford's graduates, and includes Biological Sciences, English, Music, Modern Languages, Physics, Chemistry, Theology and History: the average female Class 1 probability is 56 and the range 63 down to 51.

The bottom group, Division 3, comprises PPE [Philosophy, Politics and Economics], Engineering Science, Oriental Languages, and PPP [Psychology, Philosophy and Physiology], with an average female Class 1 probability of 42: the range is 47 down to 40 ...

It was not always so! Indeed the major driving force for the mixing of the colleges was the academic achievement of Oxford's women .... History and Modern Languages in 1974 were clearly Premiership material, with female Class 1 probabilities of [99 and 135, respectively]: today they languish in Division 2 with female Class 1 probabilities of [51 and 53].

Now there are several possible causes for this well-known, remarkable and unwelcome collapse. One identified by the Cambridge Modern and Medieval Languages Gender report is a direct result of the mixing of the colleges ... 'It seems now to be generally agreed that the ethos of many colleges is somewhat masculine and even "laddish"'.

There is another explanation ... : this is ... a relative drop in [the A-level scores of women undergraduates] since 1974, coupled with a latent propensity of most Oxford Honour Schools – women at equal A-levels perform less well in Finals than men ...

[But, in explaining different outcomes in different subjects,] the fundamental characteristic that distinguishes an ideal subject from non-ideal, speaking in general terms, is even-handedness between male and female cohorts.

3. xviii   By the 1990s all political parties were committed to university expansion. A committee chaired by the businessman and ex-civil servant Sir Ron Dearing made equality of opportunity a central concern in its recommendations for the future of higher education in Britain.

Higher Education in the Learning Society (Dearing Report).

Female students

An important element in the growth in higher education has been the increase in participation by women. The Robbins report foresaw growth in women's participation but, even by 1979/80, women made up only 37 per cent of students. Since then participation by women has increased rapidly so that they constituted 51 per cent of students in 1995/6 …

Participation by women

Women's participation overall is now in line with their demographic representation …. But they are unevenly distributed across subjects and levels of study. Women are under-represented in engineering and technology; and more than proportionately represented in the arts and humanities and in the natural sciences. As the Equal Opportunities Commission told us in its evidence, '*degree choice clearly illustrates a gender bias with more than twice as many women as men studying English and French and four times as many men as women studying Physics and Computer Studies*'. Women are under-represented at higher levels of study, especially in research degrees, where only 35 per cent of postgraduate research students are women.

List of recommendations

…. We recommend to the Government and the Funding Bodies that, when allocating funds for the expansion of higher education, they give priority to those institutions which can demonstrate a commitment to widening participation, and have in place a participation strategy, a mechanism for monitoring progress, and provision for review by the governing body of achievement.

(London: NCIHE, 1997, vol. 1, pp. 21, 102, 370).

3. xix   A study of working-class girls at a South London comprehensive school shows why there are still relatively few who go to Russell Group universities.

S. Evans, 'In a Different Place. Working-Class Girls and Higher Education', *Sociology*, 43:2, 2009.

For all the young women in this study the value of HE as a means to higher earning power was crucial but the importance of this was seldom individualistic and more usually altruistic and family centred. For example, Meg, a white working-class girl who was hoping to become a Forensic Scientist, suggested that her future income would be handed over to her mother:

> ... *I don't think it [money] is going to affect me that much, yeah, I'd have a bit of extra money – I'd just give it to my Mum or something ....* *Money really isn't important to me.....*

For this group altruism played a central role in decision-making. Keira's words were typical in this respect:

> *The one thing I want to do is just to give something back to my family really, that's the most important thing to me, and helping my Nan and all ... that's the main thing.*

Thus while the young women interviewed sought personal satisfaction through education and employment in areas they believed to be interesting, they often attempted to counterbalance their personal interests (which had the danger of being seen as selfish pursuits) through imagining how they might use their future earnings to help others. The wish to pursue a degree-level education with more predictable economic rewards led many of the girls to choose vocational subjects .... Of the seven girls from ethnic minority backgrounds five intended to pursue vocational science subjects at university and all of these girls intended to remain living at home .... As Keira put it

> *The expense has got a lot to do with it, I'm not too keen on the whole 'you're going to be in debt afterwards' – and like, that puts me off a lot ....*

There were only four girls in the total sample who intended to move away from home to study .... Given that this study took place in London this did not in itself disqualify students from application to Russell Group elite institutions, but in some other parts of the country ... the financial need to remain at home could have a major impact on student access to more highly regarded universities.

(London: Sage, 2009, pp. 345–6).

Chapter 4

Sex and Sexualities

4.i   Marie Stopes (1880–1958) was a distinguished palaeobotanist and Fellow of University College, London when she wrote this sex manual addressed to middle-class married couples. The first of its kind, it was immensely popular: six editions appeared within a year of its publication. Stopes became a more controversial figure in the 1920s as a campaigner for birth control.

Marie Carmichael Stopes, *Married Love* (1918).

To-day, particularly in the middle classes of this country, marriage is far less really happy than its surface appears. Too many who marry expecting joy are bitterly disappointed …

It is never *easy* to make marriage a lovely thing; and it is an achievement beyond the powers of the selfish, or the mentally cowardly. Knowledge is needed and, as things are at present, knowledge is almost unobtainable by those who are most in want of it …

Expressed in general terms (which , of course, will not fit everybody) my view may be formulated thus: The mutually best regulation of intercourse in marriage is to have three or four days of repeated unions, followed by about ten days without any unions at all, unless some strong external stimulus has stirred a mutual desire.

I have been interested to discover that the people known to me who have accidentally fixed upon this arrangement of their lives are *happy*: and it should be noted that it fits in with the charts I give which represent the normal, spontaneous feeling of so many women …

The supreme law for husbands is: Remember that each act of union must be tenderly wooed for and won, and that no union should ever take place unless the woman also desires it and is made physically ready for it …

To render a woman ready before uniting with her is not only the merest act of humanity to save her pain, but is of value from the man's point of view, for (unless he is one of those relatively few abnormal and diseased variants who delight only in rape) the man gains an immense increase of sensation from the mutuality thus attained, and the health of both the man and the woman is most beneficially affected.

...

It should never be forgotten that without the discipline of control there is no lasting delight in erotic feeling. The fullest delight, even in a purely physical sense, can *only* be attained by those who curb and direct their natural impulses.

(Reprinted: Oxford: World's Classics, 2004, pp. 9, 52–6, 59).

4. ii In 1885 parliament had criminalised homosexual acts between men, but an attempt by Conservative backbencher F. A. Macquisten to apply the same rule to lesbians did not succeed. Sexologists had popularised a view of same-sex relationships as the result of biological abnormalities rather than immorality.

Hansard, HC Deb, 4 Aug 1921, cc 1799–1806.

CRIMINAL LAW AMENDMENT BILL

NEW CLAUSE ... Any act of gross indecency between female persons shall be a misdemeanour and punishable in the same manner as any such act committed by male persons under section eleven of the Criminal Law Amendment Act, 1885

Mr MACQUISTEN: I beg to move, 'That the Clause be read a Second time.'
... It is one which, I think, is long overdue in the criminal code of this country. I have had professional experience of very calamitous and sad cases due to gross practices indulged in of the kind ... which are referred to in my Amendment. These moral weaknesses date back to the very origin of history, and when they grow and become prevalent in any nation ... it is the beginning of the nation's downfall .... Only tonight I was speaking with a man ... who told me how his home had been ruined by the wiles of one abandoned female, who had pursued his wife, and later some other misconduct happened with a male person which enabled him to get a divorce. But for that he would have been shackled for life to that abandoned person, who had forgotten all the dictates of Nature and morality ...

Colonel WEDGWOOD: I cannot believe that the House will really pass this Clause. In the first place, it is a beastly subject, and it is being better advertised by the moving of this Clause than in any other way. I do not suppose that there are any members of the Labour party who know in the least what is intended by the Clause. For their benefit, I will tell them that the ordinary boy who goes to a public school learns ... from the classics which he reads about what is known as Lesbian vice. He finds all about Sappho, and when he goes to college he reads Swinburne, and that is the only way decent people in this country ever get to hear of this sort of thing .... This vice ... is obviously one which cannot be suppressed by law. How on earth are people to get convictions in a case of this kind? For one conviction that could be got in ten years, you may have, on the other hand, endless blackmail ...

Lieut-Colonel MOORE-BRABAZON: ... We must remember that on this subject we are not dealing with crime at all. We are dealing with abnormalities of the brain, and we have got to look on all these cases from that point of view .... In this case we are not trying to inculcate a fear of punishment. That already exists in society to-day, because the pervert is undoubtedly despised and shunned by all grades of society ...

To adopt a Clause of this kind would do harm by introducing into the minds of perfectly innocent people the most revolting thoughts, and because of that I ask the introducers of this Clause to withdraw it.

4. iii   The journal of the National Union of Societies for Equal Citizenship presents arguments for and against contraception from two of the earliest Englishwomen to qualify as doctors, Mrs Drysdale (Alice Vickery, 1844–1929) and Dame Mary Scharlieb (1845–1930).

Woman's Leader, vol. xv, 7, March 16, 1923, pp. 52–3.

FOR BIRTH CONTROL, By Mrs Drysdale

... It is a well-known fact that all European countries save France are overcrowded, and the struggle for a bare subsistence becomes ever keener. Had it not been for a rapidly falling birth-rate in Western Europe at least, during the last thirty years, it is probable that acute distress and even war would have happened earlier than it did ...

But a most important point for civilized society to consider is: What effect has birth control, as practised, had on the quality of the people? The answer is that is has been eugenic for the individual families where practised, but dysgenic for the nation as a whole, because the more prudent citizens left the increase of the nation to be drawn almost entirely from the wage-earning, as well as from the less fit types of society ... Surely the time has arrived when we must, for the sake of the individual and the State, consider, carefully, how, when, where, and to what extent the birth-rate of the future shall be distributed ...

The strong personal and family argument in favour of birth control lies in the evidence everywhere of poverty-stricken homes, worn-out and desperate mothers, sickly, ill-fed ... children, struggling wage-earners with the allurement of the public – house as a set-off to their comfortless homes, and the overcrowded labour market.

AGAINST BIRTH CONTROL, By Dr. Mary Scharlieb

... So far as our observation and experience go we are satisfied that any artificial control of conception is likely to react injuriously on health and happiness. This evil is chiefly shown by a decadence in nervous health and vigour, and it must be remembered that not infrequently the couples who refuse to accept children during the early years of married life are unlikely to have children when they desire to do so ...

One of the moral dangers which threaten to follow artificial control of the family is that of increasing an already all too vigorous sexual instinct. A couple which has elected to enjoy the privileges of matrimony, while refusing to bear its burdens, is likely to find that want of self-control ends in satiety. The burden of this falls chiefly on the wife, who, in seeking freedom from obligation may become the slave of desire.

Artificial limitation of a family is an injury not only to the husband and wife who practise it, but also to the existing child or children. The children of a small family do not receive the mutual discipline which is inevitable when a larger family of children grow up together.

Nor is the injury confined to the individuals or the family. It affects the whole nation. Whereas in most parts of England and Wales the population is adequate to the natural resources of the land, this is not true of our Empire at large ...

4. iv   Marguerite Antonia Radclyffe-Hall (1880–1943) was already a successful novelist when her melodramatic lesbian novel *The Well of Loneliness* was published. She used her father's name as a pseudonym and felt that she was a man trapped in a woman's body. If she had lived in the later twentieth century she might well have identified as trans-sexual.

Radclyffe Hall, *The Well of Loneliness* (1928).

That night the weight against Stephen's heart, with its icy coldness, melted; and it flowed out in such a torrent of grief that she could not stand up against that torrent, so that drowning though she was she found pen and paper, and she wrote to Angela Crossby.

What a letter! All the pent-up passion of months, all the terrible, rending, destructive frustrations must burst forth from her heart: 'Love me, only love me the way I love you. Angela, for God's sake, try to love me a little – don't throw me away, because if you do I'm utterly finished. You know how I love you, with my soul and my body; if it's wrong, grotesque, unholy – have pity ... I'm some awful mistake – God's mistake – I don't know if there are any more like me, I pray not for their sakes, because it's pure hell. But oh, my dear, whatever I am, I just love you and love you ...' And so it went on for page after page ...

Two days later Anna Gordon sent for her daughter .... It seemed to Stephen that all of a sudden she saw in her mother a very old woman ...

'All your life I've felt very strangely towards you', she was saying, 'I've felt a kind of physical repulsion, a desire not to touch or be touched by you – a terrible thing for a mother to feel .... I've often felt that I was being unjust, unnatural – but now I know that my instinct was right; it is you who are unnatural, not I .... And this thing that you are is a sin against creation. Above all is this thing a sin against the father who bred you, the father whom you dare to resemble ... I can only thank God that your father died before he was asked to endure this great shame.'

(Reprinted: London: Virago, 1982, pp. 199–203).

4.v   Denounced as obscene in the *Sunday Express*, *The Well of Loneliness* was banned – despite protests from the literary world – by the Home Secretary William Joynson Hicks. It remained banned in the UK until 1948. Here the editor of a feminist literary review ridicules the policy of censorship.

'The *Well of Loneliness* Decision', *Time and Tide*, Nov 23, 1928.

It is arguable that *The Well of Loneliness* itself is neither a very wholesome book nor particularly good literature. Indeed, we should not be concerned to suggest that it is. It deals with a distasteful form of excess – and it handles its theme sentimentally, which is as distasteful a method of handling it as could well be found .... At the same time it is obviously a book written with a purpose – if, as it appears to us, a mistaken purpose – and it is impossible to withhold a mead of admiration from Miss Radclyffe Hall for the courage she has shown in publishing it ...

What in fact, has been the result of the campaign against *The Well of Loneliness*? Obviously, as several of our correspondents point out, to increase public interest in it to a phenomenal extent. Rumour has it that the first result of Mr James Douglas's [*Sunday Express*] article last August was that several hundred extra copies of *The Well of Loneliness* were immediately ordered by leading libraries. It is true that these copies have since been withdrawn from circulation, but it is also true that as a result of the protracted discussion on the whole subject there is scarcely an intelligent reader in the country who can fail to be aware of the subject which the book discusses ..., whilst we are told that booksellers in Paris and New York are doing a roaring trade. Between them, the *Sunday Express*, the Home Secretary and one of our Stipendiary Magistrates have succeeded it would appear in creating a world best-seller. It is a remarkable achievement. But is it exactly what they want? ...

The fact is that whilst there is much to be said for keeping our streets and shop windows clean from pornographic postcards (whose object is clearly merely commercial) any laws which are stretched beyond this point ... are against the public interest .... We cannot allow our literature to be purged of all books which are unsuitable for leaving upon the nursery table ...

A grown people must, for good or evil, be given the opportunity of making its own decisions.

(London: 1928, pp. 1124–5).

4. vi The causes of the decline in prostitution are reviewed by the secretary of the British Social Hygiene Council Sybil Neville-Rolfe (1885–1955), in this inter-war sequel to Charles Booth's *Life and Labour of the People of London* (1902).

Mrs C. Neville-Rolfe, 'Sex-Delinquency', in H. Llewellyn Smith (ed.), *New Survey of London Life and Labour* (1930–35), vol. IX.

Apart from unnatural practices, which are the product of abnormal physiological or psychological conditions, the form of sex-delinquency which is at once the most repugnant to modern opinion and the most anti-social in its results is undoubtedly that of prostitution, under which certain women make their living by satisfying the physical demands of men on a commercial basis. All the evidence ... points to a great reduction in the volume of prostitution in London since Charles Booth's time ...

The period which forms the subject of this survey has inevitably been affected by the abnormal war conditions from 1914 to 1918. These conditions, particularly when the population as a whole was involved, brought about, as always, the relaxation of conventions, and the prevailing psychological conditions led to widespread prostitution, and promiscuous intercourse of a non-commercial type; while for that generation, the loss and disablement of a large body of adult men seriously disturbed the balance of the sexes at marriageable age ...

The improvement in the general standard of education has undoubtedly raised women's social status, while it has increased the sense of self-respect and personal responsibility on the part of members of both sexes ...

The activities of the boy scouts, girl guides, boys' and girls' clubs, brigades, industrial welfare and similar organisations, have greatly widened the interests and reduced the isolation of the adolescent worker during leisure hours ...

The advent of the cinema, the development of popular sporting recreations, football matches, dog racing, lawn tennis, hiking, and the bicycle, provide leisure occupations in which the young person is entirely independent of family control.

The methods by which the sexes become acquainted have perforce changed, and customs that used to be limited to those of recognised lax standards are now freely followed by the normal individual. For example it is no longer an indication of the absence of moral sense if an acquaintance made at a dance hall or cinema should ripen into friendship ...

In all social classes every degree from strictness to laxity of sex-behaviour exists, but in the vast majority of cases where extra-marital sex intercourse may occur it is of a non-commercial character, and has some emotional content, and any suggestion that it is in any way allied to prostitution would be rebutted with indignation by those concerned.

Whether this relaxation of the pre-marital standard of sex behaviour on the part of women and girls has resulted in an increase or a decrease in the total volume of promiscuity it is impossible to say with certainty, but it has certainly reduced prostitution.

(London: P. S. King & Son, 1930–5, pp. 287–8, 293–6).

4. vii   The historian Jenifer Hart tells how, as an eighteen year old visiting a family friend in Geneva in the early 1930s, she was introduced to the values of the literary and intellectual world of Bloomsbury.

Jenifer Hart, *Ask Me No More. An Autobiography* (1998).

On almost my first evening, as we sat up late talking about 'life', [Elliott] questioned the value of Christian virtues such as humility and self-sacrifice. My religious faith, already waning a little, disappeared rather rapidly in the presence of his agnosticism. It would be absolutely wrong to suggest that he tried to 'convert' me aggressively to his philosophy of life. I simply changed because he opened my eyes to different value systems which can, I think, best be described broadly as those of Bloomsbury, in particular absolute candour in personal relationships and a passionate dislike of hypocrisy. Moreover, like the Bloomsbury set, Elliott and his friends did not subscribe to conventional morality in connection with sexual relations. They were not indiscriminately promiscuous, but they saw no harm in the natural consummation of loving relationships. Indeed they went further and positively advocated this kind of behaviour unless it would cause pain to others .... To me these were at first shocking attitudes, but I gradually accepted them as I came to see that the people who held these beliefs and acted on them added to the richness of life and fostered pleasure rather than pain.

Before this time I had had no experience of physical love-making. Indeed I was largely ignorant of the 'facts of life', having received no sex education at home or in school. So although I was soon deeply in love with Elliott, I tolerated rather than enjoyed the physical side of our affair, though it was by modern standards fairly restrained.

(London: Peter Halban, 1998, pp. 38–9).

4. viii   Unmarried mothers could still face harsh social sanctions. Under the 1913 Mental Deficiency Act women who became pregnant or gave birth while in receipt of poor relief could be committed to institutions as 'feeble-minded'.

Maureen Sutton (ed. Shaun Tyas), *'We Didn't Know Owt'. A Study of Sexuality, Superstition and Death in Women's Lives in Lincolnshire during the 1930s, 40s and 50s* (2012).

The study of the unmarried mother revealed the critical and sad attitude of women towards their own sex i.e., 'My daughter got herself pregnant'

rather than 'My daughter was impregnated'. 'She got herself into trouble' ....
Women took all the blame ...

A woman recalled:

> *When mother was a young girl in the 1930s, grandma would say,*
> *"Don't bring trouble home or you'll end up in the workhouse"...*

In the 1930s and early 1940s, unmarried mothers were sometimes treated
differently according to their class. Working class families tended to send
their daughter away during their pregnancy. Their babies were nearly always
adopted .... Rich families, however, might have the baby brought up by an
aunt and the unmarried mother was said to have had a 'love child'. From
the 1930s:

> *There was a lass I knew got pregnant and her mam and dad were well*
> *off, he worked in a bank.*
> *She must have been like it when she left school 'cause she went straight*
> *down to London to finish her education. She stayed with her aunt. Her*
> *mum told my mam she'd had a love child. That's what they did in them*
> *days, but folk knew it weren't education they went away for ...*

A number of homes throughout the county housed unmarried mothers.
Harmston Hall became a hospital in 1934. In its early days it was known as
Harmston Colony. A retired hospital administrator reported:

> *Girls and women who were mentally handicapped, unmarried and*
> *had given birth to an illegitimate baby were committed to the hospital*
> *under the Mental Health Act. They were termed feeble minded or moral*
> *defectives. Their babies would be born at the girls' home or one of the 'homes*
> *for unmarried women'. Babies would be taken into care soon after birth*
> *and would either be adopted or admitted to another institution .... Once*
> *admitted, the mother had no say in whether or not she left the hospital. They*
> *were examined once a year and then signed in for another year ...*

Domestic help could be hired from the hospital throughout the war
years. In 1959, the Health Act changed and the treatment of patients became
'informal'. This was a medical term for patients being released. Many were
released because there was, in fact, nothing wrong with them. Society had
defined pre-marital sex as a sign of mental illness in itself. By this time,

however, many had become institutionalised and were unable to cope with life outside.

(Donington: Shaun Tyas, 2012, pp. 173–7).

4. ix   Child sex abuse became a preoccupation in the 1970s and after but there is no way of knowing how its incidence changed over time. This account from a woman who grew up in the 1940s shows that incest was not always treated as seriously harmful by psychiatrists.

Jo Mary Stafford, *Light in the Dust. A True Story of the Triumph of the Human Spirit* (2002).

It was a lovely sunny day, a Sunday, when my education in life began in earnest. I was about seven years old and had just returned from Sunday School with my brother and sisters. Dad always had a lie-down on Sunday afternoons, after returning from the pub, and it seemed Mom joined him because the door was always locked when we got home …

On this particular Sunday … I fell … cutting my knee quite badly …. As [Mom] bandaged the wound in her rough-and-ready fashion, I heard Dad's voice rumbling from upstairs …

'Send her up here, I'll see to her' …

Up I jumped, knee temporarily forgotten, and was already up the first three stairs before Mom caught me and hauled me back into the living room …

'Joanny' Mom had begged, 'listen to me. It's very important. NEVER, NEVER goo to yer dad's bed or let 'im touch ya … stay safe. Stay away from 'im …'e might 'urt ya like my dad did me. Listen …. When I woz a little gairl, not much older'n you, me dad started to … interfere with me, when me mom wuz out. 'E told me not to tell nobody, or 'e'd kill me …. Yer dad knows what me dad done to me, and 'e says 'e'll do it to you gairls if I don't do everything 'e says … I've give 'im the rent money … e's just never satisfied. Promise me,' she whispered, 'Promise me ya'll never … I don't want it to 'appen to you.'

I recall … returning to the garden to seek out Margaret …. Her ten year old face was tired and wise and old … 'It was time yer knew, our Jo. It's safer that way. Now, when dad calls ya to go to 'is bed or anything, yer'll 'ave to act like ya ain't 'eard, like me and Josy do. Now off ya goo an' play' ….

For the record, both my father and grandfather were of above average intelligence. Both were well read and had travelled away from their narrow roots. It was not ignorance, then, that led to their crimes, but sheer animal lust. One avant-garde psychiatrist tried to tell me, when I was twenty and first sought help, that incest was 'just an excess of fatherly affection'. 'Balls', I retorted in a rare moment of coarseness ....

These experiences in my early life, and my mother's, had a devastating 'knock-on' effect. My mother never recovered, and was to spend years in and out of mental hospitals and be further violated by mind-bending drugs and electric shock treatment. And so I lost her.

(London: John Blake Publishing Ltd, 2002, pp. 81–8).

4. x   Premarital sex was still primarily associated with the lower working class, according to Gorer's mid-century survey of readers of the Sunday *People*, and women were more conservative in their attitudes to sex and marriage than men.

Geoffrey Gorer, *Exploring English Character* (1955).

Despite the importance that the majority of English people give to sexual love in marriage, the majority think that both sexes should approach marriage with no prior sexual experience. Slightly more than half the population in the case of men, and nearly two-thirds in the case of women, disapprove of any sexual experience before marriage ...

Men are markedly more in favour of some pre-marital sexual experience then are women; 40 men to 26 women approve of a young man having some experience, and 30 men to 14 women approve of a young woman doing so .... Quite a number of women support a 'double standard' of sexual morality in which what is sauce for the gander is taboo for the goose; men are much more likely to invoke a 'single standard' in which they will not deny to others what they claim for themselves ....

With one exception, social class makes remarkably little difference ... ; a far higher proportion of the lower working class are in favour of sexual experience before marriage than of any other group .... There is a folk tradition that in some of the metropolitan and rural groups of the lower working class marriage normally follows pregnancy ...

The pattern already discernible continues with the egalitarian statement 'Women really enjoy the physical side of sex just as much as men'. Sixty-three per cent of the men agree with this statement, compared with 51 per cent of the women; a mere 10 per cent of the men, but 18 per cent of the women, reject it ...

Among the young, the unmarried and the more prosperous, especially in the Midlands, there is a belief, held more strongly by men than women, that women's sexual feelings are as strong as, or stronger than, men's; this belief diminishes with marriage, increase in age, or decrease in income.

(London: Cresset Press, 1955, pp. 94–5, 116).

4. xi Improvement in the sex lives of married women was attributed mainly to socio-economic change in this study of the Potteries.

J. Sarsby, *Missuses and Mouldrunners. An Oral History of Women Pottery-Workers at Work and at Home* (1988).

By the 1970s it was possible for these women to discard brutal or feckless husbands, to live on their own wages – even with the cost of child-minding one child at £7 to £12 per week – as long as a woman had taken contraception into her own hands, or her children were grown. Social security, of course, has meant that lone women with dependent children do not have to starve, even if they do not go out to work. Increases in women's wages and changes in divorce and benefits have thus take away a lot of power from the 'manly' man with his imprisoned family. But the essential change, in the Potteries and in society in general, is in the number of families in which the husband sees himself as a man not through the number of his children but through the quality of life he can provide for the family.

To see how this is happening, let us take an example of another family in which the wife is a pottery-worker, as were her mother and grandmother before her. Born in the early 1940s, once again she was married young and a mother twice over at 20, but at that point they decided together not to have any more children:

> Me husband said, 'We've got one of each, there's no other sort to have, we've finished.' So I left it entirely into his hands, and that's been it. And we had a great relationship, we always have had, you know. I'm not afraid of sex ... I've never been on the pill. I just leave it in his hands, and he must be a good husband, that's all I can say .... He said, 'Leave it to me. We won't have no more', and we haven't had no more.
>
> (Milton Keynes: Open University Press, 1988, p. 108).

4. xii Research on girls in a 1970s Birmingham youth club throws light on the high incidence of teenage pregnancy.

Angela McRobbie, 'Working-class girls and the culture of femininity',
Women's Studies Group, Centre for Contemporary Cultural Studies,
Women Take Issue: Aspects of Women's Subordination (1978).

Age ... plays a role in structuring the girls' sexuality. That is, what is expected of them sexually is socially understood in terms of whether they are at the 'going steady' stage (fifteen onwards) or at the 'one night stand' stage (thirteen/fourteen). There are of course always exceptions, but this study suggested that between the ages of fourteen and fifteen, girls occupy a kind of twilight zone sexually. They interpret their sexuality in sub-sexual terms, in the vocabulary of a boy 'trying it on', 'trying to get it' or, more commonly, 'having "wandering" palms'. Sex education, with its emphasis on 'human biology', clinical sexuality and, as one girl put it, 'bathing babies', clearly has little to offer here. The girls cannot easily 'cash' any of its prescriptions because it completely ignores the social and brutally sexist environment within which this emergent sexuality is experienced. If you haven't got a steady then contraception is simply not an issue. Any girl who consciously 'took precautions' with a casual 'date' would be laying herself wide open to savage criticism since such calculated, premeditated action totally contravenes the dominant code of romance ....

It ... became apparent in the course of the research that girls didn't really expect the romance of marriage to last indefinitely ...

Yet despite this 'realism' the girls were still fascinated with marriage, partly because of the status it would confer on them and partly because it was the only possible means through which their sexuality could be expressed legitimately.

> Me Mum says she doesn't mind me being on the Pill if I was engaged or just about to be married, but she'd hit the roof if she thought I'd go on it just, you know, for anyone, for someone that wasn't a steady or me fiancé. I wouldn't anyway, you just get known for being like that ....

On the one hand boys naturally seek sexual experience but any girl who willingly participates sexually with them is branded and later denounced as a 'whore' or a 'tart'. This means that every time one of the Mill Lane girls goes out on a date with a boy she is confronted with a situation not easily resolved. If she gives in to the boy's demands she stands not only to become pregnant, but also to lose her reputation – still, it seems, a valuable asset on the marriage market for working-class girls. As 'Sue' put it, 'If you get known for being like that you lose all your friends. Girls don't want to know you and the boys just want the one thing. It's not worth it.'

(London: Hutchinson, 1978, pp. 98, 105–7).

4. xiii   The radical feminist academic Sheila Jeffreys reflects on the growth in acceptability of pornography.

Sheila Jeffreys, *Anticlimax: a feminist perspective on the sexual revolution* (1990).

One result of the 'sexual revolution' was that pornography was 'derepressed'. The pornography industry exploded into growth in the late 60s and early 70s and became a massive, multi-billion-dollar industry …. Pornography no longer had to be under the counter, but appeared on news-stands and at supermarket checkouts …. The sheer visibility of the porn industry had a consequence which the pornbrokers may not have intended. Women were able to look at pornography and for the first time had at their disposal a panoramic view of what constituted male sexuality. During the 1970s pornography became more and more concerned with sadomasochism and much more brutal in its portrayal of women …. The first London antipornography group was formed in 1977 because we saw double-page spreads of women's genitals, called 'split beaver' or 'salmon sandwich', in shop windows and being perused by young boys in corner newsagents' shops …. As daughters of the sexual revolution we had to overcome feelings of guilt at not liking pornography. Reprogrammed by our experience in the 1960s to see 'explicit' sex in movies and books as a positive good and nakedness as desirable, we had to overcome some powerful conditioning through consciousness-raising sessions before we could articulate our rage. Women can only seriously critique any expression of sexuality when they have thrown the junk of psychoanalytic notions of inhibitions and repression out of the window.

(London: Women's Press, 1990, pp. 250–1).

4. xiv   'Rape in Marriage Finally Illegal', declared *Spare Rib* (229, November 1991), welcoming the Law Lords' ruling of 23 October 1991 'overturning 250 years of sexual slavery'. The basis of their decision is summarised here in the Law Reports for 1992.

Lord Keith of Kinkel: Sir Matthew Hale, in his *History of the Pleas of the Crown* (vol. 1 (1736) …) wrote:

> *But the husband cannot be guilty of a rape committed by himself upon*
> *his lawful wife, for by their matrimonial consent and contract the wife hath*
> *given herself up in this kind unto her husband which she cannot retract ....*

It may be taken that the proposition was generally regarded as an accurate statement of the Common Law of England. The common law is, however, capable of evolving in the light of changing social, economic and cultural developments. Hale's proposition reflected the state of affairs in these respects at the time it was enunciated. Since then the status of women, and particularly of married women, has changed out of all recognition in various ways which are very familiar and upon which it is unnecessary to go into detail. Apart from property matters and the availability of matrimonial remedies, one of the most important changes is that marriage is in modern times regarded as a partnership of equals, and no longer one in which the wife gives her irrevocable consent to sexual intercourse with her husband under all circumstances .... In modern times any reasonable person must regard that conception as quite unacceptable.

[1992] 1 AC, 599 Regina v. R., pp. 615–16.

4. xv   Attempts by the Blair government to repeal Section 28 of the 1988 Local Government Act, which banned local authorities and schools from providing sex education that 'promoted' homosexuality, ran into prolonged opposition. Janet Young (1926–2002), a leading campaigner against liberalising the law on homosexuality, was a former Leader of the House of Lords and the only woman appointed by Margaret Thatcher to Cabinet office. Baroness Gould of Potternewton (Labour) was President of the Family Planning Association; Lady Saltoun of Abernethy a Scottish hereditary peeress and Crossbencher.

Hansard, HL Deb, 6 Dec 1999, cc 1049–50, 1079–84.

LOCAL GOVERNMENT BILL

Second Reading

Baroness Young ... I now turn to Clause 68 .... The intention is to promote homosexuality ....

Nor would it make it possible to say that marriage is best. It tells young children – remember that it applies to both primary and secondary schools – that a homosexual relationship is the same as a heterosexual one. It is not.

Nor do I believe that the overwhelming majority of people in this country believe that it is the same. But if Clause 68 is agreed it will promote something that children are far too young to understand. Above all, it goes against the tradition of family and undermines responsible parents.

The proper use of teaching and sex education – to prevent bullying and to answer proper questions from those who are worried or unhappy – can be conducted under the present law. But of one matter I am certain: if Clause 68 is agreed it will open the floodgates to very unsuitable material appearing in schools for the use of children. It will encourage many children to pursue a path which most responsible parents do not believe is right ...

Baroness Gould of Potternewton ... I wish to concentrate my brief remarks on Clause 68 of the Bill and to welcome the repeal of ... Section 28 of the Local Government Act of 1988 ....

There is no question that one of the immediate effects of the implementation of Section 28 was an increase in hate crimes against both individual gays and lesbians and organisations they were associated with. It has stopped libraries from stocking books on homosexual issues and the ambiguity it has created has meant that some teachers have used Section 28 to avoid issues of sexuality .... It has also meant that some teachers who are homophobic – and they do exist – have found Section 28 has given their prejudice a legitimacy. Furthermore, it has almost certainly meant that in many cases homophobic bullying has been tacitly tolerated.

.... There have been no prosecutions under Section 28, but its psychological impact has eliminated freedom of discussion and penalised a minority group made up of large numbers of individuals from all social classes who play a vital role in our society. That psychological impact has considerably hindered local authorities in providing support and services to the gay and lesbian communities ...

Lady Saltoun of Abernethy. The repeal of Section 28 will remove the small amount of protection which it has provided for the past eleven years against the manipulation of even quite young children against their parents' wishes by a small but vociferous and determined minority .... Section 28 needs to be strengthened, not abolished ....

I am sorry that the Christian Churches, and especially the Church of England, seem to have weakened their stance [on homosexuality] recently. There is some quite powerful stuff in the gospels about the consequences of corrupting children .... Perhaps that is why the churches are getting emptier and emptier. There is not much point in a church which has no morals and believes in nothing …

4. xvi   The philosopher Baroness Warnock, author of the 1984 Report on human fertilisation and embryology, sees no case for refusing lesbians access to artificial insemination by donor or *in vitro* fertilisation.

Mary Warnock, *Making Babies. Is There a Right to Have Children?* (2002).

Perhaps the most contentious cases in which [IVF] treatment is sought for reasons other than infertility are those of homosexuals of both genders who request assisted conception, individually or as a couple ….

As I have said, there is no positive law that confers on people the right to have children; but neither is there a law that forbids homosexuals to have children ….

There is one factual matter to be noted here …. : artificial insemination can be carried out at home, with a syringe, and without medical intervention …. There are, however, enormous advantages in having AID properly carried out, and, especially for a lesbian couple who want a child, the safeguard of screening of semen at a clinic set up for this purpose is obviously desirable …. And so the question is whether this particular kind of assisted conception should be available to everybody, regardless of his/her sexual orientation and regardless of whether any resulting child will be brought up by a homosexual couple. I do not believe that there is any reason to prohibit such a family arrangement ….

Such an outcome will seem outrageous to many people. They will argue that the good of the future child should absolutely prohibit homosexual couples from having and bringing up children …. Baroness Young and many of her supporters argued that for teachers to present homosexuality as an option, a possible and accepted alternative way of life, was to undermine the family, corrupt young people, and lead them into disastrous and permanently damaging experiments. How much worse such moralists might think it if not merely teachers at school but parents at home themselves demonstrate by their own lives that a different kind of family … is not just a possibility but an existing reality for a particular child ….

It is generally believed, by people who hold to no religious dogma on the matter, that sexual orientation is not usually a matter of choice … but of an inborn tendency …. While a child might literally inherit some 'homosexual genes' from one of her parents … she is unlikely to be so much influenced by her environment alone that she finds herself a homosexual in opposition to her natural instincts.

(Oxford: Oxford University Press, 2002, pp. 57–63; © OUP, reproduced with permission).

Chapter 5

Feminisms and Femininity

5. i Catherine Marshall (1880–1961) was among the pacifists who broke with the National Union of Women's Suffrage Societies (NUWSS) over its failure to oppose war in 1914. The WIL became the Women's International League for Peace and Freedom in 1919.

Catherine Marshall, 'The future of women in politics' (1915), in M. Kamester & J. Vellacott (eds), *Militarism Versus Feminism. Writings on Women and War* (1987).

The future of women in politics depends, more even than does the future of democracy itself, on whether the war results in the discrediting of militarism, or whether it leaves all the nations more militarist than they were before.

Conversely it is true that whether the civilised world does or does not surrender its soul to militarism will depend in no small measure on what place women are going to take in politics ….

The woman's point of view, applied to politics, would introduce a new valuation. We have become too much accustomed to talk of men as 'hands' in a factory, or 'heads' to be polled at an election; or as 'casualties'(!) by which to measure military success or failure. To a woman every man is a mother's son – not as her possession, but as her gift of great price which must not be wasted, her great adventure on which she has staked her all.

… I believe that the reaction after this war will give a tremendous impetus to the development of internationalism …

We could do much if we had the power which the vote brings. We can do something without it. As I write, a new women's organisation is being born, to be called the Women's International League, which will have as its object 'to establish the principles of Right rather than Might, and co-operation rather than conflict, in national and international affairs, and for this purpose to work for (1) the development of the ideals underlying modern democracy in the interests of constructive peace, and (2) the emancipation of women and the protection of their interests …'

The formation of this League, and of similar organisations in other countries, is the outcome of the Women's International Congress held at The Hague last April, under the presidency of Miss Jane Addams of Hull House, Chicago. That Congress marked the opening of a new chapter in the Women's Movement ...

(London: Virago, 1987, pp. 45–52).

5. ii   Founded in 1921 by Viscountess Rhondda, proprietor of *Time and Tide*, the Six Point Group stood for equal rights feminism but campaigned in the interests of women as mothers as well as wage-earners: active for over 50 years, it was dissolved in 1983.

'The Six Point Group', *Time and Tide*, 4, 19 January, 1923

We have decided to devote a series of supplements to the Six Point Group .... Whilst the objects for which the Group stands are actually of importance to every citizen in the country, they particularly and specifically affect women as women. Matters of special concern to women fall naturally into two groups .... There is the group of reforms which affects women as mothers, and the group which affects them as wage earners ...

The Six Point Group demands:-

1. Satisfactory legislation on child assault.
2. Satisfactory legislation for the widowed mother.
3. Satisfactory legislation for the unmarried mother and her child.
4. Equal rights of guardianship for married parents.
5. Equal pay for teachers.
6. Equal opportunities for men and women in the Civil Service.

.... It will ... be clear to anyone who knows the political women's world that practically all the Women's Societies are in favour of all six reforms.

5. iii   Eleanor Rathbone (1872–1946) replaced Millicent Garrett Fawcett as leader of the NUWSS, renamed the National Union of Societies for Equal Citizenship (NUSEC) in 1919. Her intellectually rigorous brand of social feminism, or 'New Feminism', provoked controversy.

'Patience and Impatience, March 6, 1923', Eleanor Rathbone, *Milestones: Presidential Addresses* (1929).

One of my good friends … said to me recently: 'You are such a good fighter: *what* a pity you are such a bad feminist!' Now my private opinion – and I told her so – is that I am a much more root and branch feminist than she is. The fact is that there are two kinds of feminism, or rather two ways of interpreting sex-equality. There are those who interpret it in terms of identity with men, and those who interpret it in terms of difference. The former school do not, I think, imagine the status achieved by man to be so ideal that all that woman needs is to climb up and stand by his side. But they see truly that one of the tricks, devices by which men have sought to lead women to acquiesce in their inferiority of status, is by pretending that it is not really an inferiority, but only a difference corresponding to a real difference of function. Hence those feminists feel that they are taking the safer course in always

11. Eleanor Rathbone in 1922, aged 50 and launched on her controversial but highly successful presidency of NUSEC, campaigning here in a chauffeur-driven car. The daughter of a wealthy Liverpool merchant and philanthropist, she was one of the few upper-middle class girls who persuaded their families to allow them to study at Oxbridge. University-educated women of her generation from similar backgrounds include Maude Royden, Lettice Fisher (nee Ilbert), Eva Hubback (nee Spielman), and Margery Fry. Courtesy of LSE Library.

demanding the identical right that men have enjoyed, just in the spirit of the housewife, who, because her grocer has repeatedly tried to palm off on her an inferior substitute for some article, will insist on having the recognised brand 'as patronised by the Royal Household.' Other feminists, while conscious of the risks they are running, are like the housewife who insists on selecting the goods that please her palate without reference to what others have preferred. I belong to the latter school. I want women to build up their own status, liberties, and opportunities free from men's restrictions, but not necessarily identical with those of men. It is a fatal thing for a woman's organisation to get the reputation of being 'anti-man', and I would not for worlds bring that reproach on the N.U.S.E.C. But I knew a wise old lady who was fond of repeating: 'The more I see of some people the better I like my dog': and after every experience of men's politics and administration my feeling is: 'The more I see of some men, especially politicians, the less I want women to adopt all their methods and standards of value.' Fortunately, on most questions of immediate practical politics, these two schools of thought think alike.

(Liverpool: privately printed, 1929, pp. 15–16).

5. iv   Rathbone's support for Family Allowances had feminist foundations, as shown in her analysis of the ways in which 'male breadwinner' ideology disadvantaged women. An Independent MP from 1929, she lived to see the introduction of Family Allowances in 1945.

Eleanor Rathbone, *The Disinherited Family. A Plea for the Endowment of the Family* (1924).

The Doctrine of a Uniform 'Living Wage'

During the last quarter of a century an uneasy conscience ... has compelled employers to allow the question of the human needs of families to intrude itself into discussions on wages .... It has gradually come to be assumed almost without discussion that a trade in a healthy condition should, under normal circumstances, yield to full-time men workers of average efficiency not only enough for their own maintenance, but for that of their wives and children ...

[But] a family consisting of husband, wife and three dependent children [generally assumed to be a typical family for purposes of calculating the 'living wage'] is in fact one of the smallest groupings .... Of men workers over twenty in England, roughly speaking,

27   per cent are bachelors or widowers without dependent children
24.7   per cent are married couples without children or with no dependent child below fourteen
16.6   per cent have one dependent child
13   per cent have two dependent children
8.8   per cent have three dependent children
9.9   per cent have more than three dependent children ...

The Woman Wage-Earner

Everyone knows that, broadly speaking, there is a double standard of pay for the two sexes. With the exception of a few occupations, of which the medical profession and the textile industry are the most conspicuous, women receive a lower rate of pay than men, even when they are engaged in the same occupation and do work which is equal in quantity and quality. Everyone knows too that there is among men workers a strong dislike and fear of the competition of women ... This dislike has no doubt been greatly intensified ... by sheer sex prejudice – by a feeling among the members of the dominant sex that it is belittling their own strength and skill to admit that any woman can attain to the like ... But there can, I think, be no doubt that the most formidable and permanent part of the opposition ... is the feeling among men workers that, as things are, the competition of women is not fair competition ....

Women are regarded as a dangerous class of blacklegs, who because they can afford to take and do take lower pay are a standing menace to the men's standard of life. [There is also] the belief that men have a better right to employment, because they represent not only themselves but their wives and children and the fact that some women have and many men have not dependants is ignored ... The married women naturally tend to share this view, though when they have themselves been wage-earners it is tempered by loyalty to their fellow workers ... It is even shared to some extent by the women wage-earners themselves, especially the young ones who expect soon to be married .... So long as the women remain in the few trades – mainly the needle trades and domestic service – which are traditionally and nearly exclusively their own, they are accepted as a matter of course, but whenever women are engaged in occupations where there is actual or potential masculine competition, they are conscious of being looked at askance ... by the whole body of organized male workers, and to a certain extent by general public opinion as expressed in the press and in social intercourse.

The Turk Complex

Among the strongest instincts of human nature is the desire of power, of domination, of being looked up to and admired. Through all ages and in all countries ... men, even the humblest and most oppressed, have found scope for the satisfaction of this desire in their power over their own wives and children. Even the slave was lord in his hut. His authority rested ultimately on the greater physical strength of the adult male, on the helplessness of infancy and the special needs of maternity ...

The last century has seen the emancipation of women and children from the most oppressive and cruel forms of marital and paternal power, as well as from the economic conditions which bound those of the poorer classes to a kind of industrial slavery ... But ... it has also seen the simultaneous and partly consequent extension of the period of their economic dependency on the male head of the family. Is it fantastic to suggest that in accepting this new burden, the unconscious mind of man was aware that he was also securing a new hold over his dependants, more subtly effective than that which he was foregoing? .... the power of the purse, the knowledge that his wife throughout her married life, his children till adolescence, would have nothing in the world but what he chose to give them? .... It is easy to see what satisfaction the institution of the dependent family gives to all sorts and conditions of men – to the tyrannous man what opportunities of tyranny, to the selfish of self-indulgence, to the generous of preening himself in the sunshine of his own generosity, to the chivalrous of feeling himself the protector of the weak .... .

This being so, it is not surprising that when the idea of direct provision [of Family Allowances] is first presented to men's minds, a large proportion of them find it distasteful, for reasons which they do not care to analyse.

(London: Edward Arnold & Co., 1924, pp. 14–16, 113–14, 269–71).

5. v   The novelist Winifred Holtby (1898–1935), a member of the Six Point Group, responds to a manifesto in favour of the New Feminism by Rathbone's ally Eva Hubback (1886–1949).

Winifred Holtby, 'Feminism Divided', *Yorkshire Post*, 26 July 1926, reprinted in P. Berry & A. Bishop (eds), *Testament of a Generation. The Journalism of Vera Brittain and Winifred Holtby* (1985).

Mrs Hubback [writing in the *Yorkshire Post* of 12 July] sees among feminists two schools of thought – the Old Feminists, who view with misgivings any 'decline from the pure milk of the word' of 'equality of liberties, status and opportunities between men and women,' and the New Feminists, who believe that 'the satisfactory solution of these points is undoubtedly in sight,' and that 'the time has come to look beyond them.' They have, therefore, included in their programme reforms such as family allowances, birth control, and similar policies affecting the lives of 'women who are doing work that only women can do,' together in some cases with causes of more general interest such as peace by arbitration.

The division concerns both the aims and policy of the feminist movement, and superficially the New Feminism appears more tolerant, sane and far-sighted. Old Feminism, with its motto 'Equality First', and its concentration upon those parts of national life where sex differentiation still prevails, may seem conservative, hysterical, or blindly loyal to old catchwords. This is not the real truth. The New Feminism emphasizes the importance of the 'women's point of view', the Old Feminism believes in the primary importance of the human being ... .

Personally, I am a feminist, and an Old Feminist, because I dislike everything that feminism implies. I desire an end of the whole business, the demands for equality, the suggestions of sex warfare, the very name of feminist. I want to be about the work in which my real interests lie, the study of inter-race relationships, the writing of novels and so forth. But while the inequality exists, while injustice is done and opportunity denied to the great majority of women, I shall have to be a feminist, and an Old Feminist, with the motto Equality First. And I shan't be happy till I get it.

(London: Virago, 1985, pp. 47–8).

5. vi   **Protective legislation for women workers in industry was a particularly divisive issue, leading to the resignation in 1927 of over half NUSEC's executive committee. Supporters of the Six Point Group formed the Open Door Council to campaign for equal treatment of women in the work-place.**

Open Door Council, First Annual Report, May 5th, 1926, to April 4th, 1927.

Those who formed the OPEN DOOR COUNCIL have for some time been viewing with increasing alarm the present tendency to legislate with the ostensible object of improving the lot of the woman worker. Not that industrial conditions do not require improvement in many ways, but that it is essential that any improvement should affect conditions for both men and women. The fact that male workers are for the most part members of Trade Unions which protect their interests does not alter the principle that conditions should by law be good, and equally good for both sexes … .

If women's freedom to work is hemmed about by restrictions and limitations (however pious their object) which do not at the same time apply to men, they will have even less chance than they have at present of securing well-paid employment. Employers will tend to employ the workers whose engagement entails the least compliance with rules and regulations …

Thus … women will be squeezed out of higher grade work and still further crowded into badly-paid jobs … .

The tradition of the delicacy of women by which so much of our factory legislation is influenced is a heritage from the days when women – the most depressed class of wage-earners – were also non-citizens … Women, so long as they were unenfranchised and unorganised, required to be legislated for. And the citizen endeavouring to do his best for them automatically classed them with his other dependants – children.

This automatic classification has continued up to the present time in industrial legislation: women are constantly grouped with children and young persons, and treated as non-adults who shall not have the same right as men to choose their work …

The proof that the first need of a woman worker is a good wage is to be found in the experience of the War, when women were not only encouraged to take up work usually considered unsuitable, but were also encouraged to work long hours by night as well as by day. The result … was a marked improvement of health among women workers – an improvement due (in spite of rationing) to the better food earned by better wages.

The real problem for the woman wage earner is poverty. Malnutrition is a far more serious evil than working after six o'clock at night.

(The Women's Library, London, GB 0106 5/ODC).

5. vii   Labour MP Margaret Bondfield (1873–1953), opposing the repeal of restrictions on women working with lead paint, defends the principle of protective legislation. A co-founder with Mary Macarthur of Britain's first general union for women, the National Federation of Women Workers (1906), she became as Minister for Labour, 1929–31, the first female cabinet minister.

Hansard, HC Deb, 19 July 1927, cc 244–5.

Miss Bondfield. The arguments to which we have just listened are exactly the same kind of arguments as were used in the eighties ... against protection for those women suffering from wrist-drop, phossy-jaw and a number of other evils which we have been nearly able to exterminate by means of protective legislation .... Regulations are not regarded as a sufficient or adequate defence for men, but even if men prefer to go on being poisoned, that is absolutely no argument why women should go on being poisoned until we have some other way of dealing with this subject ...

Let me tell the House of the manner in which this was brought vividly to my attention in connection with my own union. Women employed in painting babies' perambulators with white lead paint were taken violently ill and died .... It is surely commonsense to say that an ingredient which has proved to be so dangerous to people who have handled it, should be prohibited, just as we have prohibited phosphorus in matches ... This is one of those questions about which there is great feeling in the country, particularly among the working classes themselves ...

It seems a very amazing thing that all the objections to protective legislation should come from women who are not themselves working women. The main argument is that it is going to restrict the field of women's employment. I do not think that is a sound argument at all. Since we have ... improved the conditions of women's work by protective legislation, there are more, not fewer, women working in connection with these trades.

5. viii   **Virginia Woolf (1882–1941) criticised patriarchy in terms that appealed more to later generations than to her contemporaries. This essay was based on talks given at the Cambridge women's colleges on 'women and fiction'. Here she portrays herself researching the subject in the British Museum Reading Room.**

Virginia Woolf, *A Room of One's Own* (1929).

Have you any notion how many books are written about women in the course of one year? Have you any notion how many are written by men? ... Here I had come with a notebook and a pencil proposing to spend a morning reading ... But I should need to be a herd of elephants, I thought, and a wilderness of spiders, desperately referring to the animals that are reputed longest lived and most multitudinously eyed, to cope with all this ... .

While I pondered I had unconsciously ... been drawing a picture ... I had been drawing a face, a figure. It was the face and the figure of Professor von X engaged in writing his monumental work entitled *The Mental, Moral, and Physical Inferiority of the Female Sex* ... The professor was made to look very angry and very ugly in my sketch, as he wrote his great book ...

I strolled off to find a place for luncheon ... Some previous luncher had left the lunch edition of the evening paper on a chair, and, waiting to be served, I began idly reading the headlines. A ribbon of very large letters ran across the page. Somebody had made a big score in South Africa. Lesser ribbons announced that Sir Austen Chamberlain was at Geneva. A meat axe with human hair on it had been found in a cellar. Mr Justice – commented in the Divorce Courts upon the Shamelessness of Women ... A film actress had been lowered from a peak in California and hung suspended in mid-air ... The most transient visitor to this planet, I thought, who picked up this paper could not fail to be aware, even from this scattered testimony, that England is under the rule of a patriarchy. Nobody in their senses could fail to detect the dominance of the professor. His was the power and the money and the influence. He was the proprietor of the paper and its editor and sub-editor. He was the Foreign Secretary and the Judge. He was the cricketer ... He suspended the film actress in mid-air. He will decide if the hair on the meat axe is human: he it is who will acquit or convict the murderer, and hang him, or let him go free.

(Reprinted: Harmondsworth: Penguin, 1945, pp. 27, 31–4).

5. ix   In *Three Guineas* Woolf imagines herself responding to requests for subscriptions to three charities. She distances herself from 'feminism', and identifies with the aims of the peace movement. But she argues that women's movements of the past – including Josephine Butler's crusade against state-regulated prostitution – were fighting the same battle against tyranny as the opponents of fascism in the 1930s.

Virginia Woolf, *Three Guineas* (1938).

For the first time in English history an educated man's daughter can give her brother one guinea of her own making at his request ... That, Sir, is so momentous an occasion in the history of civilization that some celebration seems called for ... Let us invent a new ceremony for this new occasion. What more fitting than to destroy an old word, a vicious and corrupt word that has done much harm in its day and is now obsolete?

The word 'feminist' is the word indicated. That word, according to the dictionary, means 'one who champions the rights of women'. Since the only right, the right to earn a living, has been won, the word no longer has a meaning. And a word without a meaning is a dead word, a corrupt word. Let us therefore celebrate this occasion by cremating the corpse ... Observe, Sir, what has happened as a result of our celebration. The word 'feminist' is destroyed; the air is cleared; and in that clearer air what do we see? Men and women working together for the same cause. The cloud has lifted from the past too. What were they working for in the nineteenth century – those queer dead women in their poke bonnets and shawls? The very same cause for which we are working now. 'Our claim was no claim of women's rights only;' – it is Josephine Butler who speaks – 'it was larger and deeper; it was a claim for the rights of all – all men and women – to the respect in their persons of the great principles of Justice and Equality and Liberty.' The words are the same as yours; the claim is the same as yours. The daughters of educated men who were called, to their resentment, 'feminists' were in fact the advance guard of your own movement. They were fighting the same enemy that you are fighting and for the same reasons. They were fighting the tyranny of the patriarchal state as you are fighting the tyranny of the Fascist state ... You are feeling in your own persons what your mothers felt when they were shut out ... because they were women. Now you are being shut out, you are being shut up, because you are Jews, because you are democrats, because of race, because of religion ... The whole iniquity of dictatorship, whether in Oxford or Cambridge, in Whitehall or Downing Street, against Jews or against women, in England, or in Germany, in Italy or in Spain is now apparent to you. But now we are fighting together.

(Reprinted: London: Hogarth Press, 1943, pp. 183–7).

5. x   **The writer Olwen Ward Campbell (1889–1959) reports on a conference of professional women who met to discuss how women might help to improve post-war society. The focus here is on factors that restrict women's influence.**

Olwen Ward Campbell, *The Feminine Point of View* (1952).

The assumption of women's inferiority is embedded in our social attitudes. Many men, whether consciously or not, base quite a lot of their own self-valuation upon it. Mothers, moulded in the same tradition, pass it on to their daughters ... .

In the majority of homes the boy gets more pocket money than the girl. When he goes out to work he usually receives much higher pay ...

When the girl marries she has no assured economic status at all ...

Women *as a sex* are often criticised, mocked, generalised about on the smallest evidence in a way that men are not – because men are felt to represent the norm .... In almost any daily paper one may find casual and silly gibes against women occurring as a matter of course. And though women are allowed to speak with authority far oftener than ever before, they have to be specially careful how they do it. In a small volume of essays by Miss Dorothy Sayers[1] there is one written towards the end of the war which pointed out the great need that there would be to continue to work very hard if we were to survive as a nation – the kind of thing that is now said *ad nauseam*. The paper, she tells us in her preface, was written for the B. B. C., but they refused it on the ground that 'our public do not want to be admonished by a woman'. The knowledge that this attitude is common may tend to make women nervous, and sometimes as a result truculent, when they are in positions of authority.

With this kind of attitude persisting it is easy to understand why women are not admitted into Holy Orders. And as long as they are not the implication is that they are in some way – spiritually or socially – peculiar, if not definitely sub-standard.

Gross superstitions about the physical functions of women are only slowly dying out.

Whether they are much or little aware of it, it is in this atmosphere of disparagement that women grow up; and it is not surprising that many little girls wish passionately that they had been born boys, and that among grown women, according to a recent Gallup Poll in this country, 37% would rather have been men.

(London: Williams & Norgate, 1952, pp. 23–6).

5. xi   Vera Brittain (1893–1970) dwells on the need to secure equal
professional opportunities and paid maternity leave for married women;
and also on what women have gained from modern aids to beauty (a view
more fashionable in the mid-twentieth century among French than
British feminists).

Vera Brittain, *Lady Into Woman. A History of Women from Victoria to
Elizabeth II* (1953).

Women have not yet achieved equal opportunities with men, but the woman who stays single can overcome by energy and determination most of the obstacles that remain. It is the married woman who still flounders in the morass of inequality. Yet the continuation of the race depends upon mothers; their position determines its achievements, and the fate of their daughters is related to their own.

For this reason the future of all women demands a dynamic solution of the married woman's problem. How shall she bear children and yet remain a self-sufficient human being? … .

At present the idea of a 'Sabbatical year' for a mother … would appear to most communities a costly and fantastic arrangement. But why is it more important for a professor to write a book, or for a young conscript to undergo twelve months' military training, than for a woman teacher or doctor or artist to take an endowed year off duty in order to bear a child without anxiety?

Every woman who solves this problem for herself hastens the day when mothers will shed their traditional inferiority complex, and demand as a right that concern for the most fundamental of 'women's questions' which even half a century of struggle has not yet secured …

Sun, air and exercise have combined with the great cosmetics industry to create for all classes of women a standard of beauty which owes relatively little to wealth. Not the least of the many changes which transformed the 'lady' of 1901 into the 'woman' of 1952 has been the disappearance of the external contrast between the hereditary peeress and her personal maid.

Between the wars, women whether rich or poor began to treat their faces as pictures and touch them up daily – with excellent results not only for a nation's beauty but for its standards of fitness …

Some women – such as the compilers of *The Feminine Point of View* – deplore this transfiguration as either a modern variant of the old slavish desire to capture a man, or a commercial male-dominated exploitation of feminine weakness. As an habitual user of cosmetics, I do not accept this view. I have always acquired them to reinforce my own self-respect and not to please anybody …

Almost vanished today from every social class are the blotchy complexions, school-marm spectacles, bitten nails, tombstone dentures, and wispy 'buns' which in the past made British women a by-word for 'homeliness'. Dentists and even doctors, with their prescriptions for slimming and the swift restoration of normal contours after childbirth, have been compelled

to turn artist as well as scientist …. The beauty parlour, their perfumed auxiliary, has opened especially in America a vast and lucrative field of work
for women.

(London: A. Dakers, 1953, pp. 181–2, 236–7).

5. xii   Broadcaster and writer Marghanita Laski (1915–88) spoke for her
generation of socially progressive women, lamenting the frivolity of the
young, in a volume produced to mark the 50th anniversary of women's
enfranchisement. The role model she suggests, Vanessa Redgrave,
awarded a CBE in 1967, was a political activist – campaigning for nuclear
disarmament – as well as an award-winning actor.

Marghanita Laski, 'The Cult of Servility', in H. Hunkins-Hallinan
(ed.), *In Her Own Right. A Discussion Conducted by the Six Point
Group* (1968).

A couple of elections ago, when the number of women in the House of
Commons was diminished, a television interviewer went down to a
Cambridge women's college to ask undergraduates why they thought this
had happened and whether they were thinking of going into politics themselves. All but one said, No, they weren't. Pressed for the reason, one …
explained winningly, 'You see, I think men want girls to be feminine. Like it
says in the magazines.' …

  'Men like girls to be feminine' – what does being feminine mean?
Sadly I am forced to believe that *un*feminine behaviour is anything that
implies autonomous existence by a woman. It is unfeminine to speak in
public, unfeminine to be interested in ideas rather than things, unfeminine to work when you needn't because you like working. In any reasonable
definition of *feminine* no-one could accuse, say, Vanessa Redgrave of being
anything but. Yet it is not she but a model girl who is the heroine *de nos
temps* ….

  The pattern itself is pretty classless … For nearly all [girls], the goal is
marriage and retreat. Of any larger contribution to society, or, indeed, to
their own lives, there is no thought …

  'Men like girls to be feminine', and what being feminine means to a
large number of men is, it seems, being sexy and silly.

  And most women, alas, accept this definition, and what men want is
what they choose to be.

(London: Harrap, 1968, pp. 18–22).

5. xiii The Marxist feminist historian Sheila Rowbotham, working in the 1960s as a teacher in further education, places the 'women's question' within the culture of the New Left.

Sheila Rowbotham, *Women's Liberation and the New Politics* (1969).

The so-called women's question is a whole people question. It is not simply that our situation can only be fundamentally changed by the total transformation of all existing social relations, but also because without us any such transformation can only be partial and consequently soon distorted. The creation of a new woman of necessity demands the creation of a new man.

Recently E. E. Evans-Pritchard pointed out that the position of women and the relationship of the sexes called into question also those between parents and children, brothers and sisters, teachers and pupils, managers and workers, citizens of one country and citizens of another ...

The domination of women is at once the most complex and the most fundamental of links in the chain. Accordingly in moments of acute social unrest the question of our position leaps to the surface.

Consistently from the right comes the implicit commitment to the smothering of the women's revolt ... The opposition to the women is always more intense than towards any other social group .... The imagery ... becomes sexual almost immediately.

Now while the left has always included 'the women problem' and 'equal rights for women' on the agenda, it has placed them rather far down. There is a hesitancy and hopelessness about the issue ... This is expressed in a curious fear that the subject is 'diversionary'. Of course it is diversionary. It is one of the largest diversions that could possibly be made – the diversion of one half the human race towards social revolution. Partly the matter is very concrete. It is about 25p an hour and the suicide rate, about nursery schools and legal discrimination .... But there is another important aspect to 'the women problem' – how it feels in the head. If the external social situation subdues us, it is our consciousness that contains us ... .

On breaking the silence

We are fortunate to live in a time when all manner of people who had previously been trodden in the dirt, people with no place in society, people with no right to speak have audaciously lifted up their heads and taken power into their hands. We are thus able to learn from their audacity ... .

Various phases of consciousness can be observed. First there is the simple moral protest against oppression, as against religion or common humanity. Secondly there is the more material demand of the privileged among the inferior to be allowed to compete equally with the dominant group. This is conceived as equal rights. The oppressed are still able to define themselves only according to the terms of the domination. The black man must still want to be white because white represents power over the world. Thirdly there is the realisation that the real liberation of the oppressed group can only be achieved through the transformation of the economic base and of social relations – i.e. that it consequently affects others who are dissatisfied. This is the discovery of Marxism ...

Housewife

The housewife is not considered much except by those who want to make sure she stays put. Yet here social secondariness is experienced most intensely ...

A hairdressing day-release class, using the criteria of cash and respect, created a model of social stratification:

> The Queen
> pop singers (various grades)
> employers
> principal of college
> vice-principal of college
> teacher
> hairdressing students
> black people
> mothers.

It is no coincidence that mothers came at the bottom. ... Essentially the woman gives her labour to the community and the community gives her nothing in return ... .

On the whole people question

The so-called women's question is ... a whole people question not only because our liberation is inextricably bound up with the revolt of all those who are oppressed, but because their liberation is not realisable fully unless our subordination is ended.

(Reprinted in S. Rowbotham, Dreams and Dilemmas: Collected Writings. London: Virago, 1983, pp. 5–6, 15–16, 20–2, 31).

5. xiv   Ruskin College, a college for trade unionists, was the home of the socialist History Workshop movement. The first Women's Liberation Conference grew out of a proposal for a meeting there to discuss women's history.

'THE FOUR DEMANDS', *Women's Newspaper*, 1, March 6 1971.

At the first national women's conference at Ruskin College, Oxford, in February–March 1970, the following four demands were formulated.

EQUAL PAY

We have to understand *why* we don't have equal pay. It's always been said that a woman's place is in the home. We don't want to do equal work and housework as well. We don't want to do equal work when it's shitwork. Equal pay means not just the same money for the same work, but also recognising how many women work not because they want to, but because they *have* to, either for money or for friends. Equal pay is the first step not just to more money but to control over how why, and for whom we work.

EQUAL EDUCATION AND OPPORTUNITY

We don't want to demand an education equally as bad as that of men – we want equal resources, not equal repression. We want to fight for real education, to make our own jobs and opportunities.

24-HOUR NURSERIES

We need somewhere for the kids, but we have to choose as to whether the kids will be kept out of the way or given their own space, and whether, freed from children, we just manage to survive through working or make the time to discover what stops us from living.

FREE CONTRACEPTION AND ABORTION ON DEMAND

We want to be free to choose when and how many kids to have, if any. We have to fight for control over our own bodies, for even the magic pill or (in the case of mistakes) abortion on demand only gives us the freedom to get into a real mess without any visible consequences. We still can't talk of sex as anything but a joke or a battle-ground.[2]

(Reprinted in Michelene Wandor, *Body Politic: Writings from the Women's Liberation Movement, 1969–72*, London: Stage 1, 1972, p. 2).

5. xv   The WLM gave a political voice to lesbian feminists but in the late 1970s tensions within the movement over the politics of sexuality became acute.

Leeds Revolutionary Feminist Group, 'Political Lesbianism: the case against heterosexuality', *WIRES*, 81, 1979.

We know that the question of whether all feminists should be lesbians is not new ... We realise that the topic is explosive .... We would like to raise the whole issue for discussion in a workshop ...

We do think that all feminists can and should be political lesbians. Our definition of a political lesbian is a woman-identified woman who does not fuck men. It does not mean compulsory sexual activity with women ...

What part does sexuality play in the oppression of women? Only in the system of oppression that is male supremacy does the oppressor actually invade and colonise the interior of the body of the oppressed ...

Every act of penetration for a woman is an invasion which undermines her confidence and saps her strength. For a man it is an act of power and mastery which makes him stronger, not just over one woman but over all women. So every woman who engages in penetration bolsters the oppressor and reinforces the class power of men.

(Reprinted in *Love Your Enemy? The debate between heterosexual feminism and political lesbianism:* London: Onlywomen Press, 1981).

5. xvi   Dr Una Kroll (1925–2017), a leading figure in the Movement for the Ordination of Women (founded in 1978), was eventually ordained priest in 1997.

Una Kroll in 'Forum', *Spare Rib*, 80, March 1979.

I am a woman. I am a feminist. I am also a Christian. Now, many people would say that it is very difficult to be an honest feminist and a sincere Christian at one and the same time and so it is, but I find it even harder, because I am also an official representative of the Church of England as well as a practising deaconess – and my Church oppresses women .... .

The admission of women to the priesthood would enable them to have access to the symbolic rituals that are at the heart of the Church. They would make the female element in the Godhead visible to all people. But the advent of women to the priesthood might accomplish more than that .... .

Some of those who want to see women ordained are reformers. They want to see women take on the power role of the priest. They would be content to see them take on the leadership of the laity and the authority role that is presently vested in the person of male priests.

Other people, including myself, have more revolutionary ideas. We want to turn the Churches' structures upside down …. We think that lay people can exercise leadership and power jointly with priests, that priests can serve rather than govern … We want to rewrite the language used in the rituals of the Church. We would redesign the symbols which express the relationship of women and men to each other. We mean to revise the doctrines of the Church which relate to the headship of men over women. We intend to try to alter the way in which the Church relates to society and in the end we want to alter society itself.

5. xvii   **Hazel Carby, daughter of a Jamaican father and a Welsh mother, criticizes white feminism in the same vein as the black American writer bell hooks in her classic *Ain't I A Woman?* (1981). Now a professor in the African-American Studies department at Yale, she wrote this essay as a graduate student at Birmingham.**

Hazel V. Carby, 'White woman listen! Black feminism and the boundaries of sisterhood', in Centre for Contemporary Cultural Studies, *The Empire Strikes Back. Race and Racism in 1970s Britain* (1982).

Much contemporary debate has posed the question of the relation between race and gender, in terms which attempt to parallel race and gender divisions. It can be argued that as processes, racism and sexism are similar. Ideologically, for example, they both construct common sense through reference to 'natural' and 'biological' differences. It has also been argued that the categories of race and gender are both socially constructed and that, therefore, they have little internal coherence as concepts … The construction of such parallels is fruitless …. The fact that black women are subject to the *simultaneous* oppression of patriarchy, class and 'race' is the prime reason for not employing parallels that render their position and experience not only marginal but also invisible … .

Black feminists have been, and are still, demanding that the existence of racism must be acknowledged as a structuring feature of our relationships with white women. Both white feminist theory and practice have to recognize that white women stand in a power relation as oppressors of black women. This compromises any feminist theory and practice founded on the notion of simple equality.

Three concepts which are central to feminist theory become problematic in their application to black women's lives: 'the family', 'patriarchy' and 'reproduction' .... We would not want to deny that the family can be a source of oppression for us but we would also wish to examine how the black family has functioned as a prime source of resistance to oppression. We need to recognise that during slavery, periods of colonialism and under the present authoritarian state, the black family has been a site of political and cultural resistance to racism ...

The use of the concept of 'dependency' is also a problem for black feminists ... How ... can we account for situations in which black women may be heads of households, or where, because of an economic system which structures high black male unemployment, they are not financially dependent upon a black man? This condition exists in both colonial and metropolitan situations. Ideologies of black female domesticity and motherhood have been constructed, through their employment (or chattel position) as domestics and surrogate mothers to white families rather than in relation to their own families ...

Black family structures have been seen as pathological by the state and are in the process of being constructed as pathological within white feminist theory. Here, ironically, the Western nuclear family structure and related ideologies of 'romantic love' formed under capitalism, are seen as more 'progressive' than black family structures. An unquestioned common-sense racism constructs Asian girls and women as having absolutely no freedom .... .

It bears repetition that black men have not held the same patriarchal positions of power that white males have established .... Black women have been dominated 'patriarchally' in different ways by men of different 'colours' .... .

In other words, of white feminists we must ask, what exactly do you mean when you say 'WE'??

(London: Hutchinson, 1982, pp. 212–18, 233).

5. xviii   Radical feminist academics Deborah Cameron and Joan Scanlon challenge Lynne Segal's claim that late-twentieth century British feminist politics were becoming essentialist and potentially reactionary (see above, p. xlii–iii).

Deborah Cameron & Joan Scanlon, 'Trouble and Strife Magazine, 1983–2002' in *The Trouble and Strife Reader* (2010).

The *Guardian* newspaper once said of *T&S* that it was 'not for the faint-hearted feminist' (this was a reference to Jill Tweedie's *Guardian Women* column 'Confessions of a faint-hearted feminist' – and yes, we took it as a compliment) ...

A succinct summary of the magazine's political position can be found in the brief legend which appeared on the masthead:

> *Trouble and Strife is cockney rhyming slang for wife. We chose this name because it acknowledges the reality of conflict in relations between women and men. As radical feminists, our politics come directly from this tension between men's power and women's resistance ... .*

Its feminist politics were not Marxist or socialist, as is clear from the editorial with which the first issue opened:

> *We believe that men as a group benefit from the oppression and exploitation of women as a group.*
> *We do not see women's oppression as secondary in importance to class or any other oppression ... .*

Socialist feminism is not, however, the only kind from which the editorial distinguishes *T&S*'s radical feminism. The next paragraph begins:

> *Men oppress women, but not because of their (or our) biology – not because men are physically stronger, nor because ... women may bear children and breast-feed, not because men are innately more aggressive. We consider men oppress women because they benefit from doing so.*

This makes it clear that *T&S*'s radical feminism was not essentialist. Rather it was *materialist* ... .

(London: Bloomsbury Academic, 2010, pp. 5–8).

5. xix   Sociologist Mavis Bayton finds scepticism and ignorance about feminism in the world of popular music but echoes the American author Naomi Wolf in her estimate of the difference feminism has made to young women's lives.

Mavis Bayton, *Frock Rock. Women Performing Popular Music* (1998).

When I started updating my research [on women musicians], in 1995, a number of things initially struck me. In contrast to the 1970s and 1980s samples, the young women that I was interviewing generally called themselves 'girls' rather than 'women': only a minority of women described themselves as feminist ... Moreover the very question 'Are you a feminist?' seemed suddenly problematic. In the 1980s, women answered simply, 'yes' or 'no'. In the 1990s, it was either 'yes, but ...' or 'no, but ...' followed by a series of qualifications and reservations .... Often a woman would start off saying she was not a feminist and end up saying she was, the main concern expressed being a fear of being seen as anti-men. Women believed fervently in sexual equality and equal opportunities but thought that feminists wanted more than equality, and that they took it 'too far' ... Many younger women said they were not sure what feminism meant and some revealed astonishing misconceptions. Marie: 'When somebody says "feminist" you imagine someone being really dirty and not washing their hair and not wearing make-up, not wearing nice clothes and not looking after herself and burning her bra and bonking every man in sight.' .... There was also a concern that feminism was seen by the public as old-fashioned, something a popular musician, especially, would therefore wish to avoid ... .

Furthermore, feminists were seen as sexually puritanical and generally anti-fun. (In the early 1970s feminism was, conversely, seen as modern, progressive, youthful, exciting, and sexually adventurous.) Lastly, many women musicians felt that a constant focus on being female was detrimental and served only to reinforce essentialist arguments and, thereby, sexism ...

What did strike me, however, was the confidence and assertiveness of the young 1990s interviewees. I believe this is in itself an effect of feminism .... As Naomi Wolf (1994) says, there has been a 'genderquake' ... Feminism ... has profoundly affected the outlook of contemporary young women, giving them self-confidence, high expectations, and determination. They *expect* to be treated equally in a way that my generation did not.

(Oxford: Oxford University Press, 1998, pp. 206–8;
© OUP, reproduced with permission).

5. xx The founder (2002) of *The F Word* website argues that 'Third-Wave' feminism with a pluralistic and contemporary ethos is flourishing among younger women in Britain as well as the United States.

Catherine Redfern & Kristin Aune, *Reclaiming the F Word.*
The New Feminist Movement (2010).

There are many differences among today's feminists. Heated debates occur over issues like pornography, the sex industry and men's role in feminism. ...

Different kinds of inequality – ethnicity, sexuality, class, age, (dis)ability and religion – affect, and sometimes exacerbate, the disadvantages women face. The different social situations and identities of the women and men involved in today's feminism make contemporary feminism necessarily diverse ... .

As Germaine Greer wrote in *The Whole Woman*, it is the job of each generation to 'produce its own statement of problems and priorities'. As the women's liberation movement did a generation ago, we have come up with seven key themes or demands that we hope fairly represent the – frankly huge – range of activity and desires of UK feminists today ...

Feminists want:

1. Liberated bodies.
2. Sexual freedom and choice.
3. An end to violence against women.
4. Equality at work and at home.
5. Politics and religion transformed.
6. Popular culture free from sexism.
7. Feminism reclaimed.

(London: Zed Books Ltd, 2010, pp. 16–17).

Notes

1. *Unpopular Opinions* (1946).
2. Three further demands were subsequently added:
   (1974) Legal and financial independence for women.
   (1974) The right to self-defined sexuality and an end to discrimination against lesbians.
   (1978) Freedom for all women from intimidation by the threat or use of violence or sexual coercion, regardless of marital status, and an end to all laws, assumptions and institutions which perpetuate male dominance and men's aggression towards women (Editor's note).

Chapter 6

The Great War, 1914–18

6.i   A women's peace demonstration in London on 4 August 1914 coincided with Britain's entry into the war. Helena Swanwick (1864–1939) describes the effect on the NUWSS, divided between patriots led by Millicent Garrett Fawcett and pacifists. Swanwick was among the suffragists who joined the Union of Democratic Control and Women's International League for Peace.

Helena Swanwick, *I Have Been Young* (1935).

We had emerged from the Kingsway Hall meeting to hear the newsboys shouting the expiry of the British ultimatum to Germany, and I went home asking myself what was next to be done. I thought it merely futile to start a doomed 'Stop the War' movement … The National Union was far too divided on every subject but the vote to be an educative body on foreign affairs. It put its demand for the vote into cold storage, and resolved on a compromise policy of 'conserving the vital forces of the nation.' We were directed to act in conjunction with our municipal authorities, and I obediently co-operated with the Richmond Suffrage Society in forming a local Committee of Organized Women, whose chairman was Lady Nott-Bower. We set ourselves to administer help for women thrown out of work by the war, and for some months we gave out work at the Town Hall and collected and distributed relief. We also started a Day Nursery for children whose mothers had to go out to work. I was honorary secretary of both these undertakings. But the first piece of work came to a natural end, as women were absorbed in new industries, and my connection with the second came to an end when our 'patriotic' medical officer discovered from a newspaper that I desired a negotiated peace, and threatened to resign unless I did. I wonder whether he thought I was a Hun in disguise who would put arsenic into the babies' milk! …

Some Dutch Suffragists had decided to call a Congress of Women at the Hague [in April 1915] to consider what should come out of the war. None of the organised Suffrage Societies would consent to co-operate and

an *ad hoc* committee was formed to arrange a British contingent .... Objections were raised by the Government to 'the holding of so large a meeting of
a political character so close to the seat of war' ... Mr Winston Churchill at
the Admiralty ... 'closed' the North Sea for the period of the Congress and
no British ships sailed ...

The Hague Conference was finally instrumental in splitting the National
Union Executive into two nearly equal halves, because the invitation had
been addressed to it, and a considerable minority wished to accept the invitation .... When I resigned, I remained on good terms with Mrs. Fawcett ....
Years later, we were to agree heartily about the establishment of a League
of Nations.

(London: V. Gollancz, 1935, pp. 253, 258–9).

**6. ii   The diary of Vera Brittain, in later life a committed pacifist, shows
her own patriotic reaction in the first months of war. Her fiancé Roland
was to lose his life in December 1915 and her brother Edward in June 1918.**

A. Bishop & T. Smart (eds), *Chronicle of Youth. Vera Brittain, War Diary
1913–1917* **(1981).**

Wednesday September 2nd [1914]. After dinner we all discussed again
Daddy's refusal to let Edward go into the Army, & the unmanliness of it,
especially after we read in *The Times* of a mother who said to her hesitating
son, 'My boy I don't want you to go, but if I were you I should!' We saw
Mrs Ellinger later & she seems very strongly to disapprove of Daddy. Not
that other people's opinions matter to us, only they represent prestige & it
is hard luck on Edward to be misjudged for what is not his fault. ... Daddy
does not care about E's honour or courage so long as he is safe. It is left to
Edward & I to live up to our name of 'Brittain'.

(London: V. Gollancz, 1981, p. 101).

**6. iii   After a year at Oxford Brittain volunteered as a nurse, serving in
military hospitals in London and France but with an interlude in Malta
in 1916–17. Her autobiographical** *Testament of Youth* **– published like many
war memoirs over a decade later – became an international best-seller.**

Vera Brittain, *Testament of Youth* **(1933).**

The memory of my sunlit months in the Mediterranean during the War's
worst period of miserable stagnation still causes a strange nostalgia to descend

upon my spirit. For me, as for all the world, the War was a tragedy and a vast stupidity, a waste of youth and of time; it betrayed my faith, mocked my love, and irremediably spoilt my career – yet Malta remains in my recollection as an interval of heaven, a short year of glamorous beauty and delight, in which, for the time being, I came to life again after Roland's death ...

I was sorrowful, anxious, frustrated, lonely – but yet how vividly alive! ...

It is, I think, this glamour, this magic, this incomparable keying up of the spirit in a time of mortal conflict, which constitute the pacifist's real problem – a problem still incompletely imagined, and still quite unsolved. The causes of war are always falsely represented; its honour is dishonest and its glory meretricious, but the challenge to spiritual endurance, the intense sharpening of all the senses, the vitalising consciousness of common peril for a common end, remain to allure those boys and girls who have just reached the age when love and friendship and adventure call more persistently than at any later time. The glamour may be the mere delirium of fever, which as soon as war is over dies out ... , but while it lasts no emotion known to man seems as yet to have quite the compelling power of this enlarged vitality.

(Reprinted: London: Virago, 1978, pp. 290–2).

6. iv   For suffragette Sylvia Pankhurst (1882–1960), a socialist and pacifist, the war brought a complete breach with her mother and elder sister Christabel. In this account of her experiences in welfare work in East London she recalls the way working-class women were treated by the authorities.

E. Sylvia Pankhurst, *The Home Front* (1932).

The legend that the soldiers' wives had more money than they had ever had in their lives remained impregnable ... .

The War had brought into poor slumdom an unusual influx of the leisured and prosperous, to whom the bedraggled meanness of aching poverty seemed mere absence of self-respect ... To these remote ones, obtuse and obscurantist, the [separation] allowance anxious mothers craved for the nourishing of little bodies and the booting of little feet appeared merely 'money to spend in drink', which should be cut down to the sparsest limits, in the interests of sobriety and thrift ... .

In the anticipation that soldiers' wives would indulge in excessive drinking, the public houses were closed to women during certain hours open to men ...

Already in October [1914] Mrs Creighton, Adeline Duchess of Bedford and other ladies ... announced that with the Home Secretary's consent they were making arrangements 'for influencing, and if need be restraining' the behaviour of women and girls in the neighbourhood of military camps. Under the aegis of these ladies, thousands of women patrols were introduced whose efforts to control the behaviour of their sex were not seldom the subject of irritation, and also of mirth.

The busybodies of Whitehall, Scotland Yard and Mayfair were determined to establish effective control over the conduct of soldiers' wives. On October 20th an Army Council Memorandum entitled 'Cessation of Separation Allowances and Allotments to the Unworthy', and a Home Office letter to Chief Constables issued instructions for placing all women in receipt of separation allowances under surveillance .... .

Reports of alleged unworthiness, received from the relief committees, the soldiers or their commanding officers, or any other source, were to be investigated by the police, and if in their opinion proved, the separation allowance and the husband's allotment were to be discontinued, for unchastity, drunkenness, neglect of children or conviction on a criminal charge. Soldiers' wives and relatives were thus to be subject to a penalty in excess of that imposed by the ordinary law. They were placed at the mercy of secret reports, without any public or private trial or opportunity of vindication or reply.

(London: Hutchinson, 1932, pp. 98–9).

6.v   Violet Markham (1872–1959) spent the war in various public service roles. This letter of April 1915 from a Chesterfield settlement worker Jessica Smith tells of anxieties surrounding wartime rates of illegitimacy. Markham later served on a committee which investigated rumours of immoral behaviour by servicewomen stationed in France and showed them to be unfounded.

Helen Jones (ed.), *Duty and Citizenship. The Correspondence and Political Papers of Violet Markham, 1896–1953* (1994).

This awfully difficult and painful question of the number of illegitimate children to be born soon, has occupied us a good deal lately. The fact is that no one knows anything – nevertheless the wildest rumours are about. After the soldiers had been here barely a month someone said that there were 90 expectant mothers in the town! The Rescue worker here to whom I was talking on the subject one day this week, said that Miss Bruce had told her that 400 unmarried girls from Buxton had been sent to Maternity Homes. Miss Scott Smith said it was an absolute impossibility, there were not Homes to take them & it would cost £1000 a sum not likely to be collected by such a small town for the purpose. Anyone who knows anything about girls knows how they will hide the thing to the last minute ...

I do think one must be very chary about bringing any special legislation to deal with these cases. Anything that is done (& the children when they come must be cared for) should be done privately or through charitable agencies. It does seem to me that to advertise all round that illegitimate children of soldiers are different & that the irregularity is less because it is war time and so on is only to encourage the loss of self-control of which we have so little & ask for imposture.

At the same time it does fall hard on the girls in towns like ours where the custom is so prevalent of marrying just before the birth of the child that their men can't now marry them because they are abroad.

(London: Historians' Press, 1994, pp. 67–8).

6. vi   A midwife, Mrs Layton, describes how – alongside the trade unionists Margaret Bondfield and Mary Macarthur – she lobbied on behalf of the Women's Cooperative Guild for support for unmarried mothers.

M. Llewelyn Davies (ed.), *Life As We Have Known It, by Co-operative Working Women* (1931).

Another important deputation I went on during the war, and when, owing to weather conditions, I was the only one to attend with Miss Bondfield and had to do all the talking for the Guild, was to the Executive of the Prince of Wales' Fund, which had decided not to give relief to unmarried mothers. The Guild thought this was a very wrong policy, and asked the Executive to receive a deputation from the Guild to explain the reasons why they asked for that restriction to be removed. Miss Bondfield explained to me that ... some of the clerics of the Committee were of opinion that, if the unmarried mother was assisted from the fund, the feelings of all the respectable married women would be outraged ... I explained that I represented the Women's Co-operative Guild, an organisation 30,000 strong, chiefly composed of respectable married women, and that the Guild entirely repudiated the statement that married women would be resentful. I was asked a whole lot of questions, and, in asking them to reconsider their decision and give help to unmarried mothers, asked them not to forget that every time a woman fell, a man fell also. I said that when a recruiting sergeant asked young men to join up, he did not ask if they were married or unmarried, but only if strong and healthy and fit to go ... Mr. Walter Long [President of the Local Government Board] nudged Mary Macarthur and said, 'She's rubbing it in to us.' It was decided before we left the room to treat the unmarried mother with the same consideration as the married mother.

(Reprinted: London: Virago, 1977, pp. 50–2).

6. vii   A fictionalised autobiography by a former domestic servant Rosina Whyatt brings out both the attractions of munitions work and the appalling health and safety conditions.

J. Burnett (ed.), *Useful Toil. Autobiographies of working people from the 1820s to the 1920s* **(1974).**

Jenny had to clock-in at the factory at eight o'clock in the morning ... .

[It] was called Chaul End, a very large one-storey building just outside the town of Luton – for safety reasons, she learnt later ... She was given a fireproof overall and cap that must cover the head, together with rubber shoes. Not a hair of the head must be loose; no pins, brooches or rings must be worn, in fact metal of any kind was strictly prohibited. Jenny was then taken down long corridors to the room where she was to work. She was given boxes of small brass parts for fuses to be gauged and checked for rejects ...

Looking around, Jenny was puzzled to see so many girls with their fingers bandaged, but she very soon discovered the reason. The brass parts had sharp edges which cut the fingers, and she herself soon had her own fingers bandaged. In cases of septic poisoning the girls had to attend surgery to have their finger dressed each day ...

Jenny had heard that girls were earning big wages on munitions ... Her weekly wage, for the first month, was about 30s for seventy-two hours ... After a few months in the factory Jenny was asked to go on night work. This still meant a twelve-hour shift, but time-and-a-quarter pay was given, with time-and-a-half on the Sunday night shift ...

The time came when she was moved to another job, this time to a machine-shop where she was to use a press for pressing detonators, a job where special care and attention was needed because any careless move might cause an explosion, a very exacting job. The next move was to the spinning room, for an operation to test the springs of the fuses ... This operation caused dust and chemicals to fly about the room, making the skin and clothes yellow. Jenny had often noticed this among the girls ... they were in fact called 'Chaul End Canaries'. ... Not only did Jenny become yellow; she found after a time that the powder was affecting her skin. Her face, neck and legs began to swell, so much so that she could not see and had to be led home. She was ordered to stay at home for ten days on half pay. For three days she could not see anything. On being examined by the works doctor, T.N.T. poisoning was diagnosed. ...

An order was given by the works doctor that she must leave Chaul End factory, if she was ever to recover. It so happened that the firm had another and much larger works at Biscot Road, Luton, where shells and other war essentials were produced ... Here the girls were call 'Biscot Road Blackbirds', as this kind of work made them black instead of yellow. She was made an assistant forewoman, and was given a biscuit-coloured overall with red collar, cuffs and waistband; also a triangular badge bearing the words 'War Work'. She was now in charge of some fifty girl inspectors in a large machine-shop ... By now her pay had increased to £3 a week plus an allowance for assistant forewoman's duties. Her work was now intensely interesting, and she came into contact not only with her own girls but with the governors of the factory, which gave her an opportunity ... to do a lot for the girls and deal with their problems, regarding time sheets, wages and welfare – especially as she had been made a union representative ... She was never refused a reasonable request, and was always well received by the management. It was not long before her advice was being sought by all and sundry.

(London: Allen Lane, 1974, pp. 125–9).

6. viii   Agreements on wartime 'dilution' – replacing skilled union members by unskilled workers, often women – were reached with the trade unions on the understanding that they were strictly temporary. But Robert Roberts (1905–74) believed that the war had a lasting effect on relations between the sexes. His mother had kept a corner shop in Salford where he grew up.

Robert Roberts, *The Classic Slum* (1971).

Against the 'dilution of labour' skilled men felt they must fight to the death, war or no war.

The first serious clash of interests occurred at an engineering works in Essex shortly after the outbreak of war, when mechanics objected to setting up machines to be operated by women .... After months of wrangling the unions agreed to accept the new labour and relax their regulations; but only on condition that immediately after the war the 'previous rules' should be restored 'in every case' .... Dispute after dispute broke out still; but the gates of change stood open wide and the new workers poured through, to the dismay of many a conservative tradesman who saw the 'dummies' acquiring some of his own skills with disturbing ease. My father was typical. In his cups he was wont to boast that, at the lathe, he had to manipulate a micrometer and work to limits of one thousandth of an inch. We were much impressed, until one evening in 1917 a teenage sister running a capstan in the iron works remarked indifferently that she, too, used a 'mike' to even finer limits. There was, she said, 'nothing to it'. The old man fell silent. Thus did status crumble! ... . Before the end of the war more than 642,000 women had gone into government factories and engineering works of some sort, with millions more, men and women, doing manual work of almost every kind and developing new skills and new self-confidence on the way. The awe that many simpler souls had felt before the mystery of craft began to evaporate, to be replaced by at least some rational understanding ... .

With the return of peace the great mass of regulations safeguarding the status of the artisan was certainly restored ... Nevertheless, the dilution of labour and the employment of women brought communal gains of immense value, not only in engineering but in many other fields. Socially, the barriers of caste that had previously existed between the skilled worker and his family and the lower industrial grades were permanently lowered ... Women grew in social stature and gained an authority they have never lost since. Many without home ties, and often against parents' wishes, had joined one of the auxiliary forces .... Whatever war did to women in home, field, service or factory, it undoubtedly snapped strings that had bound them in so many ways to the Victorian age. Even we, the young, noticed the difference. Wives in the shop no longer talked about 'my boss', or 'my master'. Master had gone to war and Missis ruled the household, or he worked close to her in a factory, turning out shell cases on a lathe and earning little more than she did herself.

(Reprinted: Harmondsworth: Penguin, 1990, pp. 198–201).

6. ix   Lady Randolph Churchill (1854–1921), Winston Churchill's American-born mother, publicises contributions to the war effort by women of the Royal family and aristocracy. Queen Mary and nine other women, most of them titled, were honoured as 'Dames' in the first list of nominees for the Order of the British Empire, created in 1917 to recognise war work. Clementine Churchill, Winston's wife, received a CBE for her work organizing factory canteens for munitions workers.

Lady Randolph Churchill (ed.), *Women's War Work* (1916).

Every year Queen Mary knits woollen vests and other garments for the Needlework Guild, in addition to the work she pays to have done. And now, in these days of war, Her Majesty has a piece of work – vest, muffler, mitten, sock, or body-belt – in every one of the royal apartments, so that she may take up her work anywhere if she finds herself with an odd minute of leisure.

Princess Mary is said to have made 'yards and yards of mufflers' since August, 1914. It was entirely her own idea to send a Christmas present to every soldier and sailor fighting for our Empire. The brass box with her portrait embossed upon the lid, the wording of the Christmas card, the choice of the gifts – cigarettes, matches, tobacco or pipe – every little detail she thought out ...

Queen Alexandra [the Queen Mother] has also worked very hard. In our chapter about War-Nursing her name will occur again and again ...

'Queen Alexandra thinks of everything.' Early in February, 1915, she ordered betimes a great quantity of shamrock sprigs for the Front, so that our Irish fighters should be cheered by this little remembrance from her when St Patrick's Day came round .... .

At Queen Alexandra's Field Force Fund, which has its headquarters in Knightsbridge, Society women are daily at work, packing parcels for the men at the Front. The idea of this Fund is to sort out the many and varied gifts sent in and to make up useful all-round parcels that shall meet every need of the recipient .... .

Class distinction has gone for good from philanthropic work. Women have found in war-time usefulness a common platform on which they meet in friendly service.

(London: C. Arthur Pearson, 1916, pp. 20–4).

6. x   Edith Sitwell (1887–1964) wrote this poem 'during a great battle' in 1916 when her brother Osbert was in France with the Grenadier Guards.

Edith Sitwell, 'The Dancers', from *Clown's Houses* (1918).

> The floors are slippery with blood
> The world gyrates too. God is good
> That while His wind blows out the light
> For those who hourly die for us –
> We can still dance, each night.
>
> The music has grown numb with death –
> But we will suck their dying breath,
> The whispered name they breathed to chance,
> To swell our music, make it loud
> That we may dance, – may dance.
>
> We are the dull blind carrion-fly
> That dance and batten. Though God die
> Mad from the horror of the light –
> The light is mad, too, flecked with blood, –
> We dance, we dance, each night.

(Oxford: Blackwell, 1918, p. 25).

6. xi Dame Helen Gwynne-Vaughan (1879–1967), head of the botany department at Birkbeck College, London, and daughter of a Scottish military family, became in 1917 Chief Controller of the WAAC and went on to command the WRAF in 1918–19. She tackled issues of protocol with relish.

Helen Gwynne-Vaughan, *Service With the Army* (1942).

Our Standing Orders in France dealt tactfully with the question [of saluting] by laying down that 'all grades will observe the conventions of respect to persons of senior rank and grade'. Gradually at home also the need of some gesture of recognition was admitted, and women were allowed to raise their hands to their shoulders .... .

In France the women saluted officers under whom they worked, and the officials similarly saluted officers senior to them. We were usually saluted in the Army area, more rarely at the Base.

Meantime our headquarters had been temporarily established in Abbeville, and to my great advantage No. 53 Worker N. Campbell, on 13th April, had reported for duty as my clerk .... I have always been thankful for this wise and friendly young woman, who took expert charge of the office and was always on excellent terms with her opposite numbers in the offices with which we dealt. I remember the acute embarrassment of our first encounter when I broke it to her that I thought it my duty to address her by her unadorned surname …. Christian names in those days were much less used than now, and to call everyone Miss or Mrs. would have done away with the military atmosphere in which alone the work required of us could be accomplished …. Gradually we acquired an excellent little group of clerks and orderlies, of whom Campbell took charge. She was good to me and helpful in every way. She had her own methods. When we were getting into new quarters and had no light except candles she rang up the C.R.E.'s head clerk and warned him that the Director of Works (his ultimate superior) was dining in our mess. Electric light was installed in time.

(London: Hutchinson, 1942, p. 30).

6. xii   A number of medical units staffed by women were organised and financed by British suffragists. Mary Henderson served in the Scottish Women's Hospitals in Russia and Rumania with Dr Elsie Inglis (1864–1917).

Mary H. J. Henderson, *In War and Peace. Songs of a Scotswoman* (1918).

LIKE THAT

'No wonder Britain is so great if her women are like that'

Prefect of Constanza

'Like that'. -Like what? Why British to the core!
You went beyond our sheltering British shore
Out to the peril of an Arctic sea,
Bearing the Flag of British Liberty.
You laughed above the lurking submarine,
Clothing Death's terrors in a happy sheen
Of debonair lightheartedness – I've seen
How very gallant women's hearts may be
Though torn the while with deepest sympathy,
British and women – women to the core.

I've seen you kneeling on the wooden floor,
Tending your wounded on their straw-strewn bed,
Heedless the while that right above your head

The Bird of Menace scattered death around.
I've seen you guiding over shell-marked ground
The cars of succour for the shattered men,
Dauntless, clear-eyed, strong-handed, even when
The bullets flung the dust up from the road
By which you bore your anguished, helpless load.

I've seen you, oh, my sisters, 'under fire,'
While in your hearts there burned but one desire –
What British men and women hold so dear –
To do your duty without any fear.

Dedicated to the rank and file of the Scottish Women's Hospitals.
(London: Erskine Macdonald Ltd, 1918, p. 12).

6. xiii   The suffrage militants' newspaper the *Suffragette* was renamed
Britannia in 1915, and the WSPU became the 'Women's Party' in
1917 when women's suffrage was in sight. Here Christabel Pankhurst
(1880–1958) outlines its programme in a speech at the Queen's Hall. She
was narrowly defeated when she stood with coalition support as candidate
for Smethwick in the 1918 Coupon Election.

THE WOMEN'S PARTY, *Britannia*, 16 November 1917.

We believe that it is imperative to form a Women's Party in these days when
certain influences are seeking to herd the coming women voters into the
wrong political camps ...

We believe that the Women's Party may succeed in avoiding the mistakes which the men's parties have made ... (Cheers)

Our Women's Party is based upon no sort of sex antagonism. There
never could be in our minds a question of sex antagonism except in so
far as the men rear barriers of exclusion from right and responsibility
against us ... .

We stand for war till victory. (Cheers.) We are resolutely opposed to all
forms of compromise with the enemy. (Cheers.) The Allies must no more
compromise with Germany than good must compromise with evil ... .

Our Women's Programme calls for the adoption of more radical war
measures ... . Quibbling about food rations is gambling with the life of
the people in our opinion. We are tired of voluntary methods in economy.

(Cheers.) If people are not to have luxuries, don't have them there to buy. (Cheers.) …

In view of what the newspapers tell us of the effect of treachery in high places in Russia and elsewhere … it is our duty to put forward this further demand: That efficient and loyal public services be guaranteed by ridding all Government departments of officials having enemy blood or connections and of all officials having Pro-German and Pacifist leanings …

We want the authority of the national Parliament to be maintained. We do not want a League of Nations in which Germany would be included. (Cheers.) …

Let us see to it that when we women get the vote we shall use it in a sense of deep responsibility … in the true spirit of national service and consecration.

6. xiv   **Lettice Fisher (1875–1956), wife of the historian H. A. L. Fisher, President of the Board of Education in Lloyd George's coalition, looks back on child welfare work during the war. The NCUMC, which she chaired between 1918 and 1955, became the National Council for One Parent Families in 1970 and was merged with Gingerbread in 2007.**

Lettice Fisher, *Twenty-One Years and After, 1918–39* (1939).

The National Council for the Unmarried Mother and Her Child is a product of the energy released by the losses, agonies, and strain of the Great War. We were desperately anxious, wretchedly unhappy, worn, harassed, and hard pressed. There was always far more to do than could be done …. But there was also an increased clearness of vision, a determination not only to rebuild but to amend. Conferences were held, committees set up, organisations established, foundations laid …. Child welfare work went with a swing. Before long the stimulus of public opinion had placed the Maternity and Child Welfare Act of 1918 upon the Statute book, and brought into being the Ministry of Health …

Attention was soon attracted to one peculiarly difficult and unculti-vated corner of the child welfare field, partly by the vigorous reference in the Registrar General's Report for 1916,[1] and partly by the conditions of wartime. Child welfare workers … were only too familiar with the social and economic difficulties of unmarried mothers. The usual plan was to put the babies out to nurse thus automatically depriving them of their natural food and enormously diminishing their always slender chance of survival.

12. Statue of Edith Cavell in St Martin's Place, London. The director of a nurses' training school in Belgium, she was executed by the Germans (1915) for assisting an escape organization for allied soldiers. 'No single incident of the war touched and stirred the heart of the nation as did the brutal execution of the heroic nurse', claimed a *Times* editorial (18 March, 1920), paying tribute to 'the willing self-sacrifice of the whole of the great and gallant sisterhood of British nurses'. It was at the request of the National Council of Women that Edith Cavell's own last words were added as an inscription two years later: 'Patriotism is not enough ...'.

But in wartime, with its active demand for women's labour of all sorts ... foster-mothers almost ceased to exist. If no home could be found to care for the baby the mother could not work: must the baby die or the mother go upon the streets? ...

At the Mansion House on February 14th 1918 the National Council for the Unmarried Mother and her Child came into existence ... Its functions were:-

1. To obtain reform of the existing Bastardy Acts and Affiliation Acts.
2. To secure the provision of adequate accommodation to meet the varying needs of mother and babies throughout the country, with the special aim of keeping mother and child together.
3. To deal with individual enquiries from, or on behalf of, unmarried mothers.

There was complete agreement that the separation of any mother from her baby should be regarded as an exceptional and deplorable necessity, not as the normal and natural procedure temporarily interrupted by the lack of foster-mothers. And ... the natural sequence to this was that 'the responsibility of fatherhood must be recognised'.

(London: privately printed, 1946, pp. 3–5).

6. xv   The novelist (Margaret Ethel) Storm Jameson (1891–1986) speaks for a generation of women bereaved by the loss of men friends and relatives. Oxford and Cambridge-educated officers who served in the First World War had particularly high mortality rates: one in four among those who had been under 25 in 1914.

Storm Jameson, *No Time Like the Present* (1933).

For a long time I did not realise that the War had stripped my generation of its leaves and branches, leaving the bare maimed stem. Then, while it was happening, we did not notice it. Now, anyone who says that is what happened is set down as a tasteless fellow. After the long-drawn agony of the Casualty Lists, the reiterated cries and promises, the preparation and unveiling of memorials and Rolls of Honour, women crying in locked rooms and politicians mouthing to the crowds gathered to hear them, we who are left, 'the hollow men, The stuffed men'[2] look deliberately away. The other day I read a portentously stern essay in which the writer, a sort of public man, sought to prove that no generation had suffered more than another from the War. That was a kind of optical delusion, brought about by looking at old photographs and reading War books. There is (he said) no evidence that a generation was partly wiped out. Without bitterness, let me call him a liar. There are few women of my age who did not lose, by that War, if not a brother or a husband, two out of three young men who were her friends. This is only the usual thing. The exception is a woman in my generation who lost no one her own age, no relative or friend.

Notes

1. 'The ratio of illegitimate to legitimate mortality in the first week of life has increased from 170% in 1907 to 201% in 1916...'
2. 'The Hollow Men', first published in T. S. Eliot, *Poems, 1909–1925*.

Chapter 7

Franchise and After, 1918–39: The Modern Woman?

7. i   Barbara Drake (1876–1963), Fabian researcher and niece of Beatrice Webb, comments on women trade unionists' dissatisfaction with the 1918 Act, which enfranchised all men over 21 but only some women over 30. Mary Macarthur (1880–1921) was one of four women Labour candidates in 1918.

Barbara Drake, *Women in Trade Unions* (1920).

The Representation of the People Act became law in 1918. The Bill was supported by the [National] Federation [of Women Workers], but not without protest, and members did their best to abolish the absurd age-limit by which the women's vote was qualified. The absurdity was all the more glaring because this age-limit of thirty years excluded from the franchise the large majority of women war workers, to whose magnificent achievement Cabinet Ministers actually professed to owe their conversion to women's suffrage. Members pledged themselves not to rest content 'until every woman was entitled to a vote in virtue of her womanhood on exactly the same terms as every man is now in virtue of his manhood.' The Emancipation Bill of 1919, by which the Labour Party tried to remove the remaining sex anomalies, found its most active supporters amongst industrial women. As soon as the vote was granted the Federation decided by an overwhelming majority of its members in favour of political action. At the general election of 1918, Miss Macarthur was accordingly put forward as candidate for the Stourbridge Division – the seat of her early successes in the Black Country. The personal enthusiasm aroused by the Prime Minister [Lloyd George] at the hour of victory – cleverly exploited by the 'Northcliffe' Press in the interests of the Coalition – made her defeat a foregone conclusion, but few candidates of known pacifist sympathies fared better at the hands of the electors.

(Reprinted: London: Virago, 1984, pp. 104–5).

7. ii   The desire of British women for world peace was affirmed at this London meeting, chaired by the wife of the Archbishop of Canterbury, with support from all political parties and both leading suffragists and anti-suffragists.

The Woman's Leader, 13 February 1920

ALBERT HALL MEETING

The League of Nations Meeting, which was held in the Albert Hall on February 6th, was one of the most inspiring women's meetings ever held in this country; the hall was packed from floor to ceiling, about twelve thousand women being present. Mrs. Randall Davidson presided, and the speakers were Viscountess Astor, Miss Maude Royden, Miss Mary Macarthur, and Lord Robert Cecil. Mrs Davidson read the following message from their Majesties: 'Mindful of all that womanhood has sacrificed, endured, and achieved in these years of war, their Majesties feel that British idealism can have no nobler aim than that of securing to the world enduring peace.' Telegrams were also read from Mrs Fawcett and Mrs Humphry Ward ... The following resolutions were passed unanimously:-

   (1)   That this meeting regards the League of Nations as essential to the peace of the world.
   (2)   That this meeting pledges itself to support the League of Nations by every means in its power.

7. iii   Australian-born academic Dr. Marion Phillips (1881–1932), the Labour Party's first woman organiser, promoted the 'women's sections' established in the 1918 party constitution, and tried to discourage Labour women from joining non-party women's organisations.

The Woman's Leader, 30 April 1920

LABOUR WOMEN IN CONFERENCE, by a Special Correspondent
ARE NON-PARTY ASSOCIATIONS DANGEROUS?
The most controversial resolution of the Conference was that which attempted to define and limit the political work of Labour women. Dr Marion Phillips moved the resolution: 'That this Conference of working women recognises that the time is now come for a great effort to secure full political power for Labour, and therefore urges all women

in industrial organisations, to become members of the political Labour movement, and to avoid dissipating their energies in non-party political organisations.' The discussion that followed made it plain that this resolution might be diversely interpreted. The mover herself said that it should not be held to apply to temporary associations, formed for any one special object ... such as, for instance, Women's Suffrage Associations, Temperance Leagues, the League of Nations Union ... Although a good deal of opposition to the resolution was manifest, it was finally passed by a very large majority.

7. iv The treasurer of the Women's Institutes – a popular non-party movement intended to promote active citizenship among countrywomen – writes in protest against attempts to stop Labour women joining their local WI.

The Woman's Leader, 16 March 1923

Madam,

The references to the Women's Institute Movement which Dr. Marion Phillips makes ... lead me to doubt whether she has any first-hand experience or knowledge of a Women's Institute ... She enunciates the principle that Labour Women should do their Political work in their own Organizations rather than join general Political Organizations of a Non-Party character. No doubt Labour Women are doing Political work in their own Organizations where these exist, but in how many of the 2, 600 villages, which have Institutes, are there Organizations of the kind which Dr. Marion Phillips advocates?

Even where such Party Political Organizations exist, women may still find a need for social life and recreation combined with educational opportunities ... Do Labour women value opportunities for friendship, for social intercourse, for education, or artistic stimulus, less than the women of other political parties? ...

Nowhere can it be shown that the Women's Institute Movement has discouraged any women from doing Political work of whatever party character may appeal to them, but it recognizes that there is a demand among country women for things which are admittedly outside the scope of all purely Party Political Organizations. The amazing success of the Movement is the proof that it has met this demand ...

HELENA AUERBACH

7. v The physician and novelist Arabella Kenealy (1859–1938) opposed
equal citizenship on eugenic grounds. She was not unusual in worrying
about the implications of making women a majority in the electorate:
the first Conservative woman minister, Katharine Duchess of Atholl
(1874–1960), gave that as her reason for opposing equal suffrage. Giuseppe
Mazzini, the Italian liberal revolutionary cited by Kenealy, had many
admirers in the nineteenth-century women's movement.

Arabella Kenealy, *Feminism and Sex-Extinction* (1920).

The huge numerical preponderance of women must, of itself, presently
swamp all masculine power and initiative in State affairs unless the political
functions of the sexes be separated .....

In yielding his House of Parliament, man has surrendered not only
his highest and most characteristic prerogative, but he has yielded the last
exclusive stronghold of his manhood. An entrenchment indispensable to
his difficult task of holding his own against a sex overwhelmingly superior
in number, and chartered, by right of womanhood, with time-honoured
baffling privileges which handicap and defeat him at all turns. A sex
Nature has armoured with charms, moreover, and with weaknesses for
his disarming; by appeal, on the one hand, to his chivalry, on the other, to
his senses.

Entrenched in his last stronghold, he stood some chance of exert-
ing his allotted dominance in life's affairs. All his strongholds invaded, he
stands none .....

A more inspiring picture presents itself, however.

Of a Manhood, worthy of its racial and national traditions, waking timely
to a recognition of its manhood's powers and duties, and, having emancipated itself from woman's rule in all beside her natural province, reinstating
its supremacy in every virile field and function ...

Of a Womanhood re-finding itself also, and finding itself and its natural
lot upon a fairer and a nobler plane ...

And these two working for the common good, of our Anglo-Saxon Race ...

In this New Human Dispensation would be a House of Women to serve
as a second – a balancing and an uplifting – wing to the House of Men ...

Said Mazzini, '*Man and Woman are the two human Wings that lift the soul
towards the Ideal we are destined to attain.*' And the value and the effectiveness
of these two human, as of other wings, lie in the degree to which, although
they work in unison, *they move in different areas;* apart from and independent,

each of the other, but, nevertheless, each sustaining its own side of the body, Vital and Social.

(London: T. Fisher Unwin, 1920, pp. 288–91).

7. vi The Restoration of Pre-War Practices Act (1919) prompted sceptical comments from Eleanor Rathbone about politicians' commitment to equal opportunities.

Eleanor Rathbone, 'Equal Citizenship', March 9 1920, in
Milestones **(1929).**

There were some among us – happy innocents – who thought that when the vote was won (though only for some women) the need for sex solidarity was over and we might venture to behave as if we had already reached the place where 'there are neither male nor female; neither bond nor free' [*Galatians*, 3:28]. Surely those dreamers must have had a rude awakening when they realised that one of the first-fruits of the first Parliament elected partly by women voters had been the placing on the Statute Book of an Act which, without once mentioning the word 'woman' or 'female', has the effect of legally excluding women, for the first time in British history, from nearly every department of skilled industry except a few trades traditionally their own. The Pre-War Practices Act was passed in fulfilment of a pledge given in war-time under very exceptional circumstances, and women in consequence made no resistance to it. But that such a pledge should have been asked for and its literal fulfilment exacted four years later in spite of the intervening experience of the industrial capacities of women, is only one of many accumulating proofs that when any groups of men, whether grouped together as a political party, a profession or a trade, accept the formula, 'equality of opportunity between men and women', they do so with the mental reservation – 'except when it may be inconvenient to ourselves or those we want to please.' Fortunately for us, there are in every such group, of whatever party, high-minded men whose sense of justice and belief in fair play is stronger than their sectional prejudices, and their presence in our movement, enormously valuable for the practical help they give, is still more valuable because they are a living testimony to the fact that the movement is not based on sex-antagonism, but, on the contrary, seeks to remove the remaining barriers to a real comradeship.

(Liverpool: privately printed, 1929, p. 2).

7. vii   The 1919 Sex Disqualification (Removal) Act opened the legal profession to women, and also the magistracy and juries; but the courts did not interpret it as banning all discrimination on grounds of sex. This judgment confirms the legality of a Local Education Authority's decision to sack married women teachers.

Price v Rhondda Urban District Council, Chancery Division, 3 May 1923.

Lord Justice Eve

... In or about the month of July in each year a number of qualified students leave the training colleges to take up appointments as teachers, and in 1921 and 1922 the number of available qualified students was largely in excess of the demand for them. This excess, due partly ... to the reduction of teaching staff to secure economy, unfortunately involved the unemployment of a large number of capable teachers whose parents had expended considerable sums in educating them for this particular profession, and was a matter ... engaging the attention of this and other Authorities in the country.

[In July 1922 the Rhondda Education Committee voted (25 to 3) to dismiss all married women teachers, other than] widows and married women whose husbands were alive but unable, owing to accidents or ill health, to support them ...

[Various] objections were taken to the resolution. First, it was said that it is against public policy in that it is in restraint of marriage. I do not think so. It would, in my opinion, be pressing public policy to intolerable lengths to hold that it was outraged by this Authority expressing a preference for unmarried women over married women as teachers, in view of the fact that the services of the latter are frequently not available but are liable to be interrupted by absences extending over several months. Then it was argued that [it was] ... contrary to the Sex Disqualification [Removal] Act. I cannot accept that view. The Act, as appears from its title, is an Act to remove certain disqualifications arising from sex, and I am not prepared to hold that an Authority commits a breach of the Act if in some of its appointments it indicates that applications from one sex only can be received. Consider the absurdity to which such a conclusion might lead. The medical Authority might require the services of a monthly nurse. Would they be committing a breach of the Act were they to intimate that no ex-serviceman or superannuated officer need apply?

[1923] 2 Ch. 372, pp. 388–93.

7. viii   The post-war vogue for ballroom dancing lasted till the 1960s, and it remained especially popular with girls and young women. Chains of dance halls, like that owned by Mecca, became big business.

Robert Roberts, *The Classic Slum* (1971).

In the explosive dancing boom after the war, the young from sixteen to twenty-five flocked into the dance halls by the hundred thousand: some went 'jigging' as often as six times a week. The great 'barn' we patronized as apprentices held at least a thousand …

Generally, men lined one side of the hall, women the other. A male made his choice, crossed over, took a girl with the minimum of ceremony from in among and slid into rhythm. The floor lay a perfect gloss, spoilt only by a canting towards the north-west. Nowhere in the land were Great Britain's 1 ¾ million surplus women more in evidence than at the dance halls. There, when every available male had found a partner, blocs of girls either still flowered the walls or had paired themselves off in resignation to dance with each other – though in this last there was yet hope. At all 'common' halls men danced together too. For the most part, this in no way indicated homosexual inclination: a couple of males on the move could mean that they were still too shy to ask girls; but more often their mobility would give them a better chance to judge a female pair's dancing ability and charms. Having made selection, one sailed up in mid-foxtrot and 'split' the couple.

(Reprinted: Harmondsworth: Penguin, 1990, pp. 232–3).

7. ix   The Fabian social scientist Beatrice Webb, daughter of a wealthy businessman and a veteran of London Society, started the Half Circle Club for Labour MPs' wives in 1920. Her social experience was useful to the first Labour government, in which her husband Sidney was President of the Board of Trade. (Ramsay MacDonald, the Prime Minister and father of Ishbel, was a widower.)

Margaret Cole (ed.), *Beatrice Webb's Diaries, 1924–32* (1956).

January 8th [1924] … I am living a distracted life which does not please me. I have taken over S[idney]'s unofficial correspondence and dictated forty letters yesterday in twice as many minutes. What is far more troublesome is acting as the 'Doyenne' among Ministers' wives, in the organisation of their social intercourse within the Party and with outsiders like the Court. Just at present there are two questions – clothes and curtseys. A sort of underground communication is going on between Grosvenor Road and Buckingham Palace which is at once comic and tiresome … . My latest job has been to help Mrs Clynes to get her establishment fixed up at 11 Downing Street. I have provided her with house-keeper, cook and butler; no, I forgot, the *very* latest task has been to soothe the feelings of Mrs Snowden, deeply offended at being excluded from occupying the usual residence of the Chancellor of the Exchequer in favour of the wife of the Leader of the House. But the whole of the Labour world would have revolted at the bare idea of 'Ethel' established in an official residence. She is a 'climber' of the worst description, refusing to associate with the rank and file and plebeian elements in the Labour Party …. There is so little climbing in the Labour Party that one climber stands out in morbid prominence …

February 7th Ishbel MacDonald summoned a meeting at 10 Downing Street of Ministers' wives … to discuss whether or not there should be any organ-ised effort to get acquainted with the wives of Labour members and to start a common-room for the Parliamentary Party and their womenkind near the H[alf] C[ircle] C[lub], pending the establishment of a permanent Labour Club …. Ishbel is an attractive creature; charming to look at, in a pretty new frock, simple and direct in speech and manner … She announced her intention of being 'at home' one day a week and asking the Labour Members' wives to visit her and have a 'homely cup of tea' and suggested that other Ministers' wives might do likewise. Mrs Snowden also thought that the matter could be left to individuals, and that 'tea on the terrace' is what most women liked …. I should like to keep clear of the whole business and get back to my book; but I do not want the Parliamentary Labour Party to become the plaything of London Society and the despised of the more serious element in the Labour Movement.

(London: Longmans Green, 1956, pp. 3–5).

7. x   Dora Russell (1894–1986), active in the Labour Party and the Workers' Birth Control Group in the 1920s, describes a discouraging encounter with Marion Phillips. Permission for maternity clinics to give advice on contraception to women who needed it on medical grounds was given under the second Labour government in 1930. Janet Chance and Stella Browne became co-founders of the Abortion Law Reform Association in 1936.

Dora Russell, *The Tamarisk Tree*, vol.1 (1975).

Sundry requests began to be addressed to maternity clinics for birth control advice, which was always refused; the policy of the Ministry of Health being to threaten with dismissal doctors or health visitors who gave such advice …

With the coming of the [1924] Labour Government, those of us who saw the issue as political began to feel that this obscurantist attitude might be overcome ...

I found considerable support from all sorts and conditions of people. The Independent Labour Party was especially inclined towards us ... [But] the Clydeside [MPs] ... were, naturally, resentful of the attitude of the Eugenists, who implied that the working classes should not breed because they were of inferior stock ... The workers argued that they should have more money rather than less children. We Labour women fully agreed with the more money argument, but asserted that, even if we lived in Buckingham Palace, we would not want a baby every year ...

We found that the *average* death rate of mothers was then four to five per thousand births. By contrast the death rate of miners from fatal accidents was 1.1 per thousand miners actually engaged in mining. [We] then coined the slogan: 'It is four times as dangerous to bear a child as to work in a mine, and mining is men's most dangerous trade.'

We now organized a deputation to the Minister of Health of the Labour Government, Mr. Wheatley, who, unfortunately, was a Roman Catholic. There has always been a considerable Catholic vote for the Labour party ...

Mr Wheatley ... referred us to Parliament, to Parliament therefore we would go. But first of all we would obtain the verdict of the Labour Women's Conference. Several Women's Sections had sent in resolutions on birth control; as a member of the Chelsea Women's Section I was in charge of one. It was my first conference: I was excited and nervous. I dressed for the occasion in a scarlet jersey long-waisted dress with a short cape tied at the throat with dark blue braid to give myself confidence ...

In a narrow corridor of the Holborn Empire, where the conference was to take place, I was confronted by Dr Marion Phillips, Woman Organiser of the Labour Party, tall and to me appearing massive and terrifying. 'You must,' she said, 'withdraw this resolution.' 'I cannot, Dr Phillips,' I almost stammered, 'I am instructed by my Section to move it.' 'Sex should not be dragged into politics, you will split the Party from top to bottom.' ... This interview revealed to me that the Labour Woman Organiser existed, not so much to support the demands of women, as to keep them in order from the point of view of the male politicians.

The next day, 14 May 1924, Mrs K. Bruce Glasier moved the resolution of the Standing Joint Committee of Women's Organisations on motherhood, which demanded paid absence from work for women for six weeks before and six weeks after childbirth, improvement of maternity care, and some form of payment to non-wage-earning mothers. Our addendum … said:

> *This Conference, while in no way criticising the views of those who for scientific or moral reasons are opposed to the practice of birth control, expresses the opinion that the Ministry of Health should permit Public Health Authorities to provide, for those who desire it, information on the subject of birth control …*

Our addendum was carried by one thousand votes to eight … .

The supporters of abortion law reform … were at times an embarrassment to us; I did not disagree with their views, but overcoming prejudice about contraception was our first target. Janet Chance had a reassuring respectable air, but Stella Browne was a holy terror. She made no bones about raising the abortion issue in meetings and, wisps of hair floating from her untidy coiffure, would resist all efforts of a Chairman to put her down. Though I feared harm to our cause, I did glory in her intransigence.

(London: Virago, 1977, pp. 170–4).

7. xi *Home and Politics*, the Conservative Party's women's journal, made effective play with the 1924 Labour government's friendly relations with the Russian Bolshevik government.

'Over the Garden Wall', *Home and Politics*, 43, November 1924.

'That Bolshie Loan'

Mrs. Brown and Mrs. Jones have an agreeable chat about the loan to Russia

MRS. JONES: Well, Mrs. Brown, did you ever 'ear the likes of this 'ere Russian Treaty? To think as them Bolshies that 'ave robbed and murdered their own people that 'ad any money, should come over 'ere for some of ours!

MRS. BROWN: Yes, Mrs. Jones, that's bad enough! But you can understand the *Bolshies* doing that sort of thing. They're up to anything, *they* are, as long as they do all right for 'Number One.' Wot *we* must remember is that our Socialist Government, wot's supposed to look after *us*, 'as been and gone and promised to lend 'em our money – as much of it as they like to ask for, at that.

MRS. JONES: Do you mean it's *our* money they're wanting, yours and mine?

MRS. BROWN: Yes, I do, Mrs. Jones – and wot's more, the Bolshies have no call to pay it back if they don't want to. They owe us a small fortin as it is, but they ain't going to pay it back. Ho, no! Not they! …

MRS. JONES: But 'ow are *we* going to give 'em money, Mrs. Brown, when we haven't got any?

MRS. BROWN: Why, don't you see? The taxpayers 'll 'ave to pay it, and you and me is the taxpayers, and we'll have to pay more for our tea and sugar and stuff.

MRS. JONES: Goodness me! They're dear enough *now* and no mistake! As far as I can see, food's done nothing but go up since the Socialists started meddling with the country …

MRS. BROWN: …. I'm sure of one thing, I ain't going to vote for the Bolshies, whether they call themselves Socialists or not! I'm going to vote for the Party as thinks of *us* before the foreigners, and that's *the Conservative and Unionist Party!*

Mrs. JONES: You're about right Mrs. Brown. 'Safety first,' is wot I says … I'm for the Unionist candidate, every time. And I'll see my man votes the *right* way, too!

7. xii   Despite her differences with NUSEC in the 1920s over its support for Family Allowances, the veteran suffrage leader Millicent Fawcett continued to work with the movement. In this pamphlet she reflects on its achievements.

Dame Millicent Garrett Fawcett, *What the Vote Has Done* (1927).

Before women were enfranchised it was possible, after years of hard work, and persistent effort, to get through Parliament changes in the law favourable to the position of women. But this process was not rapid; and it absorbed the labour of a large number of able women. During the first eighteen years of the present century four such measures were carried, or one in every four and a-half years, whereas in the nine years since women have had the vote the rate has speeded up in a rather remarkable degree. I wish, however, to emphasise not merely the number and value of the Acts that have been passed since women had the vote, but the completely different and improved atmosphere that has been created as regards the sphere of women in national life and its responsibilities. Those of us who had worked in the Lobbies and Committee Rooms of the House of Commons for bettering the legal position of women were conscious of this improvement from the very moment when the Representation of the People Act, 1918, received the Royal Assent. We were no longer there on sufferance, but by right ... .

On April 13th, 1927, Mr. Baldwin announced his intention to place on the Statute Book next session legislation giving the vote to women on the same terms as men and from the age of 21 ...

Our long struggle for a complete measure of Women's Suffrage seems to be nearing its close ...

Perhaps I may be permitted to add, without offence, that having had opportunities of observing manners in the House of Commons, and comparing them over a period of nearly 60 years, I see an enormous, almost an incredible improvement in this respect in recent years. Democracy is a great teacher of manners. Women felt the difference and the improvement almost immediately after February, 1918.

(London: NUSEC, 1927 edition).

7. xiii   Lucy Baldwin (1869–1945) shared her husband's conviction that most women would identify with 'the nation' and against socialism. She was herself a campaigner for improved maternity services.

'"Making History". Mrs Baldwin's Faith in Women', *Home and Politics,* **97, May 1929.**

At this Election we women shall be helping to 'make history', for the great and only question to be considered is whether or not the welfare of the nation is to be handed over to a Socialist Government.

I am convinced that Socialism means the very opposite of women's ideals and hopes. That is why I feel that it cannot win the support of the women.

Socialism stands for class-war, chaos and disruption; the break-up of family life and religion; and the end of private business and individual enterprise. Our lives would be supervised at all points by State officials, and the women and children would be the first to suffer from such a changed order of society. You cannot spread the love of God by spreading discontent, and it is our women's work to spread that love ... .

I firmly believe that the Conservatives have the highest ideals, and that is why I regard them as *the* 'women's Party.' Their policy is based on a desire for the good of the whole nation; gradual progress built on firm foundations; the maintenance of justice, individual freedom and the British Constitution;

peace and co-operation in industry; the development and unity of our Empire; peace and disarmament by agreement between all countries; and the improvement of the social conditions of our people.

7. xiv Speaking for a cross-party committee 'for the Protection of Coloured Women in the Crown Colonies', Katharine Atholl represents the widely-held view that women had a special responsibility to promote the welfare of women in the British Empire. Humanitarian and feminist concerns were often expressed in language that betrayed assumptions of racial superiority.

Hansard, HC Deb, 11 Dec 1929, cc 599–608.

Duchess of Atholl ... Some Members of this House feel that there is urgent need for more consideration to be given to the social well-being, health, and education of women and girls in some of our dependencies ...

In particular we have been terribly impressed by what we have learned on ... the existence of a pre-marriage rite among young girls among many African tribes, a rite which is frequently referred to as the circumcision of girls ...

I doubt very much if ... there are many white people who realise what this rite is ... The term applied to it is totally inadequate to give an idea of what it means. Our committee has been assured by medical men and by missionaries who have attended these women in hospital that it is nothing short of mutilation. It consists of actual removal of parts connected with the organs of reproduction. The operation is performed publicly before one or two thousand people by an old woman of the tribe armed with an iron knife. No anaesthetic is given and no antiseptics are used ...

I understand the policy of British Governments of all political complexions has been to avoid interference as far as possible with native customs subject to this qualification, that they were not contrary to justice and humanity. I ask the House what could be more inhuman than the practice which I have described ...

Miss Rathbone ... We have had evidence from witnesses which has revealed to us that the position of native women in many of these tribes – I do not say all – is one of sheer slavery, accompanied by many of the worst conditions of slavery, and carried on practically without let or hindrance from the British authorities – slavery, not to Europeans, but to men of their own race ...

If we are asked to accept the principle that native self-governing institutions should be fostered ... we hope the champions of these native races will remind them that it has been an old principle that there is no slavery under the British flag .... Let them take this message to the men of the native races. There can be no equal citizenship between coloured men and white men till there is equal citizenship between coloured men and coloured women.

Colonel Wedgwood ... When I first heard of these vile things ... I think it was the cruelty to these children that horrified me. Since then, what has horrified me far more is that this thing is tolerated, not by the House – we do not know anything about it – but by the English women living in Kenya .....

7. xv   Mollie Bagot Stack (1883–1935), a pioneer of keep-fit exercises for the masses, founded the Women's League of Health and Beauty in 1930.

Mary Meta Bagot Stack, *Building the Body Beautiful* (1931).

The Body Beautiful has three ingredients: Health ... Grace ... Expression ....
    First comes Health.
    Movement is life. Stillness is the attribute of death ... A body without enough movement is like the stagnant pond: It collects the weeds of disease which will finally kill it; while the freely moving body creates its own health and exhilaration daily, and eventually becomes disease-proof .... .
    Every clumsy movement entails waste of effort and a slight unnecessary heart strain ... Thus we come to Grace ... Health Exercises, to be of any permanent value, should be graceful ...
    How, then, are we to carry out movements for Health gracefully? By remembering the third ingredient, Expression, as well. The movements should be rhythmic and musical, for rhythm is the first essential to any expression.

(London: Chapman & Hall, 1931, pp. 7–8).

7. xvi   The aviator Amy Johnson (1903–41) won press acclaim and awards for her record-breaking flights. According to the composer and former suffragette Dame Ethel Smyth (1858–1944) the man in the street was not impressed.

Ethel Smyth, *Female Pipings in Eden* (1933).

The day after Amy Johnson had finished her record flight [to South Africa] my servant asked the milkman what he thought of her, and his reply was

'Not much!' Later in the day she put the same question to the man who brought the coals, whose answer appears to have been still more uncompromising; 'I don't think about her at all,' he said gruffly, and went away, slamming the garden wicket. ''Twas easy seen,' remarked my servant, who is Irish, 'they'd made up among themselves down in Woking what they were going to say!'

But the best of all was a post-card from a niece of mine next day saying, 'I'm sure you'll like the remark of B., the Norwich bookseller, on Amy Johnson, and lest I forget the beauty of the phrasing I send this off at once from the P.O. opposite.' A customer remarked, 'Well, Mr. B., we women ought to be very proud this day because of A. J.' 'There I differ from you, Madam,' replied Mr. B 'If it had been a man I should say it was a wonderfully courageous feat and a great test of endurance. As it was a young lady I say it was sheer bravado and love of notoriety.'

(London: P. Davies Ltd, 1933, p. 21).

7. xvii Harold Nicolson (1886–1968), a National Labour MP and former diplomat, records impressions of a dinner-party with George VI and Queen Elizabeth shortly after the abdication of Edward VIII (1936); and two years later writes of the harm done by Society hostesses who encourage the policy of appeasement. Cliveden was the Berkshire home of Lady Astor.

Harold Nicolson, *Diaries and Letters, 1930–39* (1966).

17 March 1937. We ... pass on into the Picture Gallery, where we are joined by the women and by the King and Queen. Maureen Stanley is at once summoned by the King and occupies most of his attention. The Queen then goes the rounds. She wears upon her face a faint smile indicative of how much she would have liked her dinner party were it not for the fact that she was Queen of England. Nothing could exceed the charm or dignity which she displays; and I cannot help feeling what a mess poor Mrs. Simpson would have made of such an occasion ... The Queen teases me very charmingly about my pink face and my pink views ...

Thereafter ... the Queen drops us a deep curtsey which is answered by all the ladies present. We then go away, and I cadge a lift from Maureen Stanley.

10 April 1939. Does Mussolini seriously suppose that he could defeat ourselves and France? Or is he still relying upon that defeatist and pampered group in London who have for so long been assuring him that the

capitalists of England are on his side? … He must know that in the last resort our decision is embodied, not in Mayfair or Cliveden, but in the provinces. The harm which these silly selfish hostesses do is really immense. They convey to foreign envoys the impression that policy is decided in their own drawing-rooms. People such as Simon and Hore-Belisha (who are middle-class individuals flattered by the adulation of what they suppose – with extreme incorrectitude – to be the aristocracy) are also impressed by the social efficiency of silly women such as Mrs Greville and Lady Astor. Anybody who really knows the latter understands that she is a kindly but inordinately foolish woman. Yet these people have a subversive influence. They dine and wine our younger politicians and they create an atmosphere of authority and responsibility and grandeur, whereas the whole thing is a mere flatulence of spirit.

(London: Collins, 1966, pp. 298, 396–7).

7. xviii   As expectations of war mounted in 1938 the auxiliary women's services were reconstituted. Dame Helen Gwynne-Vaughan, after an academic career as a mycologist, returned to service as head of the Auxiliary Territorial Service. Here she defends it against the charge that too many officers were appointed for their social position.

Helen Gwynne-Vaughan, *Service With the Army* (1942).

The ATS had a bad start. Why? Principally, I think, because the essential preliminary of training company officers had not been attended to and because their selection had been left to well-intentioned but often inexperienced local enterprise. Also because the officers who would have been best worth having in war were by no means always those who could give most time in peace. It was natural enough that the president of the local Territorial Army Association, on whom the responsibility had been laid of nominating the county commandant, should in many cases apply to the local great lady, and that she, in her turn, should find the officers among leisured women. Indeed, she had little choice. Women who were running their own homes, looking after their children, were seldom in a position to offer full-time service in war; women in full-time jobs might abandon them for paid service on mobilization, but could not be responsible for the very considerable amount of work involved, under peace conditions, in taking up references, enrolling recruits, mastering regulations and conducting drills. The result, in spite of brilliant exceptions, was too large a proportion of the type of officer who was not accustomed to regular or exacting work …. Many of them, since September, 1938, have learnt an incredible lot but, at that time, even the best were ignorant and the less good were unaware of their deficiencies. Innumerable stories went round of lack of consideration for recruits, of delay, of unwise selection, of failures in courtesy …

Another result of the way in which officers were appointed was the titled lady outcry. This was all the more unreasonable because a title may mean so many different things; descent from belted earls, marriage off the stage to a marquis, being the wife of a soldier, doctor, historian or man of science who happens to have been knighted. These last could hardly be counted as social butterflies because their husbands had done well. It is true that a good many of the early officers had titles of one or another of these kinds. Several of them were extremely capable, completely devoted to the efficiency and well-being of their women and possessing that capacity for equal friendship with all sorts which is one of the best results of social experience. That, no doubt, was what actuated the anonymous writer of a letter from one of the south-west counties: 'I don't mind what I do to help, but please I would rather do it under a lady …'

By themselves such officers would have done the ATS nothing but good. Unfortunately, the titles and the bad manners got mixed in the minds of the public.

(London: Hutchison & Co., 1942, pp. 94–5).

7. xix   A week before the outbreak of war, as Germany prepared to invade Poland and news reached Britain of the non-aggression pact between Germany and the Soviet Union, the House of Commons debated the international situation. Ellen Wilkinson (1891–1947), MP for Jarrow and an opponent of appeasement, spoke for the Labour Left in this attack on Neville Chamberlain's foreign policy.

Hansard, HC Deb, 24 Aug 1939, cc 47–50.

Miss Wilkinson One of the tragedies of the policy of this country has been continually to under estimate what really was happening in that enormous country of Russia … We have treated that country with studied insult for as long as Members on the other side have been in power … I accept unhesitatingly the Prime Minister's word that in the last few weeks or days … he has done everything to get conclusions through the Military Mission sent to Russia, but you cannot alter the effect of years and years of insults …

I cannot enter into this general atmosphere of forgive and forget as regards the present Prime Minister ... We all admit the sincerity and high purpose of the Prime Minister, but what in fact did he do? When he came into office ... he made it his business to torpedo the system of ... collective security under the League of Nations ...

The Prime Minister, in a very good speech to-day, spoke about our obligations to small nations, to the possible victims of aggression. There was not one word that did not apply to our situation in Spain. While those gallant men were fighting for democracy in the trenches on the Ebro, and many of our own countrymen were trying to help them, the Under-Secretary for Foreign Affairs and the Prime Minister told this House over and over again things that they knew were not true about non-intervention .... There was also Czechoslovakia. We offered them a guarantee of those reduced frontiers and then did nothing to carry out our promise ...

Time after time we have had the Prime Minister doing – what? I say, putting the narrow interests of his class – [Hon. Members: 'Oh!'] – yes of his class and of the rich before the national interests ...

We talk on this side of the fifth column ... We mean those people, some of whom are Members of this House, who were so insistent, when Herr Ribbentrop was here, in telling us that we need not fight for Czechoslovakia ... What he learnt was the basis for his advice to Hitler that this country would not stand against him ...

Herr Ribbentrop learned that the real feeling of the upper classes in this country was that the Nazis had at last learned how to keep their working classes quiet.

Chapter 8

War and Reconstruction, 1939–51

8.i   General Sir Frederick Pile explains the decision to recruit women
to anti-aircraft batteries. His adviser, the electrical engineer Caroline
Haslett (1895–1957), was founder and director of the Electrical Association
for Women. Over 70,000 members of the ATS served on gun sites
during the war.

Sir Frederick Pile, *Ack-Ack. Britain's Defence against Air Attack during the
Second World War* (1949).

By the end of 1940, at a time when our organization was rapidly expanding,
we were short of no fewer than 1, 114 officers and 17, 965 other ranks. Something drastic had to be done. I suggested once more that women should be
employed in large numbers in an operational role.

13. ATS women at an Anti-Aircraft gun site at Wormwood Scrubs, West London,
October 1941. A War Office photograph. © Imperial War Museum (H14878), used
with permission.

Although this notion was new and, indeed, repugnant to a lot of people, I had been turning it over in my mind even before the War. In 1938 I had asked Miss Caroline Haslett, the distinguished engineer, to give me her opinion about women's capacity to do the work. Sunday after Sunday in that year she used to turn up, armed with mackintosh and umbrella, at sites in the Surrey hills to watch what was going on. As a result of this investigation, she had assured me that women could man searchlights and fire-control instruments, and, in fact, do almost everything except fire the guns.

As a matter of fact, I could see no logical reason why they should not fire the guns too. There is not much essential difference between manning a G.L. set or a predictor and firing a gun: both are means of destroying an enemy aircraft. However, I was not going to suggest going as far as employing them on lethal weapons. I was quite aware that there would be struggle enough to get their employment through in any operational form at all ... .

Sir James Grigg, the Under-Secretary of State for War, described the proposal as 'breathtaking and revolutionary'. There were outraged cries of horror from the diehards. But it was pure mathematics that forced everybody's hand .... The first mixed battery was to go into training in the spring [1941]. I should like to add that from the day Mr. Churchill first heard of the proposal from me he approved, and at once said that his daughter Mary would be glad to join a mixed battery ... .

It seemed that, if we didn't have a good publicity campaign, we should never get the 100,000 women we needed. The whole of the future of women soldiers needed the most careful consideration. I could not see why, if a woman was to play exactly the same part in a battery as a man, she should be controlled by a women's organization such as the A.T.S .... I wanted to make the women soldiers in the same way that men were and to give them the appropriate ranks, Gunner, Bombadier, Sergeant, and so on.

But in this laudable ambition of getting the girls equal status (and equal pay) I was more of a feminist than the members of the A.T.S. Directorate. And although the girls always wanted to feel that they were members of the Artillery, this was very actively discouraged by their own side of the house almost to the end of the War.

(Reprinted: London: Panther, 1956, 164–7).

8. ii   Frances Partridge (1900–2004), a life-long pacifist and member of
the Bloomsbury set, writes of London in the Blitz, and of the impact of
war on her Berkshire household. Virginia Woolf committed suicide in
March 1941.

Frances Partridge, *A Pacifist's War: Diaries, 1939–45* (1978).

April 4th [1941] To London, for a family business conclave …. On the way to
meet Hester (Chapman) for lunch at the Ivy I was struck with horror and
depression at the sight of the damage in small streets off Tottenham Court
Road. The sky was low and dark and London looked not like a town which
had *had* a drubbing, but one actually at war, as of course it is. I thought,
'Here I am in the war, and it's hateful,' and I shrank into the corner of my
taxi, choked with a sort of icy, leaden hatred of it all. No tables left at the
Ivy …. We went on to the Café Royal, where, as the windows had been blown
in and boarded up, we ate by electric light. Hester was amusing about her life
in the shelters with Jewish clothes-merchants, yet couldn't restrain her natural desire to boast. 'One feels magnificent the day after a raid, because one
has got through it and not shown one is afraid. But of course it is *absolutely*
terrifying – I never knew it was possible to be so terrified.'

On a bus to Harrods. Great damage all down Piccadilly gave me a series
of thwacks and thumps. In the hairdresser's warm *cellule*, I heard nothing
but talk on the eternal theme: 'There was a whistling and a groaning and
I heard my chimney-pot falling. It was a barrage balloon come down on the
roof, and there I was in the cupboard with the evacuee. "Flo," I said, "we're
finished", just like that …'

April 8th Sat out on the verandah, trying to write to Clive [Bell] about
Virginia's death. He says: ' … It became evident some weeks ago that she was
in for another of those long, agonizing breakdowns … The prospect – two
years insanity, then to wake up to the sort of world which two years of war
will have made, was such that I can't feel sure she was unwise …'

May 11th When Joan brought in the green tea this evening after dinner, she
gasped and said, 'Mrs Partridge, I want to leave and do war work, as Tim's
being sent abroad.' I went with her into the kitchen, where she told me that
he was going in about three weeks' time, and she felt she couldn't bear it
unless she was hard at work all day, so she had been to an aeroplane factory in

Newbury to see if they would take her on. I didn't know how to show her how sorry I was without upsetting her more, her white face and breathless voice were so pitiful. I came back to the sitting-room so struck by Joan's tragedy that I felt on the verge of tears ... Here was something absolutely good (Joan's relation with Tim) and it had been struck, and is crumbling away so rapidly that she has to try and drown her misery in the rumble and crash of machinery. And of course it is the happiness of not one but hundreds of Joans and hundreds of Gunner Robinsons, thousands, millions I should say – of all nationalities – that is to be sacrificed in this awful pandemonium ...

Our life gets more domestic and agricultural and when Joan goes it may get more so. If only I could cook!

(Repr. London: Phoenix Press, 1999, pp. 86–92).

8. iii   Impressions of Birmingham at war, and of shortages and rationing, from the diary of Vere Hodgson (1901–79), a London-based voluntary worker.

Vere Hodgson, *Few Eggs and No Oranges. A Diary Showing How Unimportant People in London and Birmingham Lived Through the War Years* **(1976).**

September 7th [1941] Tuesday wandered round the town [Birmingham] ... Patching up shops – because Brum is bursting with folk, and they do business even if they are blitzed again. Part of the Arcades open to the sky ...

Minnie came over from Coventry – only too glad to do a little shopping at our Woolworths. Coventry is like a city of the dead – as far as shops are concerned. They have run up a few with corrugated iron roofs. But the inhabitants are obliged to shop in Leicester, Northampton or Brum ...

Cath and I went to see the wonderful munitions procession lining up in Hagley Road. It was to attract women to the factories. All firms sent contingents in marvellously coloured overalls – on lorries containing parts of Spitfires etc. with the words: We Made These.

There never was such a talkative procession – they chattered like magpies all the time. One lorry had elderly women. We are all between 60 and 80 ... we are still working – why aren't you? How happy they all looked. They insisted on a lorry being provided for them, otherwise they said they would walk – but left out they would not be. There were some wonderful Tanks – the fastest in the world. It was a mile long, with a donkey to finish up with ...

November 28th To return to Food. My one egg during a fortnight was bad –
and they refused to give me another! Then milk rationing came in and this
has driven me nearly demented all the week. But, at last, I have got a Doctor's certificate for Miss Moyes, and she is allowed a pint a day. The rest of
us spread our miserable two pints over the week as best we can. The Cat is
being initiated into a water and milk diet ...

We are invading Libya – and seem to be marching on.

December 4th We are to economize with fuel – so there is hot water every
other day. Felt it was too good to last.

A lot of points for one tin of salmon. Sardines are 7, and baked beans
4. Pears have been seen at 3/- each. Apples are practically unobtainable.
Powdered milk has now appeared in the shops, and I bought nine penny-
worth. It does not sound very nourishing, but you can mix a few spoonfuls,
and put back the lid. Tins are a nuisance, as you must use them up rapidly.
Shall be glad when the cows are doing full time again – I am more than ever
in favour of cows.

(Repr. London: Persephone Books, 1999, pp. 208–10, 230–1).

**8. iv   After Hitler's invasion of the Soviet Union in 1941 women of the
Communist party took the lead in creating women's 'parliaments' in
London and the North of England to promote solidarity with the USSR
and discuss problems faced by working women.**

*Calling All Women! Report of the 2nd Session of the London Women's
Parliament* (1941).

The London Women's Parliament [has] definitely established itself as a
widely representative and authoritative institution, speaking with the voice
of the women of London ... Its most distinctive feature lies in the bringing
of women from the factories and trade unions, the professions and the political parties, together with the representatives of housewives', co-operators'
and women's organisations for common discussion. All sections are affected
by the overwhelming changes brought about by the war ... All alike are
menaced by the special degree of slavery and degradation which Fascism
holds for women .... .

The first Session of the Parliament met on July 13th, 1941. When the
Second Session assembled on October 26th, the numbers represented had
increased from 90,000 to over 280,000 ...

WOMAN POWER

AN OUTLINE OF PROPOSALS TO REMOVE THE OBSTACLES AT PRESENT PREVENTING THE WOMEN OF BRITAIN FROM PLAYING THEIR FULL PART IN INDUSTRIAL PRODUCTION.

The defence of our country and the defeat of German Fascism today depends as much upon the women of Britain as upon the men. The man-power position is serious, and every available person is needed to turn out the vast masses of war material so urgently awaited both by our own forces and by those of the Soviet Union, and to release the greatest possible number of able-bodied men for the fighting services ...

The Ministry of Labour estimates that half-a-million are immediately needed in industry; the requirements of the ATS. are stated to be 200,000, but compulsory registration is still a long way from providing these.

The women of this country are ready and anxious to get on with the job. They do not object to compulsion, seeing in it a way to ensure all-round equality and to prevent the few idlers from dodging their share. But thousands of women who want to volunteer find that there are a number of things which make it difficult or impossible for them to undertake a war job and to give their best to it. The most important of these are:

LOW WAGES, INSUFFICIENT DAY NURSERIES, LONG WORKING HOURS AND CONSEQUENT SHOPPING DIFFICULTIES, BAD CANTEENS and INADEQUATE TRANSPORT.

Further measures of compulsion must not be used as an alternative to the removal of these difficulties – and offer no solution.

(London: London Women's Parliament, 1941, pp. 1–4).

8. v Violet Markham, now in her seventies, passes on the Queen Mother's anxieties about black American troops in Britain to her sister-in-law in the US.

Helen Jones (ed.), *Duty and Citizenship. Correspondence and Papers of Violet Markham* (1994).

24 August 1942, Cynthia Colville, Lady in Waiting to Queen Mary, to VM.

I am writing by command of Queen Mary to bring before you a difficult but important matter. Her Majesty has been gravely concerned to hear of the unfortunate results, in many places, of association between American coloured men and English girls. You probably know that there are several negro battalions of USA Pioneer Corps etc, and these men are to be seen in large numbers in the south and west country, and elsewhere. They are friendly, generous, and have a good deal of money to spend; and there is no reason to think that they are particularly ill-behaved, though I fear there is very little doubt but that many English girls – often about fifteen years of age – do run after these men (and their money!) most persistently, especially in the big seaports, where men of colour are a familiar sight. This is not chiefly a question of morals – however important that aspect may be – but of international complications. American men refuse to allow negroes to associate with white girls, and they are ready (unpunished by their own authorities) to 'beat up', first, the offending blacks, and subsequently the white girls who encourage them. Thus, – apart from the fact that ultimate marriage would in any case be the rarest possibility … – there is a serious risk of grave ill-feeling between English and Americans, of possible lynchings, with all the disastrous consequences, not to mention the problem of half-caste births on a much bigger scale than heretofore.

The Queen feels strongly that wardens of hostels, factory welfare workers and others who are concerned with social conditions affecting girls, should give them definite instruction and enlightenment in this matter, and that it is an urgent one.

At the same time it is important that colour should *not* be stressed in writing, and that no written or printed word on this subject ever fall into the hands of those who are, after all, our country's guests. These black soldiers have come over with a tremendous sense of patriotism and determination to show that they are proud to work and fight for the USA … .

I might add that Her Majesty does *not* want her name brought into this matter …

Her Majesty felt that your knowledge and experience might be able to suggest ways & means of tackling this very thorny subject.

6 September 1942 Violet Markham to Nan Carruthers

My dear, I do wish your people hadn't sent these negroes over here. Colour is not understood in this country, and since many of the negroes are pleasant people with lots of money and good dancers silly little English girls are walking out with them. That makes your military people see red, and as a *very* reluctant House of Commons has handed over justice in American military areas to the Army things may happen. I am most uneasy about it all and so are other people. The wretched men are in a very hard position about any sort of social intercourse or leave; it's cruel to be treated as a pariah on one side or as an equal by sentimentalists who say a black man is just as good as a white. *They oughtn't to be here at all.* Please send over some black women auxiliaries as soon as possible!! It's the only alternative.

(London: Historians' Press, 1994, pp. 170–1).

8. vi The Beveridge Report, which became a blueprint for Reconstruction, set out a vision of cradle-to-grave social security based on the male-breadwinner model. It even included a proposal (not in fact implemented) that social insurance should provide benefits for housewives in cases of marriage breakdown. Beveridge's 'three assumptions' – Family Allowances, a National Health Service and full employment – were however realised in the post-war Welfare State.

Sir William Beveridge, *Social Insurance and Allied Services* (November 1942).

The census includes married women who do not work for money outside their homes among unoccupied persons .... In any measure of social policy in which regard is had to facts, the great majority of married women must be regarded as occupied on work which is vital though unpaid, without which their husbands could not do their paid work and without which the nation could not continue. In accord with facts, the Plan for Social Security treats married women as a special insurance class of occupied persons and treats man and wife as a team ... It treats a man's contributions as made on behalf of himself and his wife, as for a team, each of whose partners is equally essential, and it gives benefit as for a team ...

The principle adopted here is that on marriage every woman begins a new life in relation to social insurance. She acquires at once under a Housewife's Policy ... a right to ... marriage grant, maternity grant, widowhood and separation provision, benefit during her husband's unemployment or disability if not herself gainfully occupied. She does not carry on rights to unemployment or disability benefit in respect of contributions before marriage; she must acquire those, if at all, by fresh contributions after marriage. To mark the transition it is proposed that she should receive a marriage grant which, besides giving money when there is likely to be a felt need for it, has administrative convenience in encouraging early notification of marriage to the Security Office ...

During marriage most women will not be gainfully occupied ...

The proposal to pay less than the normal rate of unemployment and disability benefit to housewives who are also gainfully occupied is likely to be questioned, but the case for it is strong, both on practical grounds and in equity. It is undeniable that the needs of housewives in general are less than those of single women when unemployed or disabled, because their house is provided either by their husband's earnings or by his benefit ... Subsistence benefit for housewives who are also gainfully occupied need not cover their rent ... .

Three Assumptions: No satisfactory scheme of social security can be devised except on the following assumptions:-

(A) Children's allowances for children up to the age of 15, or if in full-time education up to the age of 16;

(B) Comprehensive health and rehabilitation services for prevention and cure of disease and restoration of capacity for work, available to all members of the community:

(C) Maintenance of employment, that is to say avoidance of mass unemployment.

(London: HMSO, 1942, paragraphs 107–112, 301).

8. vii   Evacuation of mothers and children from the slums focused attention on both urban poverty and the anti-social habits of 'problem families'. This study was carried out in 1939–42 by the Hygiene Committee of the WGPW, mostly professional women in social work, public health and education.

Women's Group on Public Welfare, *Our Towns. A Close-Up* (1943).

The effect of evacuation was to ... bring home to the national consciousness that the 'submerged tenth' described by Charles Booth still exists in our towns like a hidden sore, poor, dirty, and crude in its habits, an intolerable and degrading burden to decent people forced by poverty to neighbour with it.

Within this group are the 'problem families', always on the edge of pauperism and crime, riddled with mental and physical defects, in and out of the Courts for child neglect, a menace to the community, of which the gravity is out of all proportion to their numbers ...

Hostesses were entitled to look with horror upon the worst of the town mothers and children as something they could not have conceived in the England of to-day. The dreadful lesson of evacuation was the light it threw upon the home conditions of the lowest of the town dwellers. The task laid upon the authors of this book was to explore those conditions, and they have done so unsparingly. They have looked at the child who sleeps at unseemly hours and runs late and breakfastless to school; who has head lice, impetigo, scabies; who is unwashed and incontinent; who lies and pilfers. They have looked at him, as England was forced to look at him, with shame and a burning sense of neglect and wrong, and they have sought to suggest means whereby this degradation of childhood can be avoided and the home of the future made, even at its humblest, a better place. To a nation with a falling birth-rate the salvation of every child is more than ever vital.

(London: Oxford University Press, 1943, pp. xiii, xvi;

© OUP, reproduced with permission).

8. viii   Responding to an Air Ministry request for WAAF volunteers to train as Air Transport Auxiliary ferry pilots, Air Chief Marshal Sir Trafford Leigh-Mallory protests against the RAF's refusal to post women to overseas combat zones or to train them as pilots.

Leigh-Mallory to the Under-Secretary of State, Air Ministry, 3 Jan 1944.

... It is a deplorable fact that the W.A.A.F. no longer holds as high a position in public estimation as formerly, and I submit that the reason for this is its failure to attract the best and most adventurous type of woman in the country. Its pedestrian Safety First policy can make no appeal comparable with that of the A.T.S., whose members serve in large numbers in theatres of war abroad and who at home help to man A[nti] A[ircraft] batteries in the danger zone. Even the W.R.N.S. man craft at sea and, although a much smaller service, are more in evidence overseas than are the W.A.A.F., who much to their chagrin are only allowed in safe areas outside the U.K. and then in very small numbers.

Yet in the aeroplane the W.A.A.F. possess the finest medium of all three Women's Services on which to build morale, and it is astounding that the opportunity of forming its own flying branch should so long have been neglected.

It is even more deplorable, now that increasing numbers of women are required as ferry pilots, that volunteers should be called for from the ranks of a Flying Service to leave that Service in order to learn to fly.

The W.A.A.F. is, I believe, officially recognised as an integral part of the Royal Air Force. It is, therefore, difficult to see why it should be prohibited from sharing in the latter's essential function, *viz.* flying.

The excellent work done by the women pilots of the A.T.A. is fully real-ised, but there can be no reason who the two flying organisations – Service and Civilian – should not continue together for a time, though, in a year or two, amalgamation might prove advisable.

(TNA Air 8/793/100 6 WAAF – Proposal to
Form a Flying Branch).

8. ix   In debates on the 1944 Education Bill there was cross-party support from MPs of both sexes for equal pay for schoolteachers. An amendment passed, against government opposition, by 117 votes to 116; but was defeated the following day by 425 votes to 23 after Churchill made it an issue of confidence.

Hansard, HC Deb, 28–29 March, 1944, cc 1356–1390, 1452–7.

EDUCATION BILL

Clause 82 (Remuneration of teachers)

Mrs Cazalet Keir (Islington, East) In moving the Amendment ... I do not wish ... to argue the question of equal pay on general grounds today. It has often been discussed in this House, and it has been twice accepted in principle in regard to the civil service, the first time being nearly a quarter of a century ago. To-day we are discussing teachers. The teaching profession seems to be a completely clear-cut case of equality between men and women, which scarcely needs arguing. Men and women enter the training colleges at the same age, with the same entrance qualifica-tions. They take equivalent courses of training ... ; they receive the same certificates from the Board of Education or the university. When they get into the schools they are confronted with the same problems, responsibil-ities and conditions of work. In a mixed school they are, as a rule, entirely interchangeable ... .

It is difficult to see any grounds why women teachers should receive less pay for their responsibilities and work in schools than men. The argu-ment always advanced ... is that men as a rule have families to support. These arguments will be far less impressive when the Government scheme for family allowances is introduced. Let me assure the Committee that the effect of two successive wars has been to increase, by an amazing percentage, the number of women supporting dependants ...

Mrs. Tate (Frome) The hon. and gallant Member for Stafford (Major Thorneycroft) told us he was not a feminist, but I listened with great interest to him putting forward every feminist argument that I have ever used myself. I think there is a great deal of misunderstanding as to what constitutes a feminist .... I hope for once the Government will show themselves willing to keep abreast of public opinion. I do not ask too much. I do not ask that the Government should lead it. I merely ask that the Government should keep abreast of what is now really the public opinion of the country, that men and women should, when doing precisely the same work, be paid at precisely the same rate.

Dr Edith Summerskill (Fulham, West) I shall be very brief, because I think that the case for equal pay for men and women can be put much more effectively by the male Members than by the women Members .... I only draw attention to one point ... I want to ask the Minister this. Why is it that, in his Department, he pays women doctors who work for him at equal rates with the men? Why is it that he pays the women who work in his schools examining the children's bodies at the same rates as men and does not do the same justice to the women who examine the children's minds? ... I regret to say the reason why the Board of Education do justice to their women doctors is because we have been able to bring more pressure to bear on the Board than have the women teachers. We have, I may say, with due respect to representatives of the teaching profession in Parliament, been more forceful in the interests of women doctors than they have been in the interests of women teachers ...

EDUCATION BILL (GOVERNMENT DEFEAT)

The Prime Minister (Mr Churchill) ... At this very serious time in the progress of the war, there must be no doubt or question of the support which the Government enjoy in the House of Commons. Accordingly we have decided ... to resume the Committee stage of the *Education Bill*, and to delete Clause 82, as amended, entirely from the Measure. This act of deletion will be regarded as a Vote of Confidence in the present Administration. If the Government do not secure an adequate majority, it will entail the usual constitutional consequences ...

Mr. Shinwell (Seaham) May I ask the Prime Minister whether he does not think it possible to distinguish between a deliberative vote of the House on a domestic issue and any lack of confidence by the House in the Government on the general issues that are involved in the war effort? Would it not seem that hon. Members, who are 100 per cent with the Prime Minister in pursuing the war – [Interruption] – a matter upon which I should have thought there was no doubt at all – are being precluded from expressing their considered and honest opinion on a domestic matter? …

The Prime Minister No, Sir, I am afraid I cannot, in any way, alter the statement which I have made. It is really impossible to distinguish between votes on domestic policy and votes on the general policy of the war, in this country. [HON. MEMBERS: "Nonsense."] His Majesty's Government are entirely in the hands of the House, which has the fullest authority of any legislative assembly in the world, and we trust it will use it with responsibility.

8.x By 1944 the Women's Land Army employed over 80,000 women. Lady Denman (1884–1954) was its director. Novelist and gardener Vita Sackville-West (1892–1962) was on its Kent committee.

V. Sackville-West, *The Women's Land Army* (1944).

We have grown tired of hearing of the Land Army described as the Cinderella of the women's services … But this, in many ways, it really is … For the most part its members work isolated and in a mouse-like obscurity. Their very uniform seems to suggest a bashful camouflage of green-and-fawn to be lost against the grass or the stubble. It is seldom that the Land-girl emerges into the streets of great cities … Yet often in her previous occupation she has been urban enough. She has been a shop-assistant, a manicurist, a hair-dresser, a shorthand-typist, a ballet-dancer, a milliner, a mannequin, a saleswoman, an insurance-clerk. She has worn silk stockings and high-heeled shoes, pretty frocks and jaunty hats; has had plenty of fun … At a moment's notice she has now exchanged all that; instead of her silks and georgettes she wears wool and corduroy and clumping boots; her working-hours seem never definitely to end, for on the land there may always be a sudden urgent call; she lives among strangers … She gets up at an hour when other people are still warmly asleep – and although dawn in spring or summer may be a moment one should be sorry to miss, a dingy wet morning in the winter before the light has even begun to clear the eastern sky is a very different story; she goes to bed with aching muscles after a dull evening, knowing that next morning the horrible alarum will shrill through her sleep, calling her back to her damp boots, her reeking oil-skin, and the mud and numbing cold outside. All this she has done, and is doing, so that *we* may eat. Nor has she always done it under the threat of a compulsory calling-up, but often voluntarily before her age-group was reached ….

From time to time conferences are held in London, where 'the counties' meet Lady Denman and the leading officials of her staff … Information is given out … intricate legal points are reduced to elementary simplicity by the Assistant Director, and then Lady Denman as chairman, leaning back with a cigarette, invites comment. I don't know how it affects these ladies from all over the kingdom, but I do know that it made me feel very English indeed, when one after the other stood up and announced herself not by her own name but by the name of the county she represented – 'Norfolk! Devon! Warwick!' – all come together with the same purpose in the service of their country. It reminded me of the map one used to have in the schoolroom, showing one's little triangular island cut up into jig-saw patches of different colours, only here the patches were suddenly person-ified, dressed in honest tweeds and rather strong shoes. I felt how much, how very much, I liked the English; how much, how very much, how pain-fully much, I loved England.

(London: Imperial War Museum, 1944, pp. 7–8, 14).

8. xi   A baby is born just after the Normandy landings (June 1944) and while German Vis – flying bombs – are falling on London, in this novel by the Anglo-Irish writer Elizabeth Bowen (1899–1973). She was an ARP warden in London.

Elizabeth Bowen, *The Heat of the Day* (1949).

The baby, it was established, would be due about the middle of July. 'No doubt we shall be having the Second Front by that time, also,' remarked Louie … Her only pregnancy sickness was for home, for Seale-on-Sea – but ever more strictly, as with each month the invasion of Europe by us loomed nearer, was the ban on civilian entry into that area being enforced. However, now in London, it came to seem to her, *all* eyes were turning towards the coast, the sea. Spring days growing longer grew more momentous; there were calcu-lations as to the moon; day and night London shook with Invasion traffic roaring through it to unknown ports. Expectation came to its height, and stood: everybody waited …

'They're *across!*'

It had happened – under a curdled windy improbable June night. The whole of the story narrowed down to Louie, still with *her* hour ahead, heavily going to her window. Voices were in the street below; multiplied, one voice from dozens of radios came lancing across and across itself out of dozens of windows standing open. Louie leaned out and shouted: 'What – is that true?' It was …. There was at the same time being an uncoordinated movement into churches. The unexpected-expected day, with its elsewhere-ness, ran its broadcast-echoing course. You could not take back what had been done. The lucid outgoing vision, the vigil for the fighters, lasted ten days more, till the Secret Weapon started: then, it was shameful how fear wrenched thoughts home – droning *things*, mindlessly making for you, thick and fast, day and night, tore the calico of London, raising obscene dust out of the sullen bottom mind. There was no normal hour …. On and off, on and off sounded the sirens in the nightmare sunlessness …

The boy was born a little before his time.

Christened Thomas Victor, he took no notice of anything – however, Louie agreed she should take him out of London now he was born.

(Reprinted: London: Vintage, 1998, pp. 325, 328–9).

8. xii   Poems, by a Land Girl and a bereaved mother, from an anthology of women's war poetry.

Catherine Reilly (ed.), *Chaos of the Night* (1984).

Alice Coats, THE 'MONSTROUS REGIMENT', *Poems of the Land Army* (1945).

> What hosts of women everywhere I see!
> I'm sick to death of them – and they of me.
> (The few remaining men are small and pale –
> War lends a spurious value to the male.)
> Mechanics are supplanted by their mothers;
> Aunts take the place of artisans and others;
> Wives sell the sago, daughters drive the van,
> Even the mansion is without a man!
> Females are farming who were frail before,
> Matrons attending meetings by the score …
> Girls from the South and lassies from the North,
> Sisters and sweethearts bustle back and forth.
> The newsboy and the boy who drives the plough;
> Postman and milkman – all are ladies now.
> Doctors and engineers – yes, even these –
> Poets and politicians, all are shes.
> (The very beasts that in the meadows browse
> Are ewes and mares, heifers and hens and cows …)

All, doubtless, worthy to a high degree;
But oh, how boring! Yes, including me.

Vera Bax, TO BILLY, MY SON
(Killed in Action, May 15, 1945)

Now comes, indeed, the end of all delight,
The end of forward-looking on life's way,
The end of all desire to pierce the night
For gleam of hope, the end of all things gay;
The end of any promise Spring might hold,
The end of praying and, O God, the end
Of love that waited to be shared and told;
Now, evermore, shall life with sorrow blend;
That sorrow whose dark shape the months had fought,
And strictly kept in confines of the will;
Had held quiescent while each conscious thought
Searched far horizons where joy lingered still;
But, my beloved, fearless, gallant, true,
Here is fair end of sorrow, now, for you.

(London: Virago, 1984, pp. 29–30, 13).

8. xiii A cross-party committee chaired by Mavis Tate (1893–1947), Conservative MP for Frome, Somerset, continues to campaign for equal pay. A Royal Commission (1944–6) on the issue was tasked only to report on 'the social, economic and financial implications of the claim of equal pay for equal work'.

Mavis Tate MP, *Equal Work Deserves Equal Pay!* (1945).

Equal Pay for Equal Work will

Be in the NATIONAL interest
Benefit Industry
Help to bring Peace to the World
The Rate for the Job will
Maintain fair wage standards
Make certain that the right person does the job

Equal Pay for Equal Work is Right and Just
It is in the best interests of:-
The HOME

MEN – Married and Bachelors
WOMEN – Married and Spinsters
CHILDREN and Young People
EMPLOYEES and EMPLOYERS ...

POLITICALLY IT IS ACCEPTED
Because:
Each Political Party says it stands for Equal Pay for Equal Work
The House of Commons voted in favour of Equal Pay in 1936 and again in 1944
When will the Government bow to the Will of the House? – **When you make your influence felt!**
Write to your MP insisting on his support for

THE RATE FOR THE JOB

> (London: Equal Pay Campaign Committee
> pamphlet, 1945, pp. 3, 11).

8. xiv In the last months of the war the Churchill Coalition introduced Family Allowances, chiefly in order to fend off trade union pressure for inflationary wage increases. The angry reaction to proposals that they should be paid to the husband rather than the wife is voiced here by Eleanor Rathbone.

Hansard, HC Deb, 8 March 1945, cc. 2276–85.

FAMILY ALLOWANCES BILL, Second Reading

Miss Rathbone (Combined English Universities). I shall concentrate my remarks very largely on the question of the recipient of the allowance .... .

In the words of the Bill, where the man and wife are living together, the allowance will belong to the man, and that will be so even if the wife earns every penny of the income. If the man is a rotter or a total invalid and the wife is the sole wage-earner, the allowance belongs to the man. It belongs to him if the children are hers by a first marriage ...

Probably the great majority of husbands will hand over the allowance to their wives ... Say there is only one bad husband in 100. That would still be 26,000, quite a considerable number ...

Is that not a really amazing proposal, and what is the excuse for it? ... The explanation given in the White Paper is that the man is normally the head of the household ... What does the wife do? She merely risks her life to bring the children into the world, often with agonising pain, and in the vast majority of working-class homes, she spends her days and hours, as they say in my part of the world 'All the hours God makes', in washing and cleaning for the children, clothing them and feeding them ... School holidays and the week-ends bring her no remission, no time off; they actually increase the burden on the working-class mother. All that is to go for nothing, because the law holds that the man is normally the wage earner ...

What will happen if the House allows this proposal to go through unchanged? The Government have decided to leave it to a free vote of the House ... I realise perfectly well that they have blundered into this decision: it was not a stroke of Machiavellian policy to degrade the status of motherhood. But the Cabinet is composed of men, and they cannot be expected to realise how women think on this question. I want to warn them of the intensity of women's feelings about it .... The women's organisations are already planning to make sure that every politically-conscious woman in the country knows at the next election how her representative has voted. I took part in that long bitter struggle for the women's vote before the last war ... It was worth it, and we got full realisation of women's citizenship through it. But I do not want to go all through that again. It was a bitter struggle, and it caused very ugly results. During the last years, and especially during the war years, women have learned to work together with men, to play together with men, to suffer together with men. Do we want this sex grievance to raise its ugly head at the next General Election ? ...

If the Bill goes through in its present form I cannot vote for the Third Reading, although I have worked for this thing for over 25 years. It would be one of the bitterest disappointments of my political life if the Bill did not get through. But I foresee too well the consequences if it goes through in a form which practically throws an insult in the faces of those to whom the country owes most, the actual or potential mothers ... I beg Members to ... beware how they encourage sex antagonism – which we thought once was dead – to become once more an issue in a General Election.

8. xv   The National Health Service is often treated as part of a post-war political consensus, but debates on Aneurin Bevan's NHS Bill were not

without partisan conflict. Joan Davidson (1894–1985) was the only Conservative woman MP elected in 1945; a popular figure, she chaired the Party Conference in 1964–5. Alice Bacon (1909–93), a schoolteacher and daughter of a miner, was elected chairman of the Labour Party in 1950.

Hansard, HC Deb 30 Apr 1946, cc 85–91, 111–116.

Viscountess Davidson (Hemel Hempstead). On one matter hon. Members are in full agreement; namely that our health services should be so improved that all shall be able to obtain the best medical treatment. But we disagree with the Government on the best method of obtaining that treatment … We are told that many doctors are in full approval of this Bill. I have not met them … I have talked to many of them and they are deeply apprehensive of what will happen to the medical profession when this Bill becomes law, viewing it not from any selfish motive, but in the light of how it will affect their individual patients … .

I am afraid that the keen, brilliant man will not join a profession where he will have no free scope for his abilities, but will be subjected to control and interference. Very likely, he will take up other work, or will go abroad. Who will suffer then? …

I cannot see how the family doctor will remain … The personal and individual touch will be lost; the patient will not gain, the doctors will not gain …

I realise that many hon. Members opposite are most sincere in their beliefs … [But] they are gradually killing the finest characteristics of our people – the spirit of enterprise and of individual attainment … To my mind this Bill saps the very foundations on which our national character has been built … It is giving more power to the Minister … It is depriving the individual of yet more of his long-fought-for freedom …

Miss Bacon (Leeds, North-East). My experience in many parts of the country among ordinary men and women leads me to believe that the Minister has overwhelming support for this Bill … It is true that there are some defects, but the Bill, on the whole, is the greatest Measure for human well-being ever introduced into this country …. This Bill gives to thousands of people freedom they have never before enjoyed, freedom to consult a doctor or a specialist without thinking of the cost …

I have one criticism with regard to hospitals, namely the provision in public hospitals for private paying patients …. The proposals … allow specialists to treat and operate on private patients for fees, and I suggest that there might be a grave danger here ... Why should anyone pay when everyone can get the service free? There is only one answer. It is because they will obtain, or believe they will obtain, better service by paying than by using the public scheme ...

The Bill is fundamentally right ... I know that many of the defects are not due to the desire of the Minister, but to the undue pressure which has been exerted [by the medical profession] ... We on this side believe that the limit has been reached with the concessions that have been made.

8. xvi **The sociologist Michael Young, director of the Labour Party's research department between 1945 and 1951, notes that the effect of post-war welfare and fiscal policies has been to redistribute income in favour of women and children.**

Michael Young, 'The Distribution of Income within the Family', *British Journal of Sociology*, 3, 1952.

Greater opportunities for work outside the home have provided one safeguard for wives against a reduction in real income. The other and much more important safeguard has been the Welfare State. To say that inflation reduces the share in money terms of the national income received by wives and children is not to say that their share is necessarily cut down in real terms. It depends in good part upon whether the prices of things bought by men have risen more than the prices of things bought by women. That is just what happened – until 1949, at any rate. Prices of tobacco and drink have risen far more than prices in general, owing to the taxes imposed on them .... Prices of food, which bulks large in the housewives' expenditure, have, on the other hand, risen less than the average, owing to subsidies. The Welfare State has benefited wives and children in other ways as well – through Family Allowances, School Meals, Milk and Food Supplements, and through the National Health Service. Raising of the school-leaving age has, on the other hand, been paid for largely by mothers who have had to wait longer for the contribution which their children make towards housekeeping expenses when they begin to earn. But in general it is as though the taxes on tobacco and drink had been paid into a family income equalization pool, from which had been drawn the benefits provided by the State ...

All in all, the Welfare State has undoubtedly been an agency for transferring income from men to women and children.

Chapter 9

ℒ

The Fifties and Sixties

9.i In her first Christmas broadcast after the Coronation in 1953 Queen Elizabeth II – now on a Commonwealth tour – reflects on the notion of a 'new Elizabethan age'.

T. Fleming (ed.), *Voices Out of the Air. The Royal Christmas Broadcasts* (1981).

Last Christmas I spoke to you from England; this year I am doing so from New Zealand ... My husband and I left London a month ago, but we have already paid short visits to Bermuda, Jamaica, Fiji, and Tonga, and have passed through Panama .... In a short time we shall be visiting Australia and later Ceylon ...

So this will be a voyage right round the world – the first that a Queen of England has been privileged to make as Queen ...

Some people have expressed the hope that my reign may mark a new Elizabethan age. Frankly I do not myself feel at all like my great Tudor forebear, who was blessed with neither husband nor children, who ruled as a despot, and was never able to leave her native shores. But there is at least one very significant resemblance between her age and mine. For her Kingdom, small though it may have been and poor by comparison with her European neighbours, was yet great in spirit and well endowed with men who were ready to encompass the earth. Now, this great Commonwealth, of which I am so proud to be the Head, and of which that ancient Kingdom forms a part, though rich in material resources is richer still in the enterprise and courage of its peoples.

(London: Heinemann, 1981, pp. 72–3).

9.ii At a time when increasing numbers of middle-class women were marrying, the penal reformer Margery Fry (1874–1958) recalls the important contributions made by single women of her generation.

Margery Fry, *The Single Woman* (1953).

To come back to the woman active outside her home. The last sixty or seventy years has perhaps been the time (I speak deliberately) of her greatest importance in the life of the country. Women will go on proving their capacity in almost every sphere, but the changing pattern of our social life is gradually blurring the boundaries of the special territory of the unmarried woman. One of the biggest problems of today is not 'How shall women follow careers?' but 'How shall the married woman combine her career and her home?'

Going back over the last 50 years try to think of them without all the work, paid or unpaid, of single women. You will find that in transforming nursing and education, in changing the whole status of women, in bettering the position of children, they have mainly supplied, not only the leaders, but the rank and file and the enthusiasm. They have addressed the meetings and they have addressed the envelopes. Perhaps, as critics say, all this has been given to public causes because of starvation of the instincts of sex. This may be true, yet it is also true that our whole advance from animal to civilized life has proceeded on such transferences. That women have known how to achieve this sublimation is a cause for wholesome pride.

(London: Delisle, 1953, pp. 31–3).

9. iii   Baroness Wootton (1897–1988), social scientist and public intellectual, comments on the experience of the first women peers created under the 1958 Peerages Act. She was to become Deputy Speaker of the House of Lords in 1967. Voluntary public service was the background of her three colleagues, among them Stella Marchioness of Reading (1894–1971), founder of the WVS.

Barbara Wootton, *In A World I Never Made: Autobiographical Reflections* (1967).

Along with three other women, Stella Reading, now The Baroness Swanborough, Kay Elliot, now The Baroness Elliot of Harwood, and Irene Ravensdale ... I found myself amongst the first four women members of their Lordships' House.

On the first occasion that Her Majesty opened Parliament after the admission of women we waited with considerable curiosity to see whether she would vary the traditional formula. She did not. 'My Lords, pray be seated' she said, as usual .... This adherence to tradition supports the view held by the women peers that we should be described as peers and not peeresses. Indeed one at least of our masculine colleagues holds that we ought to be referred to in the House as the 'noble Lord', and not, as is the general practice, as the 'noble Lady'. Certainly it was a cause of some disappointment to us that the modes of address customarily employed make no distinction between women upon whom life peerages have been conferred in their own right, and the wives of peers or even of knights, whose titles are derived solely from their husbands. All alike are habitually addressed as 'Lady'. While the appropriate distinction could be made by the use of the title 'Baroness' in relation to women peers, attempts to popularize this have not been successful; it is apparently thought to have too foreign a sound. In any case, however, it is now accepted that a peeress is a peer's wife, as distinct from one herself who is a woman peer; and the authorities have accordingly changed the notices on our lavatories from 'Life Peeresses' to 'Women Peers' ...

Let me add that their Lordships' House has proved to be one of the (in my experience not very numerous) places where male and female alike are treated on merits. Perhaps feminine speeches are greeted with slightly more applause than they deserve or would receive if they came from manly lips, but, generally speaking, both socially and in the business of the House the atmosphere is one of comradely equality, and one is conscious neither of special favours nor of hostile discrimination.

(London: Allen & Unwin, 1967, pp. 130–3).

9. iv   **It took ten years for parliament to act on the Wolfenden Committee's recommendation that homosexual relations between adults in private should be decriminalised; but its recommendations for a crackdown on street prostitution had an immediate effect. The Street Offences Act of 1959 made it an offence 'for any common prostitute to loiter or solicit for the purposes of prostitution', without the need for a witness to testify that she had caused annoyance.**

Report of the Committee on Homosexual Offences and Prostitution.

Prostitution

We recommend:-

That the law relating to street offences be reformulated so as to eliminate the requirement to establish annoyance.

That the law be made of general application ...

That the maximum penalties for street offences be increased, and that a system of progressively higher penalties for repeated offences be introduced.

That the courts be given explicit powers to remand, in custody if need be, for not more than three weeks, a prostitute convicted for a first or second time of a street offence, in order that a social or medical report may be obtained ...
(London: HMSO, 1957, p. 116).

9.v   Opposition to the new rules on soliciting and use of the term 'common prostitute' came from two women peers with long experience of (respectively) social work and service as a magistrate. Organisations that shared their views included the National Council of Women and the Association for Moral and Social Hygiene.

Hansard, HLDeb, 5 May and 9 June, 1959, cc. 101–104, 819–821.

STREET OFFENCES BILL

Baroness Ravensdale of Kedleston ... Certain aspects of the Street Offences Bill ... make my conscience very uneasy .... .

To me the Bill deals with effects, and not causes, and it attacks only one sex, fiercely, and wants them wiped off the streets. We have already heard several times today that prostitution is not an offence in law ... ; but if I may be permitted to say so, as long as one sex, the male, desires it, it will continue in some form or shape ...

To clear the streets, as has already been said repeatedly by the noble and learned Viscount on the Woolsack, to my sorrow, we are eliminating the requirement that annoyance must be proved. Surely, that is disastrous. I thought that in this country of ours we had one law for all. In this Bill we are bringing about a double standard against one sex; and I feel very strongly that it is retrograde. To retain the words 'common prostitute' the woman in question must be charged with something: and on the 'verdict' (to my grave anxiety) of one or two policemen her name goes in a book. I wish I could see in the Bill a provision requiring evidence that annoyance had been caused to the person accosted ... If we are to clear up our streets and put the women underground, may I ask, my Lords why not clear the streets of men who solicit women as well as their own sex?

... I am not going into the question of kerb-crawlers and prostitution on wheels, about which we have heard so much, but I would point out that by clearing the streets we open a much larger field to the pimps and ponces and to absentee landlords to turn more and more rooms into brothels. These are the people, the landlords, that I should like to get hold of. I come from forty-two years of boys' and girls' club work in Stepney.

Baroness Wootton of Abinger The noble and learned Viscount the Lord Chancellor ... quotes with approbation the Report of the Wolfenden Committee as saying that the nuisance of solicitation is self-evident. If that is so, on what grounds is it necessary to label the common prostitute as a person who commits this nuisance? If the nuisance is so self-evident, it must be so apparent that any person who is taking part in it is liable ... to be charged ...

A good deal has been said this afternoon about protecting respectable women ... I think the members of my sex greatly appreciate the concern which has been shown ... for the safety of respectable women: but I would point out that this concern is not altogether shared by the most respectable women's organisations in the country, which have been singularly of one mind in expressing their alarm at the Bill in its unamended form ....

As to the use of the term 'common prostitute', there is no statutory definition. Surely we are getting into a curious position when, without a statutory definition ... this particular class of persons is to be alone in liability to this type of charge. The noble and learned Viscount quite properly says that being a common prostitute is a fact which must be proved in court ... if challenged. But I ask myself: in what is this proof going to consist? A common prostitute is a person who commonly offers her body for lewdness, and I hesitate to visualise the kind of evidence that it would be necessary to give to establish that fact in court unless we are to accept the proof of previous convictions ... As has been repeatedly pointed out, to accept that kind of evidence is contrary to the basic principles of English justice, and to accept any other kind of proof seems to me contrary to the principles of decency.

9. vi The falling age at marriage is discussed in the Crowther Report, which dealt with children who stayed at school beyond the minimum leaving age (15 from 1947, raised to 16 in 1972).

Ministry of Education, *15 to 18. A report of the Central Advisory Council for Education* (Crowther Report, 1959).

The earlier age at which women now marry has serious consequences for the education of adolescent girls. It hardly leaves time for a girl to become fully qualified professionally, and to gain experience in the exercise of her skill, before marriage and childbirth interrupt her career .... Where the intellectually abler girls are concerned, it is difficult for the schools to adjust to [the] sharpening contrast between career interests and personal demands, for most of what they learn in school is related to their professional training and to entrance into the universities and other institutions where it is pursued. There is not much scope – in school hours, at least – for giving them any education specifically related to their special interests as women.

With the less able girls, however, we think that the schools can and should make more adjustments … to the fact that marriage now looms much larger and nearer in the pupils' eyes than it has ever done before. Their needs are much more sharply differentiated from those of boys of the same age than is true of the academically abler groups. Nearly nine times as many girls as boys get married before they are 19 …

At this time, therefore, the prospect of courtship and marriage should rightly influence the education of the adolescent girl. Though the general objectives of secondary education remain unchanged, her direct interest in dress, personal appearance and in problems of human relations should be given a central place in her education. The greater psychological and social maturity of girls makes such subjects acceptable – and socially necessary. Girls must be treated, even more completely than adolescent boys, as young adults …. The increase in the number of early marriages is, in any case, creating a problem for the schools; it will be more serious when the school-leaving age is raised.

(London: HMSO, 1959, paragraphs 50–52).

9. vii   The novelist Fay Weldon looks back in her autobiography on a period of growing affluence and cultural change but traditional gender roles in the home.

Fay Weldon, *Auto da Fay* (2002).

The early Sixties were opulent, frivolous pre-feminist days … How suddenly the fashions changed. Skirts shot up, hair frothed around the face in a springy bird's-nest: look down on your shoes and they were green with satin bows, not the brown and black of the old days. Language loosened up: students took to Marxism, it became the thing to speak with the accents of the people: the young wore jeans in homage to the poor, the future was seen to lie with the workers. The schools stopped teaching by rote, and decided grammar was not important. Carrier bags were made of bright plastic not brown paper, and were everywhere, as people shopped for the fun of it ….

It was my normal female task to see to the domestic running of the house, the child-care, and do the shopping, the cooking and the laundry, as well as going out to work. I did not resent it, but took these duties for granted. The

14. Mary Quant in 1966. The writer and fashion historian Elizabeth Wilson felt that changes in clothes and hair-styles reflected a change in mood in the late fifties and early sixties: 'with the advent of the mass-market designer Mary Quant, who catered for the youth market, clothes became childish, light-hearted, *fun*, of a piece with the boom and consumerism'.[1] Among the styles associated with her were the mini-dress, white 'go-go' boots and hot pants, first sold at her 'Bazaar' shops in the King's Road and Knightsbridge. © Nijs, Jac. de / Anefo.

general assumption was that if a woman worked it was not to interfere with the household's comfort or leisure in any way. No matter how the household might depend upon her income, her working outside the home was seen as a kind of wilful, self-indulgent act: her true role was as a home-maker. A man who did housework or cooked, likewise, was despised. Male and female, we all busily gender role-played, in a way that seems extraordinary today …

I learned to cook: extravagant, murderous cooking out of Elizabeth David. Recipes from all the world, spices and herbs from everywhere: the ingredients had finally arrived: olive oil, garlic, mushrooms, avocados, aubergines, if in doubt add cream and brandy, to make up for decades of plain roast lamb and steamed cod …

(London: Flamingo, 2002, pp. 352–7).

9. viii   The anthropologist and advocate of natural childbirth,
Sheila Kitzinger (1929–2015), became a leading figure in the National
Childbirth Trust and the campaign against the medicalisation of
childbirth.

Sheila Kitzinger, *The Experience of Childbirth* (1962).

It is not then the absence or deadening of pain which gives value to the
method suggested in this book, but the addition of qualities which can make
childbirth a thrilling adventure, an achievement of the first order in which
both husband and wife can share, and a revelation for both …

This involves the conscious participation of the woman. She is no longer
a passive, suffering instrument. She no longer hands over her body to doctors and nurses to deal with as they think best. She retains the power of
self-direction, of self-control, of choice and of voluntary decision …

Some people think that natural childbirth implies a sort of hypnotic
relation between the doctor and patient and that unless a patient is unusually
suggestible this method will fail for her. Nothing could be farther from the
truth. A woman who is adequately prepared can find this method works well
for her even if the obstetrician or midwife knows nothing about it at all; all
she requires is that they shall be permissive, and, ideally, that her husband
shall be present and willing and able to take responsibility, since she should
not get involved in explanation at this time … .

The best place to have a baby, with some exceptions, is at home.

(London: Gollancz, 1962, pp. 20, 24).

9. ix.   Mary Whitehouse (1910–2001), senior mistress at a Shropshire
girls' school and member of the conservative Christian organisation Moral
Rearmament, describes the background to the foundation of the National
Viewers and Listeners Association (1965).

Mary Whitehouse, *Cleaning-Up TV: From Protest to Participation* (1967).

In her parish work Mrs Buckland [wife of the Rector of Longton,
Stoke-on-Trent] had been having experiences similar to mine at school.
Mothers in the parish came to tell her that the training they were trying to
give their children was being undermined by television.

One of them told her: 'So often in a perfectly ordinary play or programme something which runs counter to our way of thinking and training is slipped in in such a way as to make it appear normal behaviour.'

Another said after watching a documentary on unmarried mothers, 'There was no suggestion that it was wrong to become an unmarried mother – or even very regrettable – still less avoidable. No helpful advice or moral guidance was given to prevent such an occurrence, merely a plea that better arrangements should be made for the girls to have their babies.' ...

A mother came to her in great distress about a play where a man was shown unbuttoning his trousers before getting into bed with a woman (not his wife). 'There was not the slightest suggestion that it was wrong and it came straight into our family circle,' she said ...

We decided that we must do something and do it immediately. But what? It would be a waste of time taking up each point with the BBC. We had written letters in the past only to receive replies suggesting that it was we ourselves who were out of step ... So we put our heads together and produced our manifesto.

THE MANIFESTO

1. We women of Britain believe in a Christian way of life.
2. We want it for our children and our country.
3. We deplore present day attempts to belittle or destroy it, and in particular we object to the propaganda of disbelief, doubt and dirt that the BBC projects into millions of homes through the television screen.
4. Crime, violence, illegitimacy and venereal disease are steadily increasing, yet the BBC employs people whose ideas and advice pander to the lowest in human nature and accompany this with a stream of suggestive and erotic plays which present promiscuity, infidelity and drinking as normal and inevitable.
5. We call upon the BBC for a radical change of policy ...

On Monday 27 January 1964 the *Birmingham Evening News* carried a front page headline 'Mothers Campaign for Higher TV Morals'. The next day a number of the national papers picked it up, and we were away ... Within forty-eight hours the post began to arrive ... building up to a grand climax of 322 in one day and making an overall total of something like 35,000 letters up to the time of writing.

(London: Blandford Press, 1967, pp. 21–5).

9. x   *Putting Asunder* (1966), the report of a committee appointed by the
Archbishop of Canterbury, had recommended liberalisation of the divorce
laws. The feminist doctor and former Labour minister Edith Summerskill
(1901–80), since 1961 a life peer, maintained that this was not in women's
best interests and that their contribution to the family economy was not
adequately recognised in divorce settlements. The principle of marital
breakdown as grounds for divorce was to be included in the 1969 Divorce
Reform Act.

Hansard, HL Deb, 8 Nov 1967, cc 421–428

Baroness Summerskill I should like to address myself to that part of the
gracious [Queen's] Speech which relates to reforming ... family law ....
I beg the Government not to be precipitate but to give the most careful consideration to the proposition that matrimonial offences should be
replaced by the breakdown of marriage as the ground for divorce, and that
an innocent spouse should be compelled to accept divorce after a few years
of separation ...

My noble and learned friend has told us to-day that ... there is a consensus of opinion. He mentioned the Church of England, the Methodist
Church ... and the Law Reform Committee. But these are organisations
composed almost entirely of men ... Marriage means much more to a
woman that to a man. Marriage means to a woman an arrangement whereby
a man and a woman live together in order that they may have children, an
arrangement which will protect those children as long as possible ...

Surely few men can keep two families .... If a law is not enforceable it is
a bad law, and if a law is so framed that only wealthy men can take advantage
of it it is a bad law. There is a tendency in many quarters to disregard the fact
that men can earn their income and accumulate capital only by virtue of the
division of labour between themselves and their wives .... Sir Jocelyn Simon,
President of the Divorce Court ... [has] said: 'The cock bird can feather his
nest precisely because he is not required to spend time sitting on it'. This
being so, a separation of goods between married people cannot be said to do
justice to the wife ... .

My purpose to-day is simply to try to persuade the Government, before
they embark – or before a Private Member embarks – on legislation calculated to undermine the institution of marriage as we understand it in
Britain, to change the policy. However, if they find that a Private Member is
persuaded to draft a Casanova's Charter, then they must incorporate – this

is where I come back to family law – a matrimonial property law which includes community of goods, in order to protect the discarded wife.

9. xi   The Plowden Committee, best known for endorsing the progressive, child-centred methods of education that flourished in the 1960s, found less support for the expansion of state nursery education. Its recommendation that the state should provide part-time nursery school places for all 3-5-year-olds whose parents wanted it was never implemented.

Central Advisory Council for Education (England), *Children and their Primary Schools (Plowden Report)* (1967).

The under fives are the only age group for whom no extra educational provision of any kind has been made since 1944 ...

There is a wide measure of agreement among informed observers that nursery provision on a substantial scale is desirable, not only on educational grounds but also for social, health and welfare considerations. The case, we believe, is a strong one.

Our witnesses ... quoted research on the extent to which nursery education can compensate for social deprivation and special handicaps. ... There is strong support ... for the view of Bernstein and Deutsch that poverty of language is a major cause of poor achievement and that attempts to offset poverty of language are best made as early as possible. These researchers argue that thought is dependent on language and that some working class children have insufficient encouragement, example and stimulus in the situations of their daily life to build up a language which is rich and wide ranging in vocabulary, is a tool for categorisation and generalisation, and which, being complex in structure, develops concepts of time, space and contingency ...

Each of the countries we visited provides education for children before the age of compulsory entry to school on a more generous scale than we do ...

The first argument against nursery education is that the place for the young child is with his mother in the home ... Some of those who have studied the mother-child relationship in the early years hold that harm may come to some children through removal from their mother's care and companionship at too early an age before they realise that separation is only temporary ... Evidence of this kind points to the danger of allowing children to attend nursery school or class at too early an age or for too long a period each day .... .

Since it is harmful to remove a child too suddenly or for too long from his mother, part-time attendance should be the normal pattern of nursery education.

(London: HMSO, 1967, vol.i, pp. 116–23).

9. xii   Barbara Castle (1910–2002), the most influential Labour woman of her generation, resisted the label feminist, but here she defends the record of the Wilson governments from a woman's standpoint. Among the other women promoted by Wilson was Aneurin Bevan's widow Jennie Lee (1904–88), who as Minister for the Arts worked towards the foundation of the Open University.

Barbara Castle, 'No Kitchen Cabinet', in Sara Maitland (ed.), *Very Heaven: Looking Back at the 1960s* **(1988).**

I have never understood the ferment of the sixties I hear so much about. I was barely aware that it was going on. One of the reasons, I suppose, is that I was too busy … I was fulfilled. Having been a political animal all my life, here I was in 1964: unbelievably a member of the Cabinet and able to put my oar in on all the issues which were stirring people up … .

It is obviously absurd that there should not be more women in Parliament and government to voice women's needs. But this is not to say that women should be in Parliament merely to represent women's interests … It is hard for anyone, male or female, to fulfil themselves if they are poor, ill-housed, ill-educated and struggling with ill-health. Women's special problems must be grafted on to the battle against injustice wherever it may occur.

This is what we were trying to do in government. We had our quota of macho-males, but we had come into office as the standard bearers for the caring society and that was a society from which women would benefit most. And in Harold Wilson we had a Prime Minister who believed in women and positively enjoyed promoting them. So, although there were plenty of reactionary attitudes lurking in Cabinet, it was easy to win feminist arguments. It was symbolic, for instance, that David Steel was able to get his abortion law reform through Parliament and put the 1967 Abortion Act on the statute book because the government gave it time. Incidentally, seven members of the cabinet voted for the Bill on its Third Reading, including Roy Jenkins as Home Secretary, and of course myself; and one voted against. Eleven cautiously abstained.

Another symbolic achievement was when Harold Wilson persuaded me to leave my beloved Ministry of Overseas Development and become Minister of Transport ... In the event, I came to find it the most satisfying of all the ministerial jobs I had to do ... . The motor car had been a blessing to millions, but it was also snarling up our cities, damaging the environment and undermining public transport, increasing the isolation of those without a car, including the housewife left at home while her husband drove to work ... I was not going to have all the department's money swallowed up by motorways. Public transport was still the mainstay of most people's lives. I wanted to make it cheap, convenient and, not least, comfortable ...

Inevitably I aroused the resentment of the macho-motorist, who objected to my invasion of his male preserve. A woman Minister of Transport was bad enough, but one who could not drive was intolerable. Resentment turned to fury when I introduced the breathalyser. I was soon made to realise that the sex war was not dead. Publicans threatened to refuse to serve me if I visited their premises. Darts match devotees sent me abusive letters ... .

[In 1968] as Minister [for Employment] I had been outraged to discover the pay grading in industries like engineering with its descending order of categories: skilled, unskilled, labourers and women. I wanted to do something about it and women Members of Parliament gave me my opportunity. The prices and incomes policy was up for renewal in the House and they threatened to vote against the government unless the policy was amended to allow progress towards equal pay. I persuaded my male colleagues that the government would be defeated unless they allowed me to announce its phasing in. And so I was able to put the Equal Pay Act of 1970 on the statute book ...

It was the interplay between political and trade union women inside and outside government which had achieved the breakthrough.

(London: Virago, 1988, pp. 47, 52–5).

9. xiii   The militant mood of women trade unionists on the issue of equal pay was shown in the 1968 strike by sewing machinists at the Ford Dagenham plant, and at the TUC.

Report of 100th Annual Trades Union Congress (1968)

Equal Pay

Mr W. L. Kendall (Civil Service Clerical Association) moved the following composite motion:-

Congress ... fully supports the request of the United Nations that during this year the ... United Kingdom should ratify I.L.O. Conventions Nos 100 and 111 which deal respectively with equal pay for men and women and equal opportunities in employment .... .

Miss J. O'Connell (*Draughtsmen's and Allied Technicians' Association*) moved the following amendment:-

Add: Further, the General Council shall call upon all affiliated unions to support those unions who are taking industrial action in support of this principle.

She said: Our amendment deals with what is undoubtedly the oldest wage claim of the trade union Movement – equal pay for equal work. This claim affects about eight to nine million women and has been outstanding for 80 years since the T.U.C. first carried a resolution on equal pay in 1888. Similar resolutions have been carried piously and *ad nauseam* ever since. There is nothing more revolting than the annual spectacle at this Congress of women delegates going to the rostrum to beg support from the male members. It has ceased to be funny. The action of the women at Ford's bears this out. They took action as distinct from moralising about equal pay .... .

It is argued that the nation cannot afford this. I say that the women workers cannot afford it. We cannot afford to have 40 per cent of our rightful wages stolen from us .... James Connolly once said: 'All workers are slaves, but female workers are the slaves of slaves.' That is as true today as when he said it ...

The painful reality is that only 10 per cent of women working in Britain get the same pay as the men they work with. In our opinion, this position will not change until the women of Ford's are joined by thousands of other women workers up and down the country who, by taking industrial action, assert their right to the rate for the job and are supported by the male workers .... .

(London: TUC, 1968, pp. 453–5).

9. xiv   In a *New Society* article (1975) the writer Angela Carter (1940–92) reflects on the significance of sixties fashions in make-up.

Angela Carter, 'The Wound in the Face', reprinted in *Nothing Sacred; Selected Writings* (1982).

The sixties face had a bee-stung underlip, enormous eyes and a lot of disordered hair .... Its very lack of artifice suggested sexual licence in a period that had learned to equate cosmetics, not with profligacy as in the nineteenth century, but with conformity to the standard social and sexual female norm. Nice girls wore lipstick, in the fifties.

When the sixties face used cosmetics at all, it explored imports such as kohl and henna from Indian shops. These had the twin advantages of being extremely exotic and very, very cheap .....

The sixties look gloried in its open pores and, if your eye wasn't into the particular look, you probably thought it didn't wash itself much. But it was just that, after all those years of pancake make-up, people had forgotten what the real colour of female skin was. This face cost very little in upkeep ....
Nevertheless, since this face had adopted naturalism as an ingenious form of artifice, it *was* a mask, like the grease masks of cosmetics, though frequently refreshingly eccentric.

At the end of that decade, in a brief period of delirium, there was a startling vogue of black lipstick and red eyeshadow ... Dada in the boudoir! What a witty parody of the whole theory of cosmetics!

The basic theory of cosmetics is that they make a woman beautiful. Or, as the advertisers say, more beautiful. But ... black lipstick and red eyeshadow never 'beautified' anybody. They were the cosmetic equivalent of Duchamp's moustache on the Mona Lisa. They were cosmetics used as satire on cosmetics .... The best part of the joke was that the look itself was utterly monstrous ... I enjoyed it very, very much.

However, it takes a helluva lot of guts to maintain oneself in a perpetual state of visual offensiveness. Most women could not resist keeping open a treacherous little corner on sex-appeal .... We went too far, that time. Scrub it all off and start again.

And once we started again, red lipstick came back ... White-based lipsticks, colourless glosses, or no lipstick at all, were used in the 1960s. Now the mouth is back as a bloody gash, a visible wound .... Mary Quant has a shade called (of course) 'Bloody Mary', to ram the point home ...

(London: Virago, 1982, pp. 92–5).

Note

1. Wilson, E., 'Memoirs of an anti-heroine', in Bob Cant & Susan Hemmings (eds), *Radical Records: Thirty Years of Lesbian and Gay History*, 1957–1987 (London: Routledge, 1988), p. 46.

Chapter 10

Women's Lib to Post-Feminism? 1970–2000

10.i A pamphlet written by women who took part in the protest against the Miss World competition at the Albert Hall in London in November 1970.

'Why Miss World?' in M. Wandor (ed.), *The Body Politic. Writings from the Women's Liberation Movement in Britain, 1969–72* (1972).

'I felt that the event symbolised my daily exploitation. I saw the contestants being judged by men, and I know what it feels like to be judged and scrutinised every day when I am just walking down the street. I saw women being forced to compete with each other and judged by men. I felt for them. I had no intention of hurting them or attacking them in any way. We did not throw anything onto the stage when the contestants were there. We threw missiles on the stage when Bob Hope [the compère] was speaking ... We regard these contestants as unfortunate victims of the male capitalist system. This system, that makes money by persuading women to buy goods such as false eyelashes. We are sick of all this line about beauty. We are not beautiful and we are not ugly. It is a big capitalist con.' ...

The Miss World competition is not an erotic exhibition; it is a public celebration of the traditional female road to success .... The conventionality of the girls' lives and the ordinariness of their aspirations were the keynotes of all the pre and post-competition publicity, eg the example of Miss Grenada (Miss World): 'Now I'm looking for the ideal man to marry.' Their condition is the condition of all women, born to be defined by their physical attributes, born to give birth, or if born pretty, born lucky, a condition which makes it possible and acceptable within the bourgeois ethic for girls to parade, silent and smiling, to be judged on the merits of their figures and faces ...

Demonstrating against Miss World, Women's Liberation struck a blow against this narrow destiny ... .

We threw smoke bombs, flour, stink bombs, leaflets, blew whistles, waved rattles. Bob Hope freaked out, ran off the stage. We got thrown out by Mecca bouncers: Sally was arrested for assault (stubbing her cigarette out on a policeman). Jenny was done for an offensive weapon (a children's smoke bomb). Some went on the Café de Paris, where the Miss Worlds were having dinner: two more arrests – Jo and Kate for throwing flour and rotten tomatoes at the Mecca pimps. Maia was arrested for abusive language (telling a policeman to fuck off) ... .

The Miss World action and the trial which followed was the first militant confrontation with the law by women since the suffragettes ... .

(London: Stage 1, 1972, pp. 249–54).

10. ii   Mary Stott (1907–2002), editor of the *Guardian* women's page 1957–72, describes links between older feminists of the Fawcett Society and Women's Liberation, and the origins of the influential Women in Media group.

Mary Stott, *Before I Go. Reflections on my life and times* (1985).

Even before Jill Tweedie recruited me to the group that became Women in Media, in 1970, I was putting out feelers to the new liberation groups. What is the use of being a women's page editor if you aren't *listening*? I knew about that first conference at Ruskin College, Oxford, in 1970, the idea for which came from a group of women historians who rebelled against the domination of the Ruskin history workshops by men who seemed to assume that women had no part in history. They spread the word round the liberation workshops that had begun to proliferate all around London and in some universities, and hoped that 200 or 300 might turn up. In fact there were almost 600 ...

The group of women journalists who started meeting in a bleak classroom in Kingsway Hall ... included Bea Campbell and Mikki Doyle, women's page editor of the communist *Morning Star*. As Women in Media ... the group has been meeting ever since – which must be something like a record for a liberation group of the period ... .

One of our first jobs was to draw up a statement of aims ... It ... contains one clause which I would fight to the death to keep: 'Above all we must assist women to know, like and trust one another, so that the changes we seek should genuinely be the result of self-knowledge and mutual understanding'.

In those euphoric days it seemed possible for gradualist, 'liberal-minded' traditional feminists like me to work in close accord with the new young radicals ... It was agreed to launch a bi-monthly journal, *Women's Report* ... The journal was often funny as well as informative, especially in its feature 'Thanks, and a free consciousness-raising session to ... ,' a forerunner of the *Guardian* women's page's 'Naked Ape' feature ... .

'Trads' and 'Libs' ... came together to a considerable extent in the lobbying on the Sex Discrimination Act.

(London: Virago, 1985, pp. 24–7).

10. iii   An account of an early Women in Media success. Angela Rippon became BBC television's first regular woman newsreader in 1975.

Mileva Ross, 'Radio', in Josephine King and Mary Stott (eds), *Is This Your Life? Images of Women in the Media* (1977).

From nine to five every weekday – with a possible break for lunch – sound broadcasting is primarily aimed at women ...

Women in Media began pressing the BBC to use women newscasters on radio and television in 1971 ... It is important to recognize here that the effort was not just to stop job-discrimination and get jobs for the girls. As Women in Media explained in a letter to Sir Michael [Swann, Director of the BBC] on 28 March 1973: 'Our chief concern is that the present conditioning of people, children in particular, towards the view that women are seemingly incapable of certain work, for example newsreading, should be put right.' ... .

Jim Black, presentation editor of radio Four – he is in charge of all the station announcers – declared that in his experience women were just not suitable to read the news. 'If a woman could read the news as well as a man – there would be nothing to stop her doing it. But I have never found one who could,' he said. 'A news announcer needs to have authority, consistency and reliability. Women may have one or two of these qualities, but not all three.' Fortunately his particular prejudice did not prevail. In July 1974 Sheila Tracy proved it could be done ... becoming the first woman in the fifty-year history of the BBC to read the major news bulletins on national radio.

(London: Virago, 1977, pp. 9, 22–3).

10. iv   The Finer Report was the work of a departmental committee appointed by the Labour secretary of state for health and social services

Richard Crossman in 1969, at a time when births outside marriage were rising and divorce about to be made easier. It recommended a new means-tested benefit, plugging a hole in the post-war welfare system, and backing from welfare agencies to see that adequate maintenance was paid to lone mothers by the father of their children.

Finer Report on One-Parent Families (1974).

Our examination of the financial circumstances of one-parent families showed that they were, in general, much worse off than two-parent families. Two groups among them are slightly better off than the others, though still worse off than two-parent families generally: widows, who already have a State insurance benefit, and lone fathers, who can command higher earnings than lone mothers. For the rest, over half are on supplementary benefit; for most of these it is their main source of income, and some live at this level for many years. Of those not on supplementary benefit, about 15 per cent appear to be living actually below the supplementary benefit level, managing on maintenance payments and part-time earnings. Those who work full time are better off financially than the others but, because of women's low earnings and the restrictions that having to run a home and a job are likely to put on their earning capacity, they are still much less well off than two-parent families and far below the level of those where both parents are earning ....

This depressing picture of widespread family hardship, and the difficulties in modern society of bringing up children alone and in such conditions, led us to look for some means of affording these families some financial relief. ... What is wanted, we believe, is a benefit which is adapted to fit in with the idea of varying the amount of work done according to family circumstances; full-time, part-time, or none. This implies either a benefit paid at a given rate without regard to income, or one which responds to changes in earnings more gradually than does supplementary benefit. We have decided in favour of the latter ... A tapered benefit would enable more to be given to poorer families within a particular global sum. ...

We recommend that one-parent families should be entitled to a new social security benefit which we call guaranteed maintenance allowance (GMA). This benefit would be available to all one-parent families on a non-contributory basis ....

There would be title to GMA regardless of whether or not maintenance was being paid by the absent parent ... Any maintenance payment received directly by the lone mother would have to be declared and deducted from the GMA payable.

(London: HMSO, 1974, vol. 1, pp. 500–1).

10. v   Barbara Castle, now secretary of state for health and social security in the last Wilson government, observes the reaction in Scotland to the United Nations project of an International Women's Year.

Barbara Castle, *The Castle Diaries, 1974–6* (1980).

Saturday, 10 May [1975]

Off to Edinburgh for a weekend meeting of the Women's National Commission. I only agreed to go because it is International Women's Year and we must show the flag in Scotland. It was almost as dreadful as I had feared. The Lord Provost put on a reception for us and failed to turn up, leaving us to our coffee and Scotch pancakes on our own. I soon gathered that the Scots are the biggest male chauvinists of the lot and that the women there are resentful at not being treated seriously. It amuses me to see myself cast in the feminist role after a lifetime in which I have hated the whole idea, but, faced with the failure of the Secretary of State for Scotland to turn up at our functions as well as the Lord Provost, I find myself getting pretty militant.

(London: Weidenfeld & Nicolson, 1980, p. 388).

10. vi   The passage of this Sex Discrimination Bill in 1975 had far-reaching consequences: despite certain exemptions, its scope was remarkably wide.

A BILL TO

Render unlawful certain kinds of sex discrimination and discrimination on the ground of marriage, and establish a Commission with the function of working towards the elimination of such discrimination and promoting equality of opportunity between men and women generally ...

A person discriminates against a woman in any circumstances relevant for the purposes of this Act if –

(a)   on the ground of her sex he treats her less favourably than in those circumstances ... he treats or would treat a man, or

(b)   he applies to her an unfavourable requirement or condition which, although in those circumstances ... he applies or would apply it equally to a man, is such that the proportion of women who can comply with it is considerably smaller than the proportion of men who can comply with it ...

Discrimination by employers

It is unlawful for a person, in relation to employment by him which is available at an establishment in Great Britain, to discriminate against a woman –

(a) in the arrangements he makes for the purpose of determining who should be offered that employment, or
(b) in the terms on which he offers her that employment, or
(c) by refusing or deliberately omitting to offer her employment ...

Education

It is unlawful, in relation to an educational establishment ... [with certain exceptions for 'single-sex establishments'], for a person ... to discriminate against a female –

(a) in the terms on which it offers to admit her to the establishment as a pupil, or
(b) by refusing or deliberately omitting to accept an application for her admission to the establishment as a pupil, or
(c) where she is a pupil of the establishment ... in the way it affords her access to any benefits, facilities or services ... .

Goods, facilities, services and premises

[Discrimination against a woman is unlawful in relation to] –

(a) access to or use of any place which members of the public or a section of the public are permitted to enter;
(b) accommodation in a hotel, boarding house or other similar establishment;
(c) facilities by way of banking or insurance or for grants, loans, credit or finance;
(d) facilities for education;
(e) facilities for entertainment, recreation or refreshment;
(f) facilities for transport or travel;

(g) the services of any profession or trade or any local or other public
authority ...

OTHER UNLAWFUL ACTS

It is unlawful to publish or cause to be published an advertisement which
indicates ... an intention by a person to do an act which is or might be
unlawful by virtue [of this Bill].

**10. vii Working-class women take militant action in protest at housing
conditions.**

**'South Wales Association of Tenants, "Coming Alive Hurts", in Ann
Curno *et al*. (eds), *Women in Collective Action* (1982).**

In 1977 five women from near Pontypridd [in the Rhondda] chained themselves to the local town hall railings for 24 hours, to protest about the conditions on their local council estate. ...

The Glantaff Farm Estate near Pontypridd ... is quite a modern estate of
terraced houses and some maisonettes, equipped with hot air central heating systems; half the houses run on gas, half run by electricity. It was the
'electric' houses which caused problems. One of the tenants takes up the
story:

> It was beautiful when we moved in. We were absolutely thrilled.
> But no-one could keep warm in the winter. The quarterly electric-
> ity bills were up to two hundred and fifty pounds, so most people
> weren't using the heating. This meant terrible condensation. I kept
> thinking that at least we were housed and that we should be grate-
> ful. But then we got friendly with a few people and found they had
> worse problems than us, with arrears and that. So we formed a little
> Action Group.
>
> We started in the usual way, with petitions and writing letters and
> we were more or less ignored and called educationally sub-normal. So
> when the letters and petitions didn't work, we sat down one day and
> one of us said 'what we ought to do is chain ourselves to the bloody
> railings' and the next thing is, we did it.
>
> It was incredible. The press were coming, the television were com-
> ing. Suddenly, even our councillors greeted us. Then we sort of real-
> ised, that this was the key, this militant action. We chained ourselves
> to the railings for 24 hours, and the police brought us blankets in

the night and the railwaymen brought us tea. And we were stopping cars and waving and shouting that we were on T.V. tonight. It was incredible.

So after 24 hours then, we came home. We got together again and decided we would have a march. And we occupied the Council offices and took over one of the council meetings and all the councillors made a dash for the door.

They were all nervous you know, and I looked at them and thought ' if you only knew how bloody nervous I am!' ...

This is one of the songs we sang once when we disrupted the Council.

> Come to Glantaff, Come to Glantaff,
> It's a place of misery –
> If you had to live as we do,
> You'd be standing here with me.
> Build a bonfire! Build a Bonfire!
> Put the Council on the top,
> Put the officials in the middle
> and burn the bloody lot!
> (Tune Clementine) ...

Myfynwy remembers .... .

> I used to be so shy and quiet. I used to go and get [my husband] when someone came to the door, especially if it was someone in authority – I hid behind him. I had no confidence because of being a woman. The campaign seemed to tell me, 'we (as women) have an advantage – we can get away with murder'.

Sian said 'Once we'd won our campaign, we knew we couldn't just go back to our housework. We knew there was more to be done, you know, other campaigns we could help on'.

As it happened some tenants on an estate [in Penarth] about 15 miles away were just beginning to tackle a huge problem of faulty heating systems and damp in their homes ...

So some of the Penarth tenants joined up with Glantaff and it was decided to form SWAT – the South Wales Association of Tenants. We all liked the name – it signified our 'unreasonableness'.

(London: Association of Community Workers, 1982, pp. 13–20).

10. viii   In 1975 a 'pro-choice' National Abortion Committee was formed
to lobby against attempts to amend the 1967 Abortion Act. The TUC
organised a 50,000 strong demonstration in 1979 against the Corrie Bill,
which would have restricted access to abortion.

Report of the 110th Annual Trades Union Congress, 1978.

Dr. J. Gray (*Association of Scientific, Technical & Managerial Staffs: Medical Practitioners' Section*) … said: The TUC is committed to defending and
extending the 1967 abortion legislation. However … we must be clear that
attempts are still being made to move the clock back …. We must work …
hard, not only to defend what we have but to ensure that the inadequacies of
the present working of the Act are ironed out and remedied.

When I say 'we', I mean the great majority of trade unionists who understand that abortion should be a woman's right to choose …

I must stress that in no way are we suggesting that abortion should be
foisted on unwilling women, nor that doctors or nurses, whose consciences
demand otherwise, should be forced to perform abortions. Quite the reverse.
It is the opposition, the members of [the] S[ociety for] P[rotection of
the] U[nborn] C[hild] and their supporters, who want to force us to fit
their conscience.

What can we do to prevent a return to the backstreet abortions which
we all know killed and permanently damaged hundreds of women, because
it is clear that this would be the consequence of repressive legislation … ?
We are calling … on the TUC to organise a demonstration if there should be
any new attempt to restrict the present law … We trade unionists stand for
more control over our working lives; control of our fertility is one essential
part of that … .

At the moment the N[ational] H[ealth] S[ervice] only provides for less
than half the abortions necessary. The rest are either performed privately or
by charities. It is outrageous that we have a law in this country which sets
certain legal limits for abortion and yet our NHS cannot guarantee us equal
treatment under the law. It is crazy, if not criminal, that in Birmingham only
ten per cent of abortions are performed by the NHS, whereas in Newcastle
it is 96 per cent. …

Those who can pay have always been able to get round the limitations of
the NHS. Let us ensure that abortion is no longer a matter of money or luck.
Let us ensure that every woman can make that choice.

(London: TUC, 1978, pp. 510–11).

10. ix   A socialist feminist perspective on Margaret Thatcher (1925–2013) just before she became the UK's first woman prime minister in May 1979.

'Is Margaret Thatcher for women?' *Spare Rib*, 82, May 1979.

In the run-up to the election, several newspapers have asked *Spare Rib* whether we would regard a Thatcher victory as a victory for women's liberation, proof of what-the-modern-woman-can-achieve. For us as feminists the issue is not the success or failure of one individual woman, but whether the actual *policies* of Thatcher, and of the party which she leads, can promote the interests of women generally ...

Thatcher is not just a 'token woman'. She now leads her party as a representative of the strongest faction inside it – the extreme right ... Thatcher is committed to two main policies: the defeat of the trade union movement, and the running down of the welfare state, state industries, and public spending, so that the capital presently invested in them may be 'freed' for the needs of private enterprise. From the higher profits which ensure, we will all, supposedly, benefit.

The flaw in this argument is that, in a free-market economy, the only people *guaranteed* to benefit are the owners and shareholders of private industry ...

Ironically, it is on their avowed concern for the suffering housewife that the Conservatives have, traditionally captured the largest portion of the 'women's vote'. This time round, with Thatcher in the forefront, they can expect to do even better .... 'The women of Britain will bring down "dithering Jim Callaghan" and put a woman of decision into No. 10 who can cope with every problem thrown at her – like the other housewives in this country' – so prophesied Sally Oppenheim, Shadow Prices Minister, in her first speech of the election campaign.

The Tories' attempt to appeal to women across classes, via the common factor of being housewives, is calculated and very skilful. Providing praise for the housewife, however, comes cheap; providing nurseries, housing, social security benefits and adequate health care does not. Labour has already massively reduced public spending, but the Tories plan heavier cuts. The temporary inconvenience caused by strikes is negligible compared to the burden *this* will place on women, as caring for the young, the sick, the disabled and the elderly – and with minimum state aid – becomes even more our responsibility.

15. Margaret Thatcher in 1975, the year in which she unexpectedly defeated former prime minister Edward Heath in a challenge for the Conservative leadership. Industrial unrest in the 'Winter of Discontent', 1978–9, enabled her to lead the party to victory four years later.

10. x   The early 1980s brought conflict between the police and residents in poor, ethnically mixed inner-city districts of Bristol, Liverpool, Birmingham and London (Brixton). Here a black woman from Toxteth writes of the experience.

'Liverpool 8', *Spare Rib*, 110, September 1981, reprinted in Curno, *Women in Collective Action*.

The 'riots' that are taking place in Liverpool 8 (Toxteth) are the direct result of the anger and frustration and fear felt by the community at the constant harassment experienced by them at the hands of the police … .

I have spoken to several women and girls about their experiences both on the actual nights of the 'riots' and afterwards. Several women have been beaten up, some while they were actually in custody, some others simply because they were on the street, not actually participating, but often out looking for their children … .

Most of the girls were frightened by the level of violence during the incidents. I was actually chased by the police on two occasions, but the girls agree as I do that people who fought were taking the only option open to them … Last night during the latest incident the mothers were out supporting their youths. A television set was thrown over the balcony onto the police officers who were beating someone up.

Since the 'riots' all started, one of the worst effects on the community has been the increase (although it has always been high) in police activity ... Their new tactic is to drive their transit vans and landrovers at high speed straight at you, whether or not you are taking action against them. They don't stick to the roads – they drive over pavements, and over grass landscaping – anywhere. I was actually *behind* the police lines, and a van came straight at me ... .

Whenever anyone is out now, your family is terrified, thinking you will never get home. It's always been bad here, but we've never known it as bad as this.

(London: Association of Community Workers, 1982, pp. 96–7).

10. xi   **Women were prominent in the Campaign for Nuclear Disarmament when it revived in the 1980s. The Greenham Common air base in Berkshire became the site of a women's peace camp in 1981. Opinion polls showed that two-thirds of women opposed the stationing of US Cruise missiles in Britain.**

Maggie Lowry, 'A voice from the Peace Camps ... ', in Dorothy Thompson (ed.), *Over Our Dead Bodies. Women Against the Bomb* (1983).

On Sunday, 21 March 1982, coaches sped to Greenham Common from far and wide in eager anticipation of a festival 'to celebrate the unity of all life', organised by the Women's Peace Camp ... After a great festival, enjoyed by all the family, more than 150 women chained themselves in groups to each of the eight main gates of the air base, and began the first ever twenty-four-hour women's blockade of a military base in the history of CND.

Huddling under the stars in the dark, on the edge of a devastatingly bleak military base, guarded constantly by US Army personnel, might have been a daunting experience, but the women were sustained by their convictions, and unified by a fervent desire to forward the cause of peace by resisting the installation of Cruise missiles on our soil. Throughout the night, the discomfort of the cold ground, the weight of the heavy chains shackling us to the fence were forgotten as support groups rallied round with hot food and drink. Theatre and music groups provided entertainment, and in between we sang peace songs, watched the smouldering camp fire and talked ... Sixteen hours into the protest, the Ministry of Defence, the Military Police and the United States Airforce conceded moral defeat, having been prevented from gaining access to the site. So far we had achieved total victory and had halted all work inside the fence. In a mood of euphoria we tucked into well-cooked porridge – difficult to eat with both arms shackled!

Suddenly police numbers doubled, and three vanloads of protesters were swept off to the local police station to face a charge of 'obstruction'. In the meantime, a hole had been cut in a section of the fence to give access to the base. Thirty-nine brave women raced to fill the gap, and were promptly arrested while traffic carrying base personnel and supplies queued up to drive in. Frightened but determined, a group of us unchained ourselves from the fence and hurried through the police barricades to refill the gap and prevent them from getting in .... We did not prevent all traffic from gaining access to the site, but we made its passage inconvenient and difficult by our presence. With forty of us at the gap and another hundred and more chained to the gates we had proved that women could cause a great deal of embarrassment to the authorities and could unite to make an effective protest against the increasing danger of nuclear war. Our parting words were – 'We'll be back soon!'

(London: Virago, 1983, pp. 73–4).

10. xii   The TUC, fighting a rearguard action in the 1980s against the anti-union policies of the Thatcher governments, came under pressure from women members to tackle the sexist traditions of the trade union movement itself.

Report of the 115th Annual Trades Union Congress, 1983.

Ms K. Holman (*National Union of Journalists*) ... I have in my hand the TUC's new leaflet on sexual harassment. I present it to Congress for the benefit of delegates who were on holiday in Outer Mongolia and did not read the hysterical response of the Press to its appearance. I think it was described as the sex commandments of the TUC. That is how the Daily Mirror referred to it. Despite the ability of some NUJ members to trivialise the issue, the union welcomes the booklet and congratulates the Women's Advisory Committee on its work. However we believe there is much more to be done. What is sexual harassment? The term is relatively new but the situation is as old as the relationship between employer and employee. It arises when a worker receives repeated and unwelcome comments, looks or jokes about her sex, or physical approaches that can lead to assault .... .

Sexual harassment can be irritating, humiliating or downright frightening. It can destroy the victim's morale, job satisfaction, relationships, security or prospects. A recent survey that was undertaken by the Inland Revenue Staff Federation revealed that three out of four women suffered sexual harassment at work. It can happen to men as but women are much more often the victims. It reflects the position of inequality that women still hold in society and in the work force. Only 8.5 per cent of British managers are female and most women are still restricted to low paid, unskilled and low status jobs. Sexual harassment is often practised by someone in a position of power or superiority, whether an employer or another worker ... It is high time that the trade union Movement took it seriously.

Ms J. Webber *(National Union of Public Employees)* .... The TUC has many good policies on women and women's rights, child care, equal opportunities and a minimum legal wage, and it is now time to pull these policies together into one strong policy and to act on it in our working lives .... Apart from fighting the Government's cuts and fighting for jobs, that means fighting for ourselves and defending ourselves. It means that delegates and their members must change their attitudes and take their share in child care and work in the home. It means that delegates must consider what they are doing when they maintain and increase the differentials between men and women by keeping women in the lowest grades ... .

Sexual harassment is not a matter for jokes and sniggers. How many isolated women members are driven back into the home after having been mauled or abused by their brothers in and outside the Movement? Very often they are too frightened to say anything so they leave quietly and go home. It is no joke. Delegates, have the courage to tackle your own attitudes and those of your brothers.

Ms J. Tinsley *(Transport Salaried Staffs Associations)* ... Attitudes have to change within our Movement ... You are going to ask, 'What's in it for me?' Earlier this year ... women flocked to the polls to put Margaret Thatcher back in power, and they did this because they were not politically aware ... It is your job to go home to your mothers, sisters, wives and daughters and involve them in our Movement. You do not need to look very far to tell you what committed women can do. You saw the women at Lee Jeans, and Ken has already told you about the magnificent women at Greenham Common.

It is not enough for the TUC to issue excellent leaflets, like the one on Sexual Harassment, whilst their own male staff post sexist cartoons on the noticeboard at Congress House. So I would ask you, please, to wholeheartedly support the Women's Action Day, and maybe we just might find a day when the women can come to this Congress and not feel like gatecrashers at a stag party ...

(TUC Annual Report, 1983, pp. 544–6).

10. xiii   Women in coalmining communities mobilised in support of the strike of 1984–5 against pit closures, in the process raising expectations of better representation for women in the parliamentary Labour party. In Scotland, but not in England or Wales, the National Union of Mineworkers allowed women to become associate members.

Jean Stead, *Never the Same Again: Women and the Miners' Strike* **(1987).**

At Polmaise [at Fallin, Stirlingshire], in August 1984, as in the coalfields throughout Britain, the women's support groups had reached a critical phase. The support ... was strengthened by a mass meeting and march in London of 15,000 women on 11 August which brought new strength to the strike and by the enormous efforts of the women's leaders to get the campaign to switch into a new gear, ready for the long haul through the winter months, with only a barren Christmas to look forward to. They were, of course, successful. When the strike ended in March, it was against the wishes of the women, who protested that they had not come so far, nor endured such hardship, only to be defeated at that point.

The Polmaise women had started collecting their own funds for the food and had taken over work at the miners' welfare food kitchen. The hire purchase, the pension subscriptions, the new carpets, the rent and, in some cases, the mortgage – all these preoccupations had been put aside until after the strike. They did not bother about clothes any more – how could they?

They were out with the collecting boxes in the streets of Glasgow, and soon, like miners' wives and relatives all over the country, they were standing up on platforms to make speeches to raise funds and flying abroad on fund-raising campaigns .... .

The fight for jobs was at the core of the women's support, without which the strike could never have kept going for more than a few months. By 1984, women knew what the face of unemployment looked like. The picture was depression and despair, which destroyed the life of a family. It was drink, degradation, homelessness and drugs for the young, the slow destruction of self-sufficient communities, illness, suicide and the drawn-out extinction of hope … .

A year after the strike ended in March 1985, the fight for women's representation in the Labour Party had scarcely even begun. There were no more than a sprinkling of women Parliamentary candidates through the country and women had no effective voice on the Labour Party National Executive. The Labour Party was going into the next election with the same old male middle-class image … .

(London: Women's Press, 1987, pp. 4–7, 25).

10. xiv   **The Hansard Society, which aims to strengthen parliamentary democracy, sponsored this influential critique of under-representation of women in Britain's elites.**

Report of the Hansard Society Commission on Women at the Top (1990).

Summary of Conclusions and Recommendations

Public Philosophy and Legal Framework

1. As a nation, we are committed by our public philosophy and by law to eliminate discrimination against women in the political and public life of the country, and to ensure genuine equality of opportunity for women in all aspects of life.

Need for Voluntary Measures

2. Good laws are essential, but not by themselves sufficient to change the practices and attitudes which maintain the profoundly unequal status of women in this country today. …

Women's Contribution and Wasted Talent

3. By 1995, over half the labour force will be women. But today only a tiny minority have reached positions of influence and power. Most women remain clustered in positions that do not make full use of their abilities. Generally, they are in badly paid, low status jobs, and their opportunities for training and promotion are severely restricted.

The 1990s: An Opportunity for Change

4. The 1990s offer an opportunity for change. Eighty per cent of new workers in the next five years will be women, most of whom will have major family

responsibilities. This, together with the creation of more high-level jobs, will compel employers to compete more strongly for the best candidates for their companies, irrespective of gender. These facts of life may mean that the best man for the job in the 1990s is a woman ... .

The Glass Ceiling

5. For many women, there is a glass ceiling blocking their aspirations, allowing them to see where they might go but stopping them from arriving there. In any given occupation, and in any given public office, the higher the rank, prestige or influence, the smaller the proportion of women.

The Barriers to Equality for Women

6. The barriers to equality are general and pervasive:

outmoded attitudes about the role of women;
direct and indirect discrimination;
the absence of proper childcare provision;
inflexible structures for work and careers.

7. Discrimination against women is still widespread. Too often organisations who say they do not discriminate have not properly considered how their normal policies and practices affect women. Discrimination assumes many forms: direct and overt; indirect and disguised:

subjective and informal selection procedures;
stereotyped assumptions about the ability, character, suitability and 'natural' role of women;
the use of 'insider', word-of-mouth and old-boy networks;
unnecessary age bars;
excessive mobility requirements.

Women are discouraged by attitudes at work expressed in everything from outright sexual harassment to a refusal to take them seriously ...

Women in Parliament

11. Women are seriously under-represented in Parliament. In the General Election of 1987, 609 men were returned to the House of Commons. In the years since women's suffrage in 1918, only 139 individual women have taken up seats in the House. We are almost at the bottom of the league table of modern democracies, whether in terms of the proportion of women in the legislature or in the Cabinet ... .

12. The present position is wholly unacceptable in a modern democracy.

(London: Hansard Society, pp. 1–4).

10. xv   A historian's perspective on Diana, Princess of Wales (1961–97) after her divorce in 1996 and death the following year in a car crash in Paris with her lover Dodi Fayed.

June Purvis, 'Diana, Princess of Wales', editorial in *Women's History Review,* **6:3, 1997.**

For me, the short life of Diana revealed ….that despite her wealth, her status and privileges, some of her experiences were the common lot of women in any society and in any social class.

Diana was a modern, vulnerable, sensitive, and insecure woman who married into a traditional, autocratic family. Young and inexperienced, she ... was expected to fulfil her 'royal duty' by bearing sons and tolerating a loveless marriage and her husband's infidelities. Instead of understanding her post-natal depression, her eating disorders and her general unhappiness, she was seen as mentally unstable and difficult ... The Press hounded her, eager for any story or picture that would expose cracks in her marriage, capture her love life, reveal her cellulite or portray her as a glamorous pin-up ...

The scenario of Diana's life is familiar to historians of women. That she found the strength to fight back, to analyse her illnesses and to build up her self esteem in ways that she thought appropriate (and which some of us would shun) reveals that streak of steely independence that women have found through the ages when they attempt to define their lives on their own terms. For us today, her life laid painfully bare many of those contradictions and complexities that women face in the late twentieth century.

(London: Taylor and Francis, 1997, p. 315).

10. xvi   The Blair government was criticised for refusing to restore welfare cuts made by Conservatives before the 1997 General Election. Harriet Harman here defends New Labour policy for lone parents as a package, including subsidised child care, to reduce welfare dependency and raise living standards.

Hansard, **HC Deb, 8 June 1998, cc 695–6.**

Oral answers to questions

Income support (Lone Parents)

Mr Tony McNulty (Harrow, East) What action have the Government taken to help lone parents of children to get into work?

The Secretary of State for Social Security and Minister for Women (Ms Harriet Harman). We have established a new deal for lone parents to help them get off income support and into work so that they and their children can have a better standard of living than they could have on benefits .... More parents are going into work and lone parents and their children are better off by, on average, £39 a week and the taxpayer is better off by, on average, £42 a week ....

Mr David Rendel (Newbury) I welcome any efforts the Government may make to encourage opportunities for lone parents to get back into work where they wish to do so. However, is there not a problem for lone parents who have children under five and who may wish to choose not to go into work? Given the benefit cuts for lone parents – partly offset, admittedly, by child benefit increases – what further effort does the Secretary of State intend to make to allow such lone parents a real choice of whether to go back into work?

Ms Harman The problem in the past was not that lone parents did not have the choice to stay at home – more than 1 million of them stayed at home on income support, bringing up 2 million children – but that too few lone parents were able to go out to work. The Government's policies of giving advice and support to help them into work, ensuring help with the costs of child care and ensuring that quality child care is available, provide the choice that was previously not available. The new deal for lone parents is directed at those with children over five. If the hon. Member examines the figures, he will find that more than half the number of married mothers with children under five go out to work. No one is forcing them to do so. They have the choice, and they are taking the opportunities. We are making sure that lone parents can do the same, be better off and save the taxpayer money.

10. xvii   In this review a panel chaired by Trevor Phillips placed more emphasis on ethnic than on gender inequalities in early twenty-first century Britain. Violence against women remained, however, a major concern.

Fairness and Freedom: the Final Report of the Equalities Review (2007).

While men and women experience similar levels of violent crime the nature of the violence they experience can be very different. The majority of violent

crime experienced by men is likely to be as a consequence of stranger violence linked to excessive drinking in pubs and clubs .... For women, the
majority of the violence experienced is in the home and the offender is
known to them ...

Domestic violence accounts for 16 per cent of all violent crime .... It
is often a repeated crime which claims the lives of two women each week.
It will be experienced by one in four women in their lifetime. It is all too
often a closely held, painful secret. Recent research reveals that 31 per cent
of female victims had not told anyone about their experience of domestic
violence .... On average there will have been 35 assaults before a victim of
domestic violence calls the police. For ethnic minority victims of domestic
violence, the effects are often compounded by the effects of racism. Domestic violence may manifest differently in these communities. Forced marriage,
so called 'honour' based violence and female genital mutilation are all aspects
of domestic violence ... .

Between 75 and 95 per cent of rape crimes are never reported to the
police; for those victims who do come forward, between half and two thirds
of cases will not proceed beyond the investigation stage and where cases are
referred to prosecutors for a charging decision, a significant proportion will
not proceed. Of the cases that do reach court, between one third and a half
will result in acquittal.

(London: HMSO, 2007, pp. 80–1).

A History of Women in Britain.
Sources and Readings from the Twentieth Century

Chapter 1   Class, Region and Ethnicity

   i. Atkinson, M., *The Economic Foundations of the Women's Movement* (Fabian Tract no. 175, 1914) repr. in Alexander, S. (ed.), *Women's Fabian Tracts* (London: Routledge, 1988), pp. 270–1.

  ii. Mitchison, N., *You May Well Ask. A Memoir, 1920–1940* (London: Victor Gollancz, 1979), pp. 19, 27–8.

 iii. Firth, V., *The Psychology of the Servant Problem* (London: The C. W. Daniel Company, 1925), pp. 18–22.

  iv. Lennon, M., McAdam, M. & O'Brien, J. (eds), *Across the Water. Irish Women's Lives in Britain* (London: Virago, 1988), pp. 48–50.

   v. Troubridge, L. G., Lady, *The Book of Etiquette* (Kingswood, Surrey: The World's Work, 1931), pp. 80, 83–4, 152, 159.

  vi. Gibbon, L. G., *A Scots Quair: A Trilogy of Novels* (Jarrolds Publishing, 1932–4; Repr. London: Penguin, 1998), pp. 407–8.

 vii. Priestley, J. B., *English Journey* (London: W. Heinemann in association with V. Gollancz, 1934; repr. London: Mandarin, 1994), pp. 332–4, 401.

viii. Andrews, E., 'Wales and Her Poverty', *Labour Woman*, July 1939, repr. in Masson, U. (ed.), Andrews, E., *A Woman's Work is Never Done* (Dinas Powys: Honno, 2006), pp. 110–11.

  ix. Madge, C., *War-time Patterns of Saving and Spending* (Cambridge University Press, 1943), pp. 52–3.

   x. Zweig, F., *Women's Life and Labour* (London: Gollancz, 1952), pp. 121–5.

  xi. Gorer, G., *Exploring English Character* (London: Cresset Press, 1955), pp. 34, 37–8.

 xii. Stacey, M., *Tradition and Change. A Study of Banbury* (Oxford University Press, 1960), pp. 104–6.

xiii. Lewis, G., 'From Deepest Kilburn', in Heron, L. (ed.), *Truth, Dare or Promise. Girls Growing Up in the 50s* (London: Virago, 1985), pp. 213–16, 221–6.

xiv. Wilson, A., *Finding a Voice. Asian Women in Britain* (London: Virago, 1978), pp. 16–17, 20–1, 25–7.

xv. Oakley, A., *Subject Women* (Oxford: Martin Robertson, 1981), pp. 285–6, 289–90.

xvi. Abbott, P. & Sapsford, R., *Women and Social Class* (London: Tavistock, 1987), pp. 122–3.

xvii. Steedman, C., *Landscape for a Good Woman* (London: Virago, 1986), pp. 1–2.

xviii. Kay, J., *Other Lovers* (Newcastle upon Tyne: Bloodaxe, 1993), p. 24.

Chapter 2   Family and Work

i. Black, C., *Married Women's Work* (London: G. Bell & Sons Ltd, 1915; repr. Virago, 1983), pp. 1–7.

ii. Mackworth, M. H. T., Viscountess Rhondda, *This Was My World* (London: Macmillan, 1933), pp. 263–7.

iii. Burnett, J. (ed.), *Useful Toil: Autobiographies of Working People from the 1820s to the 1920s* (London: Allen Lane, 1974; repr. Routledge, 1994), pp. 221–4.

iv. Priestley, J. B., *English Journey* (London: W. Heinemann, 1934; repr. Mandarin, 1994), pp. 128–30.

v. Sarsby, J., *Missuses and Mouldrunners. An Oral History of Women Pottery Workers at Work and at Home* (Milton Keynes: Open University Press, 1988), p. 70.

vi. Pilgrim Trust, *Men Without Work* (Cambridge University Press, 1938), pp. 231–2.

vii. Cole, M., *Marriage Past and Present* (London: J. M. Dent, 1938), pp. 193–200.

viii. Law Reports, [1943] 2 AC, 579 Blackwell v Blackwell.

ix. Zweig, F., *Women's Life and Labour* (London: Gollancz, 1952), pp. 18–19.

x. Dennis, N., Henriques, F. & Slaughter, C., *Coal is Our Life* (London: Eyre & Spottiswoode, 1956), pp. 180–2.

xi. Titmuss, R., 'The Position of Women', in *Essays on 'The Welfare State'* (London: Allen & Unwin, 1958), pp. 91–3, 99–103.

xii. Myrdal, A. & Klein, V., *Women's Two Roles: Home and Work* (London: Routledge & Kegan Paul, 1956), p. xv.

xiii. Stacey, M. *et al.*, *Power, Persistence and Change. A Second Study of Banbury* (London: Routledge & Kegan Paul, 1975), pp. 105–8.

xiv. Oakley, A., *Housewife* (London: Allen Lane, 1974), pp. 2–4.

xv. Seabrook, J., *What Went Wrong? Working People and the Ideals of the Labour Movement* (London: Victor Gollancz, 1978), pp. 122–5.

xvi. Campbell, B., *Wigan Pier Revisited. Poverty and Politics in the Eighties* (London: Virago, 1984), pp. 59–61.

xvii. Dench, G., Gavron, K. & Young, M., *The New East End* (London: Profile Books Ltd, 2006), p. 125.

Chapter 3   Education

i. Burnett, J. (ed.), *Destiny Obscure. Autobiographies of Childhood, Education and Family from the 1820s to the 1920s* (London: Allen Lane, 1982, repr. Routledge 1994), pp. 207–9.

ii. *Hansard*, HCDeb, 22 June 1921, cols 1395–6.

iii. *Report of the Consultative Committee on the Differentiation of the Curriculum for Boys and Girls Respectively in Secondary Schools* (London: HMSO, 1922), pp. 94–5, 132, 139–40.

iv. Mackworth, M. H. T., Viscountess Rhondda, *Leisured Women* (London: Hogarth Press, 1928), pp. 20–4, 29–30.

v. Chamberlain, M., *Fenwomen* (London: Virago, 1978), pp. 93–6.

vi. Miles, M., ... *And Gladly Teach: The Adventure of Teaching* (Reading: Educational Explorers, 1966), pp. 19–24, 35–6.

vii. Jewish Women in London Group, *Generations of Memories. Voices of Jewish Women* (London: Women's Press, 1989), pp. 85–9.

viii. Okely, J. M., 'Privileged, Schooled and Finished', in *Own or Other Culture* (London: Routledge, 1996), pp. 150–1.

ix. Hubback, J., *Wives Who Went to College* (London: Heinemann, 1957), pp. 25–6, 29, 159.

x. Mitchison, L., 'The price of educating women', *Guardian*, 8 January 1960.

xi. *15 to 18 (Crowther Report)* (London: HMSO, 1959), vol. 1, pp. 33–5.

xii. *Robbins Report on Higher Education* (London: HMSO, 1963) pp. 17, 40, 167–8.

xiii. Mitchell, J., 'Women: The Longest Revolution', *New Left Review*, 1966.

xiv. Newson, J. & E., *Four Years Old in an Urban Community* (London: George Allen & Unwin, 1968), pp. 433–4, 441.

xv. Department of Education and Science, Education Survey 21, *Curricular Differences for Boys and Girls* (London: HMSO, 1975).

xvi. Spender, D. & Sarah, E. (eds), *Learning to Lose. Sexism and Education* (London: Women's Press, 1980), pp. 91–3.

xvii. McCrum, N. G., 'The Gender Gap at Oxford', *Oxford Magazine*, 143 (1997).

xviii. *Higher Education in the Learning Society (Dearing Report)* (London: NCIHE, 1997), vol.1, pp. 21, 102, 370.

xix. Evans, S., 'In a Different Place. Working-Class Girls and Higher Education', *Sociology*, 43 (London: Sage, 2009), pp. 345–6.

Chapter 4   Sex and Sexualities

i. Stopes, M., *Married Love* (London: A. C. Fifield, 1918; repr. Oxford, World's Classics, 2004), pp. 9, 52–6, 59.

ii. *Hansard*, HC Deb, 4 August 1921, cols 1799–1806. Debate on Criminal Law Amendment Bill.

iii. *Woman's Leader*, 16 March 1923, pp. 52–3. Debate on Birth Control.

iv. Hall, R., *The Well of Loneliness* (London: J. Cape, 1928; repr. Virago 1982), pp. 199–203.

v. 'The Well of Loneliness Decision', *Time and Tide*, 9, 23 November 1928.

vi. Neville-Rolfe, Mrs C., 'Sex Delinquency', in Llewellyn Smith, H. (ed.), *New Survey of London Life and Labour*, vol IX, *Life and Leisure* (London: P. S. King & Son, 1935), pp. 287–8, 293–6.

vii. Hart, J., *Ask Me No More. An Autobiography* (London: Peter Halban, 1998), pp. 38–9.

viii. Sutton, M., (ed. Tyas, S.), *'We Didn't Know Owt'. A Study of Sexuality, Superstition and Death in Women's Lives in Lincolnshire During the 1930s, 40s and 50s* (Donington: Shaun Tyas, 2012), pp. 173–7.

ix. Stafford, J. M., *Light in the Dust. A True Story of the Triumph of the Human Spirit* (London: John Blake Publishing Ltd, 2002), pp. 81–8.

x. Gorer, G., *Exploring English Character* (London: Cresset Press, 1955), pp. 94–5, 116.

xi. Sarsby, J., *Missuses and Mouldrunners* (Milton Keynes: Open University Press, 1988), p. 108.

xii. McRobbie, A., 'Working-Class Girls and the Culture of Femininity', in Women's Studies Group, Centre for Contemporary Cultural Studies, *Women Take Issue: Aspects of Women's Subordination* (London: Hutchinson, 1978), pp. 98, 105–7.

xiii. Jeffreys, S., *Anticlimax: A Feminist Perspective on the Sexual Revolution* (London: Women's Press, 1990), pp. 250–1.

xiv. [1992] 1 AC, 599 Regina v. R., pp. 615–16. The Law Lords declare rape in marriage illegal.

xv. *Hansard*, HL Deb, 6 December 1999, cols 1049–50, 1079–84. House of Lords debate on proposed repeal of section 88 of the 1988 Local Government Act.

xvi. Warnock, M., *Making Babies. Is There a Right to Have Children?* (Oxford University Press, 2002), pp. 57–63.

Chapter 5   Feminisms and Femininity

i. Marshall, C., 'The Future of Women in Politics' (1915), in Kamester, M. & Vellacott, J. (eds), *Militarism versus Feminism. Writings on Women and War* (London: Virago, 1987), pp. 45–52.

ii. 'The Six Point Group', *Time and Tide*, 4, 19 January 1923.

iii. Rathbone, E., 'Patience and Impatience' (1923) in *Milestones: Presidential Addresses* (Liverpool: privately printed, 1929), pp. 15–16.

iv. Rathbone, E., *The Disinherited Family. A Plea for the Endowment of the Family* (London: Edward Arnold & Co, 1924), pp. 14–16, 113–14, 269–71.

v. Holtby, W., 'Feminism Divided' (1926), in Berry, P. & Bishop, A. (eds), *Testament of a Generation. The Journalism of Vera Brittain and Winifred Holtby* (London: Virago, 1985), pp. 45–7.

vi. Open Door Council, *First Annual Report*, 5 May 1926 to 4 April 1927 (London: The Women's Library, GB 0106 5/ODC).

vii. *Hansard*, HCDeb, 19 July 1927, cols 244–5. Margaret Bondfield speaks in House of Commons debate on protective legislation.

viii. Woolf, V., *A Room of One's Own* (London: Hogarth Press, 1929, repr. Harmondsworth, Penguin, 1945), pp. 27, 31–4.

ix. Woolf, V., *Three Guineas* (London: Hogarth Press, 1938; new edn 1943), pp. 183–7.

x. Campbell, O. W., *The Feminine Point of View* (London: Williams & Norgate, 1952), pp. 23–6.

xi. Brittain, V., *Lady into Woman. A History of Women from Victoria to Elizabeth II* (London: A. Dakers, 1953), pp. 81, 236–7.

xii. Laski, M., 'The Cult of Servility', in Hunkins-Hallinan, H. (ed.), *In Her Own Right. A Discussion Conducted by the Six Point Group* (London: Harrap, 1968), pp. 18–22.

xiii. Rowbotham, S., *Women's Liberation and the New Politics* (London: May Day Manifesto, 1969; repr. in her *Dreams and Dilemmas: Collected Writings*, London: Virago, 1983), pp. 5–6, 15–16, 20–2, 31.

xiv. Wandor, M. (ed.), *Women's Newspaper*, 6 March 1971, 'The Four Demands', repr: in *Body Politic: Writings from the Women's Liberation Movement, 1969–72* (London: Stage 1, 1972), p. 2.

xv. Leeds Revolutionary Feminist Group, 'Political Lesbianism: The Case Against Heterosexuality', *WIRES*, 81, 1979, repr. in *Love Your Enemy? The Debate Between Heterosexual Feminism and Political Lesbianism* (London: Onlywomen Press, 1981).

xvi. Kroll, U., 'Forum', *Spare Rib*, 80, March 1979.

xvii. Carby, H. V., 'White Woman Listen! Black Feminism and the Boundaries of Sisterhood', in Centre for Contemporary Cultural Studies, *The Empire Strikes Back. Race and Racism in 1970s Britain* (London: Hutchinson, 1982), pp. 212–18, 233.

xviii. Cameron, D. & Scanlon, J., 'Trouble and Strife Magazine, 1983–2002', in *The Trouble and Strife Reader* (London: Bloomsbury Academic, 2010), pp. 5–8.

xix. Bayton, M., *Frock Rock. Women Performing Popular Music* (Oxford University Press, 1998), pp. 206–8.

xx. Redfern, C. & Aune, K., *Reclaiming the F Word. The New Feminist Movement* (London: Zed Books, 2010), pp. 16–17.

Chapter 6   The Great War, 1914–18

i. Swanwick, H., *I Have Been Young* (London: V. Gollancz, 1935), pp. 253, 258–9.

ii. Bishop, A. & Smart, T. (eds), *Chronicle of Youth. Vera Brittain, War Diary 1913–1917* (London: V. Gollancz, 1981), p. 101.

iii. Brittain, V., *Testament of Youth* (London: V. Gollancz, 1933; repr. Virago, 1978), pp. 290–2.

iv. Pankhurst, E. S., *The Home Front* (London: Hutchinson, 1932; repr. Cresset Library, 1987), pp. 98–9.

v. Jones, H. (ed.), *Duty and Citizenship. The Correspondence and Political Papers of Violet Markham, 1896–1953* (London: Historians' Press, 1994), pp. 67–8.

vi. Llewellyn Davies, M. (ed.), *Life as We Have Known it, by Cooperative Working Women* (London: L. and V. Woolf, 1931; repr. Virago, 1977), pp. 50–2.

vii. Burnett, J. (ed.), *Useful Toil* (London: Allen Lane, 1974), pp. 125–9.

viii. Roberts, R., *The Classic Slum* (Manchester University Press, 1971; repr. Penguin, 1990), pp. 198–201.

ix. Churchill, Lady R. (ed.), *Women's War Work* (London: C. Arthur Pearson Ltd, 1916), pp. 20–4.

x. Sitwell, E., 'The Dancers', *Clowns' Houses* (Oxford: Blackwell, 1918), p. 25.

xi. Gwynne-Vaughan, H., *Service With the Army* (London: Hutchinson, 1942), p. 30.

xii. Henderson, M., *In War and Peace. Songs of a Scotswoman* (London: Erskine Macdonald, Ltd, 1918), p. 12.

xiii. Christabel Pankhurst, 'The Women's Party', *Britannia*, 16 November 1917.

xiv. Fisher, L., *Twenty-One Years and After, 1918–39* (London: privately printed, 1946), pp. 3–5.

xv. Jameson, S., *No Time Like the Present* (London: Cassell & Co., 1933), pp. 94–5.

Chapter 7   Franchise and After: The Modern Woman? 1918–39

i. Drake, B., *Women in Trade Unions* (London: Labour Research Dept, 1920; repr. Virago, 1984), pp. 104–5.

ii. 'Albert Hall Meeting', *Woman's Leader*, 13 February 1920.

iii. 'Labour Women in Conference', *Woman's Leader*, 30 April 1920.

iv. Auerbach, H., letter in the *Woman's Leader*, 16 March 1923.

v. Kenealy, A., *Feminism and Sex-Extinction* (London: T. Fisher Unwin, 1920), pp. 288–91.

vi. Rathbone, E., 'Equal Citizenship', 9 March 1920, in her *Milestones* (Liverpool: privately printed, 1929), p. 2.

vii. Price v Rhondda District Council, [1923] 2 Ch.372, pp. 388–93.

viii. Roberts, R., *The Classic Slum* (Manchester University Press, 1971; repr. Penguin 1990), pp. 232–3.

ix. Cole, M. (ed.), *Beatrice Webb's Diaries 1924–32* (London: Longmans Green, 1956), pp. 3–5.

x. Russell, D., *The Tamarisk Tree*, vol 1 (London: Virago, 1977), pp. 170–4.

xi. 'Over the Garden Wall', *Home and Politics*, 43, November 1924.

xii. Fawcett, Dame M. G., *What the Vote Has Done* (London: NUSEC, 1927 edn).

xiii. '"Making History". Mrs Baldwin's Faith in Women', *Home and Politics*, 97, May 1929.

xiv. *Hansard*, HC Deb, 11 Dec 1929, cc 599–608. Katharine Duchess of Atholl and Eleanor Rathbone on the position of women in British East African colonies.

xv. Bagot Stack, M. M., *Building the Body Beautiful* (London: Chapman & Hall, 1931), pp. 7–8.

xvi. Smyth, E., *Female Pipings in Eden* (London: P. Davies Ltd, 1933), p. 21.

xvii. Nicolson, H., *Diaries and Letters, 1930–39* (London: Collins, 1966), pp. 298, 396–7.

xviii. Gwynne-Vaughan, H., *Service With the Army* (London: Hutchinson & Co, 1942), pp. 94–5.

xix. *Hansard*, HC Deb, 24 Aug 1939, cc 47–50. Ellen Wilkinson on the foreign policy of Neville Chamberlain.

Chapter 8   War and Reconstruction, 1939–51

i. Pile, Sir F., *Ack-Ack. Britain's Defence Against Air Attack During the Second World War* (London: Harrap, 1949; repr. London: Panther, 1956), pp. 164–7.

ii. Partridge, F., *A Pacifist's War: Diaries, 1939–45* (London: Hogarth Press, 1978; repr. Phoenix Press, 1999), pp. 86–92.

iii. Hodgson, V., *Few Eggs and No Oranges. A Diary Showing How Unimportant People in London and Birmingham Lived Through the War Years* (London: D. Dobson, 1976; repr. Persephone books, 1999), pp. 208–10, 230–31.

iv. *Calling All Women!* (London: London Women's Parliament, 1941; Bodleian Library, 24741e197), pp. 1–5.

v. Jones, H. (ed.), *Duty and Citizenship. Correspondence and Papers of Violet Markham* (London: Historians' Press, 1994), pp. 170–1.

vi. Beveridge, W., *Social Insurance and Allied Services* (London: HMSO, 1942), paras 107–13, 302.

vii. Women's Group on Public Welfare (England), *Our Towns. A Close-Up* (Oxford University Press, 1943), pp. xiii, xvi.

viii. Air Chief Marshal Leigh-Mallory, 'W.A.A.F. Proposal to Form a Flying Branch', TNA Air 8/793/100/6.

ix. *Hansard*, HC Deb, 28–29 March 1944, cc. 1356–90, 1452–57. Debates on equal pay amendment to Education Act.

x. Sackville-West, V., *The Women's Land Army* (London: Michael Joseph, 1944; repr. Imperial War Museum, 1944), pp. 7–8, 14.

xi. Bowen, E., *The Heat of the Day* (London: J. Cape, 1949; repr. London: Vintage, 1998), pp. 325–9.

xii. Reilly, C. (ed.), *Chaos of the Night* (London: Virago, 1984), pp. 29–30, 13 (Poems by Alice Coats and Vera Bax).

xiii. Tate, M., *Equal Work Deserves Equal Pay!* (London: Equal Pay Campaign Committee pamphlet, 1945; Bodleian Library, 24741e.204), pp. 3, 11.

xiv. *Hansard*, HC Deb, 8 March 1945, cols 2276–85. Debate on Family Allowances Bill, Second Reading.

xv. *Hansard*, HC Deb, 30 Apr 1946, cc 85–91, 111–116. Debate on National Health Service Bill.

xvi. Young, M., 'The Distribution of Income within the Family', *British Journal of Sociology*, 3, 1952 (London: Routledge & Kegan Paul), pp. 318–19.

Chapter 9   The Fifties and Sixties

i. Fleming, T. (ed.), *Voices Out of the Air. The Royal Christmas Broadcasts, 1932–1981* (London: Heinemann, 1981), pp. 72–3.

ii. Fry, M., *The Single Woman* (London: Delisle, 1953), pp. 31–3.

iii. Wootton, B., *In a World I Never Made: Autobiographical Reflections* (London: Allen & Unwin, 1967), pp. 130–3.

iv. Recommendations on prostitution, *Report of the Committee on Homosexual Offences and Prostitution (Wolfenden)* (London: HMSO, 1957), p. 116.

v. *Hansard*, HL Deb, 5 May & 9 June 1959, cc. 101–104, 819–821. House of Lords debates on the Street Offences Bill.

vi. Central Advisory Council for Education (England), *15 to 18* (London: HMSO, 1959), paras 50–2.

vii. Weldon, F., *Auto Da Fay* (London: Flamingo, 2002), pp. 352–7.

viii. Kitzinger, S., *The Experience of Childbirth* (London: Gollancz, 1962), pp. 20, 24.

ix. Whitehouse, M., *Cleaning-Up T.V.: From Protest to Participation* (London: Blandford Press, 1967), pp. 21–5.

x. *Hansard*, HL Deb, 8 Nov 1967, cc 421–8. Baroness Summerskill criticises proposals for reform of the divorce laws.

xi. Central Advisory Council for Education (England), *Children and Their Primary Schools (Plowden Report)* (London, 1967), pp. 116–23.

xii. Castle, B., 'No Kitchen Cabinet', in Maitland, S. (ed.), *Very Heaven: Looking Back at the 1960s* (London: Virago, 1988), pp. 47, 52–5.

xiii. *Report of the 100th Annual Trades Union Congress, 1968* (London: TUC, 1968), pp. 453–5.

xiv. Carter, A., 'The Wound in the Face', *New Society*, 1975 repr. in *Nothing Sacred: Selected Writings* (London: Virago, 1982), pp. 92–5.

Chapter 10 Women's Lib to Post-Feminism? 1970 to the Present

i. Wandor, M. (ed.), *The Body Politic. Writings from the Women's Liberation Movement in Britain, 1969–72* (London: Stage 1, 1972), pp. 249–54.

ii. Stott, M., *Before I Go. Reflections on My Life and Times* (London: Virago, 1985), pp. 24–7.

iii. Ross, M., 'Radio', in King, J. & Stott, M. (eds), *Is This Your Life? Images of Women in the Media* (London: Virago, 1977), pp. 9, 22–3.

iv. *Finer Report on One-Parent Families* (London: HMSO, 1974), vol 1, pp. 500–1.

v. Castle, B., *The Castle Diaries, 1974–6* (London: Weidenfeld & Nicolson, 1980), p. 338.

vi. 1975 Bill to render unlawful certain kinds of sex discrimination.

vii. Curno, A. *et al.* (eds), *Women in Collective Action* (London: Association of Community Workers, 1982), pp. 13–20.

viii. *Report of the 110th Annual Trades Union Congress, 1978* (London: TUC, 1978), pp. 510–11.

ix. 'Is Margaret Thatcher for Women?' *Spare Rib*, 82, May 1979.

x. 'Liverpool 8', *Spare Rib*, 110, September 1981, repr. in Curno, *Women in Collective Action*, pp. 96–7.

xi. Lowry. M., 'A Voice from the Peace Camps ...', in Thompson, D. (ed.), *Over Our Dead Bodies. Women Against the Bomb* (London: Virago, 1983), pp. 73–4.

xii. *Report of the 115th Annual Trades Union Congress, 1983* (London: TUC, 1983), p. 544–6.

xiii. Stead, J., *Never the Same Again: Women and the Miners' Strike* (London: Women's Press, 1987), pp. 4–7, 25.

xiv. *Women at the Top* (London: Hansard Society), pp. 1–4.

xv. Purvis, J., 'Diana, Princess of Wales', editorial in *Women's History Review*, 6 (Wallingford: Triangle Journals, 1997), p. 315.

xvi. *Hansard*, HC Deb, 8 June 1998, cc 695–6. Question on Income Support (Lone Parents).

xvii. *Fairness and Freedom: The Final Report of the Equalities Review* (London: HMSO, 2007), pp. 80–1.

Select Bibliography

Abbreviations: *CSH*: Cultural and Social History; *EHR*: English Historical Review; *G&H*: Gender and History; *HJ*: Historical Journal; *HR*: Historical Research; *HWJ*: History Workshop Journal; *JBS*: Journal of British Studies; *JCH*: Journal of Contemporary History; *JMH*: Journal of Modern History; *P&P*: Past and Present; *TCBH*: Twentieth-Century British History; *WHR*: Women's History Review.

General

Addison, P., *No Turning Back. The Peaceful Revolutions of Post-War Britain* (Oxford: Oxford University Press, 2010).

Addison, P. & H. Jones (eds), *A Companion to Contemporary Britain, 1939–2000* (Oxford: Blackwell, 2005).

Breitenbach, E. & P. Thane (eds), *Women and Citizenship in Britain and Ireland in the Twentieth Century* (London: Continuum, 2010).

Carnevali, F. & J.-M. Strange (eds), *Twentieth-Century Britain: Economic, Cultural and Social Change* (Harlow: Pearson Longman, 2007).

Cowman, K., *Women in British Politics, c. 1689–1979*, part 3 (Basingstoke: Palgrave Macmillan, 2011).

Ewan, E., S. Innes, S. Reynolds & R. J. Pipes, *Biographical Dictionary of Scottish Women* (Edinburgh: Edinburgh University Press, 2006).

Francis, M., 'Labour and Gender' in D. Tanner, P. Thane & N. Tiratsoo (eds), *Labour's First Century* (Cambridge: Cambridge University Press, 2000).

Hall, L. A., *Sex, Gender and Social Change in Britain since 1880* (Basingstoke: Macmillan, 2000).

Halsey, A. H. & J. Webb (eds), *Twentieth-Century British Social Trends* (Basingstoke: Macmillan, 2000).

Jones, H., *Women in British Public Life, 1914–50. Gender, Power and Social Policy* (Harlow: Longman, 2000).

Lovenduski, J., P. Norris & C. Burness, 'The Party and Women', in A. Seldon & S. Ball (eds), *Conservative Century. The Conservative Party Since 1900* (Oxford: Oxford University Press, 1994).

Matthew, H. G. C. & B. H. Harrison (eds), *The Oxford Dictionary of National Biography* (Oxford: Oxford University Press, 2004).

McCarthy, H., 'Gender Equality', in P. Thane & L. Filby (eds), *Unequal Britain: Equalities in Britain since 1945* (London: Continuum, 2010).

McKibbin, R., *Classes and Cultures. England 1918–1951* (Oxford: Oxford University Press, 1998).

Noakes, L., *Women in the British Army: War and the Gentle Sex, 1907–48* (London: Routledge, 2006).

Norris, P., 'Gender: A Gender-Generation Gap?', in G. Evans & P. Norris (eds), *Critical Elections: British Parties and Voters in Long-Term Perspective* (London: Sage, 1999).

Pugh, M., *Women and the Women's Movement, 1914–1999* (Basingstoke: Macmillan, 2000 edn).

Purvis, J. (ed.), *Women's History. Britain, 1850–1945: an introduction* (London: UCL Press, 1995).

Rowbotham, S., *A Century of Women. The History of Women in Britain and the United States* (London: Viking, 1997).

Wilson, E. & L. Taylor, *Through the Looking Glass. A history of dress from 1860 to the present day* (London: BBC Books, 1989).

Zweiniger-Bargielowska, I. (ed.), *Women in Twentieth-Century Britain* (Harlow: Longman, 2001).

Class, Region and Ethnicity

Abrams, L., *Myth and Materiality in a Woman's World. Shetland 1800–2000* (Manchester: Manchester University Press, 2005).

Abrams, L. *et al.*, *Gender in Scottish history since 1700* (Edinburgh: Edinburgh University Press, 2006).

Beddoe, D., *Out of the Shadows. A History of Women in Twentieth-Century Wales* (Cardiff: University of Wales Press, 2000).

Bourke, J., *Working-Class Cultures in Britain, 1890–1960: Gender, Class and Ethnicity* (London: Routledge, 1994).

Breitenbach, E. & E. Gordon (eds), *Out of Bounds: Women in Scottish Society, 1800–1945* (Edinburgh: Edinburgh University Press, 1990).

Bryan, B. *The Heart of the Race. Black Women's Lives in Britain* (London: Virago, 1985).

Chinn, C., *They Worked All Their Lives. Women of The Urban Poor in England, 1880–1939* (Manchester: Manchester University Press, 1988).

Dabydeen, D., J. Gilmore & C. Jones (eds), *The Oxford Companion to Black British History* (Oxford: Oxford University Press, 2007).

Davies, R., *People, Places and Passions: 'Pain and Pleasure'. A Social History of Wales and the Welsh, 1870–1945* (Cardiff: University of Wales Press, 2015).

Delap, L., *Knowing Their Place: Domestic Service in Twentieth-Century Britain* (Oxford: Oxford University Press, 2011).

Dench, G., K. Gavron & M. Young, *The New East End. Kinship, Race and Conflict* (London: Profile Books Ltd, 2006).

Gilroy, P., *There Ain't No Black in the Union Jack* (London: Routledge, 2002 edn).

Goldthorpe, J. H. *et al.*, *The Affluent Worker in the Class Structure* (Cambridge: Cambridge University Press, 1969).

Gregson, N. & M. Lowe, *Servicing the Middle Classes. Class, Gender and Waged Domestic Labour in Contemporary Britain* (London: Routledge, 1994).

Gunn, S. & R. Bell, *Middle Classes: Their Rise and Sprawl* (London: Phoenix, 2003).

Guy, F., R. Burman & B. Williams, *Women of Worth: Jewish Women in Britain* (Manchester: Manchester Jewish Museum, 1992).

Hanley, L., *Respectable. The Experience of Class* (London: Allen Lane, 2016).

Hoggart, R., *The Uses of Literacy. Aspects of Working-Class Life* (London: Chatto & Windus, 1957).

Horn, P., *Life Below Stairs in the 20th Century* (Stroud: Amberley, 2010).

Howkins, A., *The Death of Rural England. A Social History of the Countryside Since 1900* (London: Routledge, 2003).

Jackson, A. A., *The Middle Classes, 1900–1950* (Nairn: David St John Thomas, 1991).

John, A. V. (ed.), *Our Mothers' Land: Chapters in Welsh Women's History, 1830–1939* (Cardiff: University of Wales Press, 2011).

———— *Rocking the Boat. Welsh Women who Championed Equality, 1840-1990* (Cardigan: Parthian, 2018).

Lewis, R. and A. Maude, *The English Middle Classes* (London: Phoenix House, 1949).

McDowell, L., *Working Lives. Gender, Migration and Employment in Britain, 1945–2007* (Chichester: Wiley Blackwell, 2013).

Moulton, M., *Ireland and the Irish in Inter-War Britain* (Cambridge: Cambridge University Press, 2014).

Rees, T., 'Women in Post-war Wales', in T. Herbert & G. Elwyn Jones, *Post-War Wales* (Cardiff: University of Wales Press, 1995).

Roberts, E., *A Woman's Place: An Oral History of Working-Class Women, 1890–1940* (Oxford: Basil Blackwell, 1984).

Summers, A., 'Public Functions, Private Premises: Female Professional Identity and the Domestic Service Paradigm in Britain, c.1850–1930', in B. Melman (ed.) *Borderlines: Genders and Identities in War and Peace, 1870–1930* (London: Routledge, 1998).

Todd, S., 'Domestic Service and Class relations in Britain, 1900–50', *P&P*, 203 (2009).

———— *The People: the Rise and Fall of the Working Class, 1910–2010* (London: John Murray, 2014).

Webster, W., *Imagining Home. Gender, 'Race' and National Identity, 1945–64* (London: UCL Press, 1998).

Welshman, J., *Underclass. A History of the Excluded since 1880* (London: Bloomsbury, 2013).

Williams, A. S., *Ladies of Influence. Women of the Elite in Interwar Britain* (London: Allen Lane, 2000).

Wilson, A., *Dreams, Questions, Struggles. South Asian Women in Britain* (London: Pluto, 2006).

Wilson, N., *Home in British Working-Class Fiction* (Farnham: Ashgate, 2015).

Young, M. and P. Willmott, *Family and Kinship in East London* (London: Routledge & Kegan Paul, 1957).

Family and Work

Anderson, G., *The White-Blouse Revolution: Female Office Workers since 1870* (Manchester: Manchester University Press, 1989).

Ardener, S. & H. Callan (eds), *The Incorporated Wife* (London: Croom Helm, 1984).

Charles, N., C. A. Davies & C. C. Harris, *Families in Transition. Social Change, Family Formation and Kin Relationships* (Bristol: Policy Press, 2008).

Connolly, S. & M. Gregory, 'Women and Work since 1970', in N. F. R. Crafts, I. Gazely & A. Newell (eds), *Work and Pay in Twentieth-Century Britain* (Oxford: Oxford University Press, 2007).

Davis, A., *Modern Motherhood. Women and Family in England, 1945–2000* (Manchester: Manchester University Press, 2012).

—— *Pre-School Childcare in England, 1939–2010. Theory, Practice and Experience* (Manchester: Manchester University Press, 2015).

Giles, J., 'Good Housekeeping: Professionalizing the Housewife, 1920–50', in K. Cowman & L. Jackson (eds), *Women and Work Culture in Britain, c.1850–1950* (Aldershot: Ashgate, 2005).

Glucksman, M., *Women Assemble: Women Workers in the New Industries in Inter-War Britain* (London: Routledge, 1990).

Holden, K., *The Shadow of Marriage. Singleness in England, 1914–60* (Manchester: Manchester University Press, 2007).

Holloway, G., *Women and Work in Britain Since 1840* (London: Routledge, 2005).

Kiernan, K., J. Lewis & H. Land, *Lone Motherhood in Twentieth-Century Britain: from footnote to front page* (Oxford: Clarendon Press, 1998).

Lewis, J., *The End of Marriage? Individualism and Intimate Relations* (Cheltenham: Elgar, 2001).

—— 'The Failure to Expand Childcare Provision and to Develop a Comprehensive Childcare Policy in Britain During the 1960s', *TCBH*, 24:2 (2013).

McCarthy, H., 'Social Science and Married Women's Employment in Post-War Britain', *P&P*, 233:1 (2016).

—— 'Women, Marriage and Paid Work in Post-War Britain', *WHR* 26:1 (2017).

McDowell, L., 'Changing Cultures of Work: Employment, Gender, and Lifestyle', in D. Morley & K. Robins (eds), *British Cultural Studies: Geography, Nationality, and Identity* (Oxford: Oxford University Press, 2001).

McIvor, A. 'Women and Work in Twentieth-Century Scotland', in T. Dickson & J. Treble (eds), *People and Society in Scotland: a Social History of Modern Scotland*, vol iii, 1914–90 (Edinburgh: John Donald, 1992).

Nicholson, V., *Singled Out: How Two Million Women Survived Without Men After the First World War* (London: Viking, 2007).

Rees, T., 'Women and Paid Work in Wales', in J. Aaron (ed.), *Our Sisters' Land. The Changing Identities of Women in Wales* (Cardiff: University of Wales Press, 1997).

Roberts, E., *Women and Families: An Oral History, 1940–70* (Oxford: Blackwell, 1995).

Thane, P., 'Unmarried Motherhood in Twentieth-Century England', *WHR*, 20:1 (2011).

Thane, P. & T. Evans, *Sinners? Scroungers? Saints?: Unmarried Motherhood in Twentieth-Century England* (Oxford: Oxford University Press, 2012).

Todd, S., *Young Women, Work and Family in England, 1918–1950* (Oxford: Oxford University Press, 2005).

Young, M. & P. Willmott, *The Symmetrical Family: a Study of Work and Family in the London Region* (London: Routledge, 1972).

Education

Arnot, M., 'A cloud over coeducation', in S. Walker & L. Barton (eds), *Gender, Class and Education* (Lewes: Falmer, 1983).

Arnot, M., M. David & G. Weiner (eds), *Closing the Gender Gap. Post-war Education and Social* Change (Cambridge: Polity, 1999).

Avery, G., *The Best Type of Girl. A History of Girls' Independent Schools* (London: Deutsch, 1991).

Betts, S. (ed.), *Our Daughters' Land: Past and Present* (Cardiff: University of Wales Press, 1996).

Blandford, L., 'The Making of a Lady', in G. M. Fraser, *The World of the Public School* (London: Weidenfeld & Nicolson, 1977).

Bunkle, P., 'The 1944 Education Act and Second Wave Feminism', *WHR* 25:6 (2016).

Dyhouse, C., *No Distinction of Sex? Women in British Universities, 1870–1939* (London: UCL Press, 1995).

———— *Students: a gendered history* (London:Routledge, 2006).

Edwards, E., *Women in Teacher Training Colleges, 1900–1960: A Culture of Femininity* (London: Routledge, 2001).

Fewell, J. & F. Paterson (eds), *Girls in their Prime. Scottish Education Revisited* (Edinburgh: Scottish Academic Press, 1990).

Goodman, J., 'Class and Religion: Great Britain and Ireland' in J. C. Albisetti, J. Goodman & R. Rogers (eds), *Girls' Secondary Education in the Western World: from the Eighteenth to the Twentieth Century* (Basingstoke: Palgrave Macmillan, 2010).

Howarth, J., 'Women', in B. H. Harrison (ed.), *History of the University of Oxford*, vol viii, *The Twentieth Century* (Oxford: Oxford University Press, 1994).

Hunt, F. (ed.), *Lessons for Life. The Schooling of Girls and Women, 1850–1950* (Oxford: Basil Blackwell, 1987).

———— *Gender and Policy in English Education: Schooling for Girls, 1902–44* (London: Harvester Wheatsheaf, 1991).

Lowe, R., *Schooling and Social Change, 1964–1990* (London: Routledge, 1997).

Mahony, P., *Schools for the Boys? Coeducation Reassessed* (London: Hutchinson, 1985).

Martin, J., 'Gender, Education and Social Change: a study of feminist politics and practice in London, 1870–1990', *Gender and Education*, 25:1 (2013).

Maxtone Graham, Y., *Terms and Conditions: Life in Girls' Boarding-Schools, 1939–1979* (London: Abacus, 2016).

McWilliams Tullberg, R., *Women at Cambridge* (2nd edn, Cambridge: Cambridge University Press, 1998).

Moore, L., 'Educating for the "Woman's Sphere": Domestic Training Versus Intellectual Discipline', in Breitenbach and Gordon, *Out of Bounds*.

Oram, A., *Women Teachers and Feminist Politics, 1900–1930* (Manchester: Manchester University Press, 1996).

Peel, M., *The New Meritocracy. A History of UK Independent Schools, 1979–2015* (London: Elliott & Thompson, 2015).

Plummer, G., *Failing Working-Class Girls* (Stoke on Trent: Trentham Books, 2000).

Reay, D., 'Compounding Inequalities: Gender and Class in Education', in C. Skelton, B. Francis & L. Smulyan, *The Sage Handbook of Gender and Education* (London: Sage, 2006).

Sharpe, S., *Just Like a Girl'. How Girls Learn to be Women. From the Seventies to the Nineties* (London: Penguin, 1994).

Spencer, S., *Gender, Work, and Education in Britain in the 1950s* (Basingstoke: Palgrave Macmillan, 2005).

Thane, P., 'Girton Graduates: Earning and Learning, 1920s to 1980s', *WHR*, 13:3 (2004).

Walkerdine, V. *et al.*, *Growing Up Girl. Psychosocial Explorations of Gender and Class* (Basingstoke: Palgrave, 2001).

Watts, R., 'Pupils', in R. Aldrich (ed.), *A Century of Education* (London: Routledge/Falmer, 2002).

Weiner, G. *et al.*, 'Is the Future Female? Female Success, Male Disadvantage and Changing Gender Patterns in Education', in A. H. Halsey (ed.), *Education, Culture, Economy, and Society* (Oxford: Oxford University Press, 1997).

Sexualities

Alexander, S., 'The Mysteries and Secrets of Women's Bodies: Sexual Knowledge in the First Half of the Twentieth Century', in M. Nava & A. O'Shea (eds), *Modern Times. Reflections on a Century of English Modernity* (London: Routledge, 1995).

Bingham, A., *Family Newspapers?: Sex, Private Life, And the British Popular Press, 1918–1978* (Oxford: Oxford University Press, 2009).

Bingham, A., L. Delap, L. Jackson & L. Settle, 'Historical Child Abuse in England and Wales: The Role of Historians', *History of Education*, 45:4 (2016).

Bland, L., *Modern Woman on Trial: Sexual Transgression in the Age of the Flapper* (Manchester: Manchester University Press, 2013).

Brooke, S., 'Bodies, Sexuality and the "Modernization" of the British Working Classes, 1920s to 1960s', *International Labor and Working-Class History*, 69 (2006).

Cant, B. & S. Hemmings (eds), *Radical Records: Thirty Years of Lesbian and Gay History, 1957–1987* (London: Routledge, 1988).

Collins, M., *Modern Love. An Intimate History of Men and Women in Twentieth-Century Britain* (London: Atlantic, 2003).

Cook, H., *The Long Sexual Revolution: English Women, Sex and Contraception. 1800–1975* (Oxford: Oxford University Press, 2004).

Feminist Review (ed.), *Sexuality. A Reader* (London: Virago, 1987).

Fisher, K., *Birth Control, Sex and Marriage in Britain, 1918–60* (Oxford: Oxford University Press, 2006).

Gittins, D., *Fair Sex: Family Size and Structure, 1900–39* (London: Hutchinson, 1982).

Hall, L. A., *Sex, Gender and Social Change in Britain since 1880* (Basingstoke: Macmillan, 2000).

———— *Outspoken Women: An Anthology of Women's Writing on Sex, 1870–1969* (London: Routledge, 2005).

Hampshire, J. & J. Lewis, '"The Ravages of Permissiveness": Sex Education and the Permissive Society', *TCBH*, 15:3 (2004).

Harris, A. & T. W. Jones (eds), *Love and Romance in Britain, 1918–1970* (Basingstoke: Palgrave Macmillan, 2015).

Humphries, S. & P. Gordon (eds), *Forbidden Britain. Our Secret Past, 1900–1960* (London: BBC Books, 1994).

Jennings, R., *Tomboys and Bachelor Girls: A Lesbian History of Post-War Britain, 1945–71* (Manchester: Manchester University Press, 2007).

Jivani, A., *It's Not Unusual: A History of Lesbian and Gay Britain in the Twentieth Century* (London: Michael O'Mara, 1997).

Langhamer, C., *The English in Love. The Intimate Story of an Emotional Revolution* (Oxford: Oxford University Press, 2013).

Oram, A., 'Repressed and Thwarted, or Bearer of the New World? The Spinster in Inter-War Feminist Discourses', *WHR*, 1:3 (1992).

Oram, A. & A. Turnbull (eds), *The Lesbian History Sourcebook* (London: Routledge, 2001).

Stanley, L., *Sex Surveyed, 1949–94: from Mass Observation's Little Kinsey to the National Survey and the Hite Report* (London: Taylor & Francis, 1995).

Szreter, S. & K. Fisher, *Sex Before the Sexual Revolution. Intimate life in England, 1918–1963* (Cambridge: Cambridge University Press, 2010).

Weeks, J., *Sex, Politics and Society* (3rd edn, Harlow: Pearson, 2012).

Wellings, K., *Sexual Behaviour in Britain. The National Survey of Sexual Attitudes and Lifestyles* (Harmondsworth: Penguin, 1994).

Feminisms and Femininity

Alberti, J., *Beyond Suffrage. Feminists in War and Peace, 1914–28* (Basingstoke: Macmillan, 1989).

Andrews, M., *The Acceptable Face of Feminism: the Women's Institute as a social movement* (2nd edn, London: Lawrence & Wishart, 2015).

Beaumont, C., *Housewives and Citizens. Domesticity and the Women's Movement in England, 1928–64* (Manchester: Manchester University Press, 2013).

Berry, P. & M. Bostridge, *Vera Brittain. A Life* (London: Virago, 2008 edn).

Birmingham Feminist History Group, 'Feminism as Femininity in the 1950s?', *Feminist Review*, 3 (1979).

Bolt, C., *Sisterhood Questioned? Race, Class and Internationalism in the American and British Women's Movements, c. 1880s–1970s* (London: Routledge, 2004).

Browne, S. F., *The Women's Liberation Movement in Scotland* (Manchester: Manchester University Press, 2014).

Caine, B., *English Feminism, 1780–1980* (Oxford: Oxford University Press, 1997).

Cameron, D. & J. Scanlon (eds), *The Trouble and Strife Reader* (London: Bloomsbury Academic, 2010).

Delap, L., 'Feminist Bookshops, Reading Cultures and the Women's Liberation Movement in Great Britain, c. 1974–2000', *HWJ*, 81:1 (2016).

Dyhouse, C., *Feminism and the Family in England, 1880–1939* (Oxford: Basil Blackwell, 1989).

———— *Glamour: Women, History, Feminism* (London: Zed, 2010).

Gillis, S. & R. Munford, 'Genealogies and Generations: The Politics and Praxis of Third Wave Feminism', *WHR*, 13:2 (2004).

Gupta, R. (ed.), *From Homebreakers to Jailbreakers. Southall Black Sisters* (London: Zed, 2003).

Harrison, B., *Prudent Revolutionaries: Portraits of British Feminists Between the Wars* (Oxford: Clarendon Press, 1987).

James, S., M. Rediker & N. Lopez, *Sex, Race and Class- the Perspective of Winning: A Selection of Writings, 1952–2011* (Oakland, California: PM Press, 2012).

Klein, V., *The Feminine Character: History of an Ideology* (3rd edn, London: Routledge, 1989).

Lee, H., *Virginia Woolf* (London: Chatto & Windus, 1996).

Liddington, J., *The Long Road to Greenham. Feminism and Anti-militarism in Britain Since 1820* (London: Virago, 1989).

Mirza, H. S. (ed.), *Black British Feminism. A Reader* (London: Routledge, 1997).

Mitchell, J., *Woman's Estate* (Harmondsworth: Penguin, 1971).

Moyse, C., *A History of the Mothers' Union. Women, Anglicanism and Globalisation, 1876–2008* (Woodbridge: Boydell Press, 2009).

Murray, J., *The Woman's Hour: 50 Years of Women in Britain* (London: BBC Books, 1996).

Offen, K., *European Feminisms, 1700–1950: A Political History* (Stanford: Stanford University Press, 2000).

Owen, N., 'Men and the 1970s British Women's Liberation Movement', *HJ*, 56:3 (2013).

Pedersen, S., *Eleanor Rathbone and the Politics of Conscience* (London: Yale University Press, 2004).

Redfern, C. & K. Aune, *Reclaiming the F Word. The new feminist movement* (London: Zed Books, 2013).

Rowbotham, S., *Woman's Consciousness, Man's World* (Harmondsworth: Penguin, 1973).

Rupp, L. J., *Worlds of Women. The Making of an International Women's Movement* (Princeton: Princeton University Press, 1997).

Schulz, K., (ed.), *The Women's Liberation Movement. Impacts and Outcomes* (New York: Berghahn Books, 2017).

Scott, G., *Feminism and the Politics of Working Women: the Women's Cooperative Guild from the 1880s to the Second World War* (London: UCL Press, 1998).

Segal, L., *Is the Future Female? Troubled Thoughts on Contemporary Feminism* (London: Virago, 1987).

Setch, E., 'The Face of Metropolitan Feminism: the London Women's Liberation Workshop, 1969–79', *TCBH*, 13:2 (2002).

Smith, H. L. (ed.), *British Feminism in the Twentieth Century* (Aldershot: Elgar, 1990).

———— 'British Feminism in the Second World War', in P. Levine & S. Grayzel (eds), *Gender, Labour, War and Empire. Essays on Modern Britain* (Basingstoke: Palgrave Macmillan, 2009).

Spender, D., *There's Always Been a Women's Movement this Century* (London: Pandora Press, 1983).

Stott, M. (ed.), *Women Talking. An anthology from the Guardian Women's Page, 1922–35, 1957–71* (London: Pandora, 1987).

Strachey, R., *'The Cause': a Short History of the Women's Movement in Great Britain* (London: G. Bell & Sons, 1928).

Thomlinson, N., *Race, Ethnicity and the Women's Movement in England, 1968–1993* (Basingstoke: Palgrave Macmillan, 2016).

Walkowicz, J., 'The Politics of Prostitution and Sexual Labour', *HWJ*, 82:1 (2016).

Walter, N., *The New Feminism* (London: Little Brown, 1998).

Wandor, M. (ed.), *Once A Feminist: stories of a generation* (London: Virago, 1990).

Wilson, E., 'Feminism and Fashion', in *Adorned in Dreams. Fashion and Modernity* (London: Virago, 1985).

The Great War, 1914–18

Braybon, G., *Women Workers in the First World War: the British Experience* (London: Croom Helm, 1981).

———— (ed.), *Evidence, History and the Great War: Historians and the Impact of 1914–18* (Oxford: Berghahn, 2003).

Braybon, G. & P. Summerfield, *Out of the Cage: Women's Experience in Two World Wars* (London: Routledge, 2013).

Brock, M. G. & E. Brock (eds), *Margot Asquith's Great War Diary, 1914–1916: the View from Downing Street* (Oxford: Oxford University Press, 2014).

de Groot, G., *Back in Blighty: the British at Home in World War One* (London: Vintage Books, 2014).

Dwork, D., *War is Good for Babies and Other Young Children* (London: Tavistock Publications, 1987).

Grayzel, S. R., *Women's Identities at War: Gender, Motherhood and Politics in Britain and France During the First World War* (Chapel Hill, NC: University of N. Carolina Press, 1999).

Gullace, N. F., 'White Feathers and Wounded Men. Female Patriotism and the Memory of the Great War', *JBS*, 36 (1997).

———— *The Blood of Our Sons: Men, Women and the Renegotiation of British Citizenship During the Great War* (New York: Palgrave Macmillan, 2002).

Hunt, K., 'A Heroine at Home: the Housewife on the First World War Home Front', in M. Andrews & J. Lomas (eds), *The Home Front in Britain. Images, Myths and Forgotten Experiences since 1914* (Basingstoke: Palgrave Macmillan, 2014).

Levine, P., 'Walking the Streets in a Way No Decent Woman Should: Women Police in World War One', *JMH* 66:1 (1994).

Liddington, J., 'The Women's Peace Crusade', in D. Thompson (ed.), *Over Our Dead Bodies: Women Against the Bomb* (London: Virago, 1983).

Marlow, J. (ed.), *The Virago Book of Women and the Great War, 1914–18* (London: Virago, 1998).

Meyer, J. (ed.), *British Popular Culture and the First World War* (Leiden: Brill, 2008).

Oldfield, S., *Women Against the Iron Fist. Alternatives to Militarism, 1900–1989* (Oxford: Basil Blackwell, 1989).

Pedersen, S., 'Gender, Welfare and Citizenship in Britain during the Great War', *American History Review*, 95 (1990).

Potter, J., '"Peace Could Not Give Back Her Dead": Women and the Armistice', in M. Howard (ed.), *A Part of History. Aspects of the British Experience of the First World War* (London: Continuum, 2009).

Purvis, J., 'The Women's Party of Great Britain (1917–1919): A Forgotten Episode in British Women's Political History', *WHR*, 25:4 (2016).

Thom, D., *Nice Girls and Rude Girls. Women Workers in World War I* (London: I.B.Tauris, 1998).

Twinch, C., *Women Of the Land: Their Story During Two World Wars* (Cambridge: Lutterworth, 1990).

Wiltshire, A., *Most Dangerous Women: Feminist Peace Campaigners of the Great War* (London: Pandora, 1985).

Woollacott, A., *On Her Their Lives Depend. Munitions Workers in the Great War* (London: University of California Press, 1993).

Franchise and After, 1918–39 – the Modern Woman

Alexander, S., 'Becoming a Woman in London in the 1920s and 30s', in *Becoming a Woman and other essays in Nineteenth and Twentieth Century Feminist History* (London: Virago, 1994).

Andrews, M. & M. Talbot (eds), *All the World and Her Husband. Women in Twentieth-century Consumer Culture* (London: Cassell, 2000).

Beauman, N., *A Very Great Profession: The Woman's Novel, 1914–39* (London: Virago, 1983).

Bingham, A., '"An Era of Domesticity"? Histories of women and gender in inter-war Britain', *CSH*, 1:2 (2004).

———— *Gender, Modernity, and the Popular Press in Inter-War Britain* (Oxford: Oxford University Press 2004).

Beers, L., *Red Ellen: The Life of Ellen Wilkinson, Socialist, Feminist, Internationalist* (London: Harvard University Press, 2016).

Bowden, S. & A. Offer, 'Household Appliances and the Use of Time: The United States and Britain Since the 1920s', *Economic History Review*, 47 (1994).

Flinn, A., ' "Mothers for Peace", Co-operation, Feminism and Peace: the Women's Co-operative Guild and the Anti-War Movement between the Wars', in L. Black & N. Robertson, *Consumerism and the Co-operative Movement in Modern British History: Taking Stock* (Manchester: Manchester University Press, 2009).

Giles, J., *Women, Identity and Private Life in Britain, 1900–50* (Basingstoke: Macmillan, 1995).

Gottlieb, J. V., *Feminine Fascism. Women in Britain's Fascist Movement, 1923–45* (London: I.B.Tauris, 2000).

—— *'Guilty Women', Foreign Policy, and Appeasement in Inter-war Britain* (Basingstoke: Palgrave Macmillan, 2015).

Gottlieb, J. V. & R. Toye (eds), *The Aftermath of Suffrage. Women, Gender and Politics in Britain, 1918–1945* (Basingstoke: Palgrave Macmillan, 2013).

Graves, P. M., *Labour Women. Women in British Working-Class Politics, 1918–39* (Cambridge: Cambridge University Press, 1994).

Hannam, J., 'Women and Labour Politics', in M. Worley (ed.), *The Foundations of the British Labour Party: Identities, Cultures & Perspectives, 1890–1939* (Aldershot: Aldgate, 2009).

Harrison, B., 'Women in a Men's House: The Women MPs, 1919–45', *HJ*, 29 (1986).

Honeyball, M., *Parliamentary Pioneers. Labour Women MPs, 1918–1945* (Chatham, Kent: Urbane Publications, 2015).

Humble, N., *The Feminine Middlebrow Novel, 1920s to 1950s. Class, Domesticity and Bohemianism* (Oxford: Oxford University Press, 2001).

Jarvis, D., 'The Conservative Party and the Politics of Gender, 1900–39', in M. Francis & I. Zweiniger-Bargielowska, *The Conservatives and British Society, 1880–1990* (Cardiff: University of Wales Press, 1996).

—— 'Behind Every Great Party', in A. Vickery (ed.), *Women, Privilege and Power* (Stanford: Stanford University Press, 2001).

John, A. V., *Turning the Tide. The Life of Lady Rhondda* (Cardigan: Parthian, 2013).

Langhamer, C., *Women's Leisure in England, 1920–1960* (Manchester: Manchester University Press, 2000).

Law, C., *Suffrage and Power: The Women's Movement, 1918–28* (London: I.B.Tauris, 1997).

Light, A., *Forever England: Femininity, Literature and Conservatism between the Wars* (London: Routledge, 1991).

McCarthy, H., 'Parties, Voluntary Associations, and Democratic Politics in Interwar Britain', *HJ*, 50 (2007).

—— 'Service Clubs, Citizenship and Equality: Gender Relations and Middle-Class Associations in Britain Between the Wars', *HR*, 81:213 (2008).

McKibbin, R., 'Class and Conventional Wisdom: The Conservative Party and the "Public" in inter-war Britain', in *The Ideologies of Class* (Oxford: Oxford University Press, 1990).

Melman, B., *Women and the Popular Imagination in the Twenties: Flappers and Nymphs* (London: Macmillan, 1988).

Miller, C., '"Geneva – the Key to Equality". Inter-War Feminists and the League of Nations', *WHR*, 3:2 (1994).

Nott, J., *Going to the Palais. A Social And Cultural History of Dance Halls in Britain, 1918–60* (Oxford: Oxford University Press, 2015).

Pedersen, S., *Eleanor Rathbone and the Politics of Conscience* (London: Yale University Press, 2004).

Perry, M., *'Red Ellen' Wilkinson. Her Ideas, Movements, and World* (Manchester: Manchester University Press, 2014).

Proctor, T., '(Uni)Forming Youth: Girl Guides and Boy Scouts in Britain, 1908–39', *HWJ*, 45 (1998).

Strachey, R. (ed.), *Our Freedom and Its Results* (London: Hogarth Press, 1936).

Tanner, D., 'Gender, Civic Culture and Politics in South Wales: explaining Labour Municipal policy, 1918–39', in M. Worley (ed.), *Labour's Grass Roots: Essays on the experiences and activities of local Labour parties and members, 1918–45* (Aldershot, Ashgate, 2005).

Thane, P., 'What difference did the vote make?', in A. Vickery (ed.), *Women, Privilege and Power* (Stanford University Press, 2001), pp. 253–87.

Tinkler, P., *Constructing Girlhood: Popular Magazines for Girls Growing Up in England, 1920–50* (London: Taylor & Francis, 1995).

Tinkler, P. & C. Warsh, 'Feminine Modernity in Interwar Britain and North America: Corsets, Cars, and Cigarettes', *Journal of Women's History*, 20:3 (2008).

White, C. L., *Women's Magazines, 1693–1968* (London: M. Joseph, 1970).

Zweiniger-Bargielowska, I., 'The Making of a Modern Female Body: Beauty, Health and Fitness in Interwar Britain', *WHR*, 20:2 (2011).

World War Two and Reconstruction, 1939–51

de Groot, G., & C. Peniston-Bird (eds), *A Soldier and a Woman: Sexual Integration in the Military* (Harlow: Longman, 2000).

Gledhill, C. & G. Swanson (eds), *Nationalising Femininity. Culture, Sexuality and British Cinema in the Second World War* (Manchester: Manchester University Press, 2011).

Harris, J., *William Beveridge* (Oxford: Clarendon Press, revised edn 1997).

Hennessy, P., *Never Again: Britain 1945–51* (London: Cape, 1992).

Hinton, J., 'Militant Housewives: the British Housewives' League and the Attlee Government', *HWJ*, 38 (1994).

———— *Women, Social Leadership and the Second World War. Continuities of Class* (Oxford: Oxford University Press, 2002).

———— *Nine Wartime Lives. Mass-Observation and the Making of the Modern Self* (Oxford: Oxford University Press, 2010).

Kynaston, D., *Austerity Britain, 1945–51* (London: Bloomsbury, 2007).

Morelli, C. & J. Tomlinson, 'Women and Work after the Second World War: a Case Study of the Jute Industry, c. 1945–54', *TCBH*, 19:1 (2000).

Nicholson, V., *Millions Like Us: Women's Lives in War and Peace, 1939–49* (London: Viking, 2011).

Noakes, L. & J. Pattinson (eds), *British Cultural Memory and the Second World War* (London: Bloomsbury Academic, 2013).

Parkin, D., 'Women in the Armed Services, 1940–45', in R. Samuel (ed.), *Patriotism. The Making and Unmaking of British National Identity* (London: Routledge, 1989).

Purnell, S., *First Lady. The Life and Wars of Clementine Churchill* (London: Aurum Press, 2015).

Rose, S. O., *Which People's War? National Identity and Citizenship in Britain, 1939–1945* (Oxford: Oxford University Press, 2003).

Schwarzkopf, J., 'Combatant or Non-Combatant? The Ambiguous Status of Women in British Anti-Aircraft Batteries during the Second World War', *War and Society*, 28:2 (2009).

Smith, H. L., 'The Effect of War on the Status of Women', in H. L. Smith (ed.), *War and Social Change. British Society in the Second World War* (Manchester: Manchester University Press, 1986).

Summerfield, P., *Reconstructing Women's Wartime Lives: Discourse and Subjectivity in Oral Histories of the Second World War* (Manchester: Manchester University Press, 1998).

—— 'Women, War and Social Change: Women in Britain in World War Two', in A. Marwick (ed.), *Total War and Social Change* (Basingstoke: Macmillan, 1988).

Summerfield, P. & C. Peniston-Bird, *Contesting Home Defence. Men, Women and the Home Guard in the Second World War* (Manchester: Manchester University Press, 2007).

Summers, J., *Stranger in the House. Women's stories of Men Returning from the Second World War* (London: Simon & Schuster, 2008).

Thane, P., 'Visions of Gender in the Making of the British Welfare State: The Case of Women in the British Labour Party and Social Policy 1906–45', in G. Bock & P. Thane (eds), *Maternity and Gender Politics: Women and the Rise of European Welfare States, 1880s–1950* (London: Routledge, 1991).

Welshman, J., 'Evacuation, Hygiene, and Social Policy: The *Our Towns* Report of 1943', *HJ*, 42 (1999).

Zweiniger-Bargielowska, I., *Austerity in Britain: Rationing, Controls, and Consumption, 1939–55* (Oxford: Oxford University Press, 2000).

The Fifties and Sixties

Akhtar, M. & S. Humphries, *The Fifties and Sixties: A Lifestyle Revolution* (London: Boxtree, 2001).

Aldgate, A., J. Chapman & A. Marwick (eds), *Windows on the Sixties: Exploring Key Texts of Media and Culture* (London: I.B.Tauris, 2000).

Black, L., *Redefining British Politics: Culture, Consumerism and Participation, 1954–70* (Basingstoke: Palgrave Macmillan, 2010).

—— 'Reactionaries: There Was Something About Mary: the National Viewers' and Listeners' Association and Social Movement History', in N. J. Crowson,

M. Hilton & J. McKay (eds), *NGOs in Contemporary Britain: Non-State Actors in Society and Politics since 1945* (Basingstoke: Palgrave Macmillan, 2009).

Brooke, S., 'Gender and Working Class Identity in Britain During the 1950s', *Journal of Social History*, 34:4 (2001).

Brown, C. G., *The Death of Christian Britain. Understanding Secularisation, 1800–2000, Chapter 8* (London: Routledge, 2001).

Collins, M. (ed.), *The Permissive Society and Its Enemies: Sixties British Culture* (London: Rivers Oram, 2007).

Conekin, B., *The Autobiography of a Nation. The 1951 Festival of Britain* (Manchester: Manchester University Press, 2003).

Conekin, B., F. Mort & C. Waters (eds), *Moments of Modernity. Reconstructing Britain, 1945–1964* (London: Rivers Oram, 1999).

Curtis, H. & M. Sanderson, *The Unsung Sixties. Memoirs of Social Innovation* (London: Whiting and Birch, 2004).

Gardiner, J., *From the Bomb to The Beatles* (London: Collins & Brown, 1999).

Giles, J., *The Parlour and The Suburb: Domestic Identities, Class, Femininity and Modernity* (Oxford: Berg, 2004).

Green, J., *All Dressed Up: the Sixties and the Counter-Culture* (London: Jonathan Cape, 1998).

Harrison, B., *Seeking a Role: the UK, 1951–70* (Oxford: Oxford University Press, 2011).

Hennessy, P., *Having It So Good: Britain in the Fifties* (London: Allen Lane, 2006).

Heron, L. (ed.), *Truth, Dare or Promise: Girls Growing Up in the Fifties* (London: Virago, 1985).

Hilton, M., 'The Female Consumer and the Role of Consumption in Twentieth-Century Britain', *HJ*, 45:1 (2002).

Hollis, P., *Jennie Lee. A Life* (Oxford: Oxford University Press, 1997).

Kynaston, D., *Family Britain, 1951–1957* (London: Bloomsbury, 2009).

Laite, J. A., 'The Association for Moral and Social Hygiene: Abolitionism and Prostitution Law in Britain, 1915–1959', *WHR*, 17:2 (2008).

Langhamer, C., 'The Meanings of Home in Postwar Britain', *JCH*, 40:2 (2005).

MacCarthy, F., *Last Curtsey: The End of the Debutantes* (London: Faber & Faber, 2006).

Maitland, S. (ed.), *Very Heaven. Looking Back at the 1960s* (London: Virago, 1988).

Marquand, D. & A. Seldon (eds), *The Ideas that Shaped Post-War Britain* (London: Fontana, 1996).

Marwick, A., *The Sixties. Cultural Revolution in Britain, France, Italy and the United States, c.1958–c.1974* (Oxford: Oxford University Press, 1998).

McLeod, H., *The Religious Crisis of the 1960s, Chapter 8* (Oxford: Oxford University Press, 2007).

Mort, F., *Capital Affairs. London and The Making of the Permissive Society* (London: Yale University Press, 2010).

———— 'The Permissive Society Revisited', *TCBH* 22:2, 2011.

Oakley, A., *A Critical Woman. Barbara Wootton, Social Science and Public Policy in the Twentieth Century* (London: Bloomsbury Academic, 2011).

Obelkevich, J. & P. Catterall (eds), *Understanding Post-war British Society* (London: Routledge, 1994).

Perkins, A., *Red Queen. The authorised biography of Barbara Castle* (London: Macmillan, 2003).

Pimlott, B., *The Queen. Elizabeth II and the Monarchy* (London: HarperCollins, 2001).

Reeves, R. & R. Carr, *Alice in Westminster. The political life of Alice Bacon* (London: I.B.Tauris, 2017).

Rowbotham, S., *Promise of a Dream. Remembering the Sixties* (London: Penguin, 2000).

Sandbrook, D., *Never Had It So Good. A History of Britain from Suez to The Beatles* (London: Little Brown, 2005).

————— *White Heat: a History of Britain in the Swinging Sixties* (London: Little Brown, 2006).

Summerfield, P., 'Public Memory or Public Amnesia? British Women of the Second World War in Popular Films of the 1950s and 60s', *JBS*, 48:4 (2009).

Spencer, S., *Gender, Work and Education in Britain in the 1950s* (Basingstoke: Palgrave Macmillan, 2005).

Wilson, E., *Only Halfway to Paradise. Women in Post-war Britain 1945–68* (London: Tavistock Publications, 1980).

Women's Liberation to Post-feminism? 1970 to the Present

Addison, P., *No Turning Back. The Peaceful Revolutions of Post-War Britain* (Oxford: Oxford University Press, 2010).

Bale, T., *Margaret Thatcher* (4 vols, London: Routledge, 2015).

Banyard, K., *The Equality Illusion. The Truth About Women and Men Today* (London: Faber, 2010).

Barry, J., *The Women's Movement and Local Politics: the Influence on Councillors in London* (Aldershot: Avebury, 1991).

Black, L., H. Pemberton & P. Thane, *Reassessing 1970s Britain* (Manchester: Manchester University Press 2013).

Blaxhill, L. & K. Beelen, 'A Feminized Language of Democracy? The Representation of Women at Westminster since 1945', *TCBH* 27:3 (2016).

Breitenbach, E. & P. Thane (eds), *Women and Citizenship in Britain and Ireland in the Twentieth Century. What Difference did the Vote Make?* (London: Continuum, 2010).

Brown, C. G., 'Secularization, the Growth of Militancy and the Spiritual Revolution: Religious Change and Gender Power in Britain, 1901–2001', *HR*, 80:209 (2007).

Bruley, S., 'Women's Liberation at the Grass Roots: a View from some English Towns', *WHR*, 25:5 (2016).

Byrne, P., 'The Politics of the Women's Movement', in J. Lovenduski & P. Norris (eds), *Women in Politics* (Oxford: Oxford University Press, 1996).

Coote, A. & B. Campbell, *Sweet Freedom: The Struggle for Women's Liberation* (2nd edn, Oxford: Basil Blackwell, 1987).

Dixon, J., 'Separatism: A Look Back at Anger', in B. Cant & S. Hemmings (eds), *Radical Records. Thirty Years of Lesbian and Gay History, 1957–87* (London: Routledge, 1988).

Driver, S. & L. Martell, *Blair's Britain* (Oxford: Polity, 2002).

Harman, H., *A Woman's Work* (London: Allen Lane, 2017).

Jackson, B. & R. Saunders (eds), *Making Thatcher's Britain* (Cambridge: Cambridge University Press, 2012).

Lent, A., *British Social Movements since 1945: Sex, Colour, Peace and Power* (Basingstoke: Palgrave, 2001).

Lovenduski, J. & V. Randall, *Contemporary Feminist Politics. Women and power in Britain* (Oxford: Oxford University Press, 1993).

McBride, D. E. (ed.), *Abortion Politics, Women's Movements, and the Democratic State* (Oxford: Oxford University Press, 2001).

McKibbin, R., 'Mass Observation in the Mall', in M. Merck (ed.), *After Diana: Irreverent Elegies* (London: Verso, 1998).

McRobbie, A., *Feminism and Youth Culture: from 'Jackie' to 'Just Seventeen'* (Basingstoke: Macmillan, 1991).

———— *The Aftermath of Feminism* (London: Sage, 2009).

Moore, C., *Margaret Thatcher* (2 vols, London: Allen Lane, 2013).

Morgan, S., '"Stand by Your Man": Wives, Women and Feminism During the Miners' Strike, 1984–5', *Llafur*, 9 (2005).

Norris, P. (ed.), *Women, Media, and Politics* (Oxford: Oxford University Press, 1997).

Purvis, J., 'What was Margaret Thatcher's legacy for women?', *WHR*, 22:6 (2013).

Rees, J., 'A Look Back at Anger: the WLM in 1978', *WHR*, 19:3 (2010).

Rees, T., 'The Politics of "Mainstreaming" Gender Equality' in E. Breitenbach *et al.*, *The Changing Politics of Gender Equality in Britain* (Basingstoke: Palgrave, 2002).

Sandbrook, D., *State of Emergency: The Way We Were. Britain, 1970–74* (London: Allen Lane, 2010).

———— *Seasons in the Sun: The Battle for Britain 1974–1979* (London: Allen Lane, 2012).

Saunders, R., 'The Many Lives of Margaret Thatcher', *EHR* 82:556 (2017).

Spence, J. & C. Stephenson, '"Side by Side with Our Men?" Women's Activism, Community, and Gender in the 1984–5 Miners' Strike', *International Labor and Working-Class History*, 75 (2009).

Thomlinson, N., *Race, Ethnicity and the Women's Movement in England, 1968–1993* (Basingstoke: Palgrave Macmillan, 2016).

Vinen, R., *Thatcher's Britain. The Politics and Social Upheaval of the Thatcher Era* (London: Simon & Schuster, 2009).

Walby, S. & C. Short (eds), *New Agendas for Women* (Basingstoke: Macmillan, 1999).

Walter, N., *Living Dolls: The Return of Sexism* (London: Virago, 2010).

Williams, S., *Climbing the Bookshelves: The Autobiography of Shirley Williams* (London: Virago, 2009).

Williamson, A., 'The Law and Politics of Marital Rape in England, 1945–94', *WHR*, 26:3 (1917).

Young, H., *One of Us: A Biography of Margaret Thatcher* (London: Macmillan, 1991).

Electronic Resources

Bibliography of British and Irish History. Available at www.brepolis.net/

British Library Sisterhood Project. Available at www.bl.uk/sisterhood

COPAC Library Catalogue – free access to online catalogues of major UK libraries including the British Library. Available at http://copac.ac.uk/

The F Word. Available at www.thefword.org.uk (founded 2001 by Catherine Redfern).

Fawcett Society. Available at https://www.fawcettsociety.org.uk/

Glasgow Women's Library. Available at www.womenslibrary.org.uk

Margaret Thatcher archive. Available at www.margaretthatcher.org/archive/thatcher-archive.asp

Mass-Observation Online. Available at www.massobs.org.uk

The National Archives. Available at www.nationalarchives.gov.uk/. For guidance on material on women see *Women in The National Archives. A finding aid and digital resource* (Adam Matthew Publications); or TNA in-depth research guides on topics including *First World War: women's military service; Gay and Lesbian History; Health between the Wars, 1919–39; Labour History; Second World War: Home Front.*

Online photographic archives. Available at http://pro.corbis.com/ and www.getty images.com/

Oxford Dictionary of National Biography. Available at www.oxforddnb.com/

University of Sussex, 'Observing the 80s'. Available at http://blogs.sussex.ac.uk/observingthe80s

Women's Archive of Wales. Available at www.womensarchivewales.org

The Women's Library. Available at www.lse.ac.uk/Library/Collections/Collection-highlights/The-Womens-Library/

Women, War and Society, 1914–1918. Available at http://gdc.gale.com/archives unbound/archives-unbound-women-war-and-society-1914–1918/

Permission Notes and Acknowledgements

This section details acknowledgements and permissions for extracts used in the book, where relevant, and with wording as requested by the rights holder or licensor. Any omissions will be rectified in future printings.

Chapter 1   Class, Region and Ethnicity
The publisher gratefully acknowledges the permission granted by David Higham on behalf of the estate of Naomi Mitchison to publish the extract from Mitchison, Naomi, *You May Well Ask. A memoir, 1920–1940* (London: Victor Gollancz, 1979).

The publisher gratefully acknowledges the permission granted by Mary Lennon, Marie McAdam, Joanne O'Brien and the Little, Brown Book Group to publish the extract from Lennon, Mary, McAdam, Marie and O'Brian, Joanne, *Across the Water. Irish Women's Lives in Britain* (London: Virago, 1988).

The publisher gratefully acknowledges the permission granted by United Agents on behalf of The Estate of J. B. Priestley to publish the extract from Priestley, J. B., *English Journey* (London: W. Heinemann in association with V. Gollancz, 1934; repr. London: Mandarin, 1994).

Andrews, E., 'Wales and Her Poverty', Labour Woman, July 1939, repr. in Masson, U. (ed.), Elizabeth Andrews, *A Woman's Work is Never Done* (Dinas Powys: Honno, 2006) with permission from Honno Press and the Estate of Elizabeth Andrews. *A Woman's Work is Never Done* is available from www.honno.co.uk.

The publisher gratefully acknowledges the permission granted by Cambridge University Press to publish the extract from Madge, Charles, *War-time Patterns of Saving and Spending* (Cambridge: CUP, 1943).

The publisher gratefully acknowledges the permission granted by David Higham on behalf of the estate of Geoffrey Gorer to publish the extract from Gorer, Geoffrey, *Exploring English Character* (London: Cresset Press, 1955).

The publisher gratefully acknowledges the permission granted by Gail Lewis to publish the extract from Heron, Liz (ed.), *Truth, Dare or Promise. Girls Growing Up in the 50s* (London: Virago, 1985).

The publisher gratefully acknowledges the permission granted by the Little, Brown Book Group and Amrit Wilson to publish the extract from Wilson, Amrit, *Finding a Voice. Asian Women in Britain* (London: Virago, 1978).

The publisher gratefully acknowledges the permission granted by Ann Oakley to publish the extract from Oakley, Ann, *Subject Women* (Oxford: Martin Robertson, 1981).

The publisher gratefully acknowledges the permission granted by Pamela Abbott to publish the extract from Abbott, P. & Sapsford, R, *Women and Social Class* (London: Tavistock, 1987).

The publisher gratefully acknowledges the permission granted by Carolyn Steedman, Rutgers University Press and the Little, Brown Book Group to publish the extract from Steedman, Carolyn, *Landscape for a Good Woman* (London: Virago, 1986).

The publisher gratefully acknowledges the permission granted by Bloodaxe Books to publish the extract from Kay, Jackie, *Other Lovers* (Newcastle upon Tyne: Bloodaxe, 1993).

Chapter 2 Family and Work

Burnett, John (ed.), *Useful Toil: autobiographies of working people from the 1820s to the 1920s* (London: Allen Lane, 1974) is reproduced by permission of Taylor & Francis Books UK. Copyright © John Burnett 1974.

The publisher gratefully acknowledges the permission granted by United Agents on behalf of The Estate of J. B. Priestley to publish the extract from Priestley, J. B., *English Journey* (London: W. Heinemann in association with V. Gollancz, 1934; repr. London: Mandarin, 1994).

The publisher gratefully acknowledges the permission granted by Jacquie Sarsby to publish the extract from Sarsby, Jacquie, *Missuses and Mouldrunners. An oral history of women pottery workers at work and at home* (Milton Keynes: Open University Press, 1988).

The publisher gratefully acknowledges the permission granted by Cambridge University Press to publish the extract from Pilgrim Trust, *Men Without Work* (Cambridge, CUP, 1938).

The publisher gratefully acknowledges the permission granted by Margaret Cole and J M Dent (as granted by David Higham) to publish the extract from Marriage Past and Present (London: J. M. Dent, 1938).

Law Reports, [1943] 2 AC, 579 Blackwell v Blackwell is covered by the Open Government Licence: http://www.nationalarchives.gov.uk/doc/open-government-licence/version/3/.

The publisher gratefully acknowledges the permission granted by Ann Oakley to publish the extract from Titmuss, R., 'The position of women', in *Essays on 'The Welfare State'* (London: Allen & Unwin, 1958).

Myrdal, A. & Klein, V., *Women's Two Roles: Home and Work* (London: Routledge & Kegan Paul, 1956) is reproduced by permission of Taylor & Francis Books UK. Copyright © Myrdal & Klein 1956.

The publisher gratefully acknowledges the permission granted by Ann Oakley to publish the extract from Oakley, Ann, *Housewife* (London, Allen Lane, 1974).

The publisher gratefully acknowledges the permission granted by David Higham to publish the extract from Seabrook, J, *What Went Wrong? Working people and the ideals of the Labour Movement* (London: Victor Gollancz, 1978).

The publisher gratefully acknowledges the permission granted by Beatrix Campbell and the Little, Brown Book Group to publish the extract from Campbell, Beatrix, *Wigan Pier Revisited. Poverty and politics in the eighties* (London: Virago, 1984).

The publisher gratefully acknowledges the permission granted by Profile Books to publish the extract from Dench, G., Gavron, K. & Young, M., *The New East End* (London: Profile Books Ltd, 2006).

Chapter 3 Education
Burnett, John (ed.), *Destiny Obscure* (London: Allen Lane, 1974, repr. Routledge 1994) is reproduced by permission of Taylor & Francis Books UK. Copyright © John Burnett 1974.

Hansard, HC Deb, 22 June 1921, cc 1395–6 is covered by the Open Parliament Licence: http://www.parliament.uk/site-information/copyright-parliament/open-parliament-licence/.

Report of the Consultative Committee on the Differentiation of the Curriculum for Boys and Girls Respectively in Secondary Schools (London: HMSO, 1922) is covered by the Open Government Licence: http://www.nationalarchives.gov.uk/doc/open-government-licence/version/3/.

The publisher gratefully acknowledges the permission granted by Mary Chamberlain to publish the extract from Chamberlain, Mary, *Fenwomen* (London, Virago, 1978).

Okely, J. M., 'Privileged, Schooled and Finished', in *Own or Other Culture* (London: Routledge, 1996) is reproduced by permission of Taylor & Francis Books UK. Copyright © Judith Okely 1996.

15 to 18 (Crowther Report), vol. 1 is covered by the Open Government Licence: http://www.nationalarchives.gov.uk/doc/open-government-licence/version/3/.

The publisher gratefully acknowledges the permission granted by *New Left Review* to publish the extract from Mitchell, Juliet, 'Women: the Longest Revolution', *New Left Review*, 1966.

The publisher gratefully acknowledges the permission granted by Routledge to publish the extract from Newson, J. & E., *Four Years Old in an Urban Community* (London: George Allen & Unwin, 1968).

The publisher gratefully acknowledges the permission granted by Carolyn McCrum to publish the extract from N. G. McCrum, 'The Gender Gap at Oxford', *Oxford Magazine* 143 (1997).

The publisher gratefully acknowledges the permission granted by Sage to publish the extract from Evans, S., 'In a Different Place. Working-Class Girls and Higher Education', *Sociology*, 43 (London: Sage, 2009).

Chapter 4   Sex and Sexualities

Stopes, Marie, *Married Love* (London, A. C. Fifield, 1918; repr Oxford, World's Classics, 2004), © The Galton Institute London, reproduced with permission.

Ask Me No More. An Autobiography by Jenifer Hart, Halban Publishers London 1998, Copyright © 1998 by Jenifer Hart, reproduced with permission.

The publisher gratefully acknowledges the permission granted by Shaun Tyas for the reproduction of Sutton, M. (ed. Shaun Tyas), *'We Didn't Know Owt', A Study of Sexuality, Superstition and Death in Women's Lives in Lincolnshire during the 1930s, 40s and 50s* (Donington: Shaun Tyas, 2012).

The publisher gratefully acknowledges the permission granted by Jo Mary Stafford and Faith Pentland for the reproduction of the extract from Stafford, Jo Mary, *Light in the Dust. A True Story of the Triumph of the Human Spirit* (London, John Blake Publishing, Ltd, 2002).

The publisher gratefully acknowledges the permission granted by David Higham to publish the extract from Gorer, Geoffrey, *Exploring English Character* (London: Cresset Press, 1955).

The publisher gratefully acknowledges the permission granted by Jacquie Sarsby to publish the extract from Sarsby, Jacquie, *Misuses and Mouldrunners. An oral history of women pottery workers at work and at home* (Milton Keynes: Open University Press, 1988).

The publisher gratefully acknowledges the permission granted by Angela McRobbie to publish the extract from McRobbie, A., 'Working-class girls and the culture of femininity', in Women's Studies Group, Centre for Contemporary Cultural Studies, Women Take Issue: aspects of women's subordination (London: Hutchinson, 1970).

The publisher gratefully acknowledges the permission granted by Sheila Jeffreys to publish the extract from Jeffreys, Sheila, *Anticlimax: a feminist perspective on the sexual revolution* (London: Women's Press, 1990).

[1992] 1 AC 599 Regina v R is covered by the Open Government Licence: http://www.nationalarchives.gov.uk/doc/open-government-licence/version/3/.

Hansard, HL Deb, 6 December 1999, cc 1049–50, 1079–84 is covered by the Open Parliament Licence: http://www.parliament.uk/site-information/copyright-parliament/open-parliament-licence/.

Chapter 5   Feminisms and Femininity

The publisher gratefully acknowledges the permission granted by Jenny Rathbone on behalf of the estate of Eleanor Rathbone to publish the extract from Rathbone, Eleanor, 'Patience and Impatience' (1923) in *Milestones: Presidential Addresses* (Liverpool: privately printed, 1929).

The publisher gratefully acknowledges the permission granted by Jenny Rathbone on behalf of the estate of Eleanor Rathbone to publish the extract from Rathbone, Eleanor, *The Disinherited Family* (London: Edward Arnold & Co., 1924).

Hansard, HC Deb, 19 July 1927, cols 244–5 is covered by the Open Parliament Licence: http://www.parliament.uk/site-information/copyright-parliament/open-parliament-licence/.

The extract from Brittain, Vera, *Lady into Woman. A History of Women from Victoria to Elizabeth II* (London: A. Dakers, 1953) is included by permission of

Mark Bostridge and T. J. Brittain-Catlin, Literary Executors for the Estate of Vera Brittain 1970.

The publisher gratefully acknowledges the permission granted by David Higham on behalf of the estate of Marghanita Laski to publish the extract from Laski, Marghanita, 'The Cult of Servility', in H. Hunkins-Hallinan (ed.), *In Her Own Right. A Discussion Conducted by the Six Point Group* (London: Harrap, 1968).

The publisher gratefully acknowledges the permission granted by Sheila Rowbotham to publish the extract from Rowbotham, Sheila, *Women's Liberation and the New Politics* (London: May Day Manifesto, 1969).

The publisher gratefully acknowledges the permission granted by Michelene Wandor to publish the extract from *Women's Newspaper*, March 6 1971, 'The Four Demands' in Wandor, Michelene (ed.), *Body Politic: Writings from the Women's Liberation Movement* (London: Stage 1, 1972).

The publisher gratefully acknowledges the permission granted by Florence Kroll to publish the extract from Una Kroll, 'Forum', *Spare Rib*, 80, March 1979.

The publisher gratefully acknowledges the permission granted by Hazel Carby to publish the extract from Carby, Hazel V., 'White Woman Listen! Black feminism and the boundaries of sisterhood', in Centre for Contemporary Cultural Studies, *The Empire Strikes Back. Race and Racism in 1970s Britain* (London: Hutchinson, 1982).

The Trouble and Strife Reader © Deborah Cameron and Joan Scanlon, 2010, 'The Trouble & Strife Reader' Bloomsbury Academic, an imprint of Bloomsbury Publishing Plc, and reproduced with permission.

The publisher gratefully acknowledges the permission granted by Zed Books to publish the extract from Redfern, Catherine & Aune, Kristin, *Reclaiming the F Word. The New Feminist Movement* (London: Zed Books, 2010).

Chapter 6   The Great War, 1914–18

The extract from Bishop, A. & Smart, T. (eds), *Chronicle of Youth. Vera Brittain, War Diary 1913–1917* (London: V. Gollancz, 1981) is included by permission of Mark Bostridge and T. J. Brittain-Catlin, Literary Executors for the Estate of Vera Brittain 1970.

The extract from Brittain, V., *Testament of Youth* (London: V. Gollancz, 1933; repr Virago, 1978) is included by permission of Mark Bostridge and T. J. Brittain-Catlin, Literary Executors for the Estate of Vera Brittain 1970.

The publisher gratefully acknowledges the permission granted by Helen Pankhurst to publish the extract from Pankhurst, E. Sylvia, *The Home Front* (London: Hutchinson, 1932).

The publisher gratefully acknowledges the permission granted by Helen Jones to publish the extract from Jones, Helen (ed.), *Duty and Citizenship. The correspondence and political papers of Violet Markham, 1896–1953* (London: Historians' Press, 1994).

Llewelyn Davies, M. (ed.), *Life as We Have Known It, by Cooperative Working Women* (London: L. and V. Woolf, 1931; repr Virago, 1977), pp. 50–2.

Burnett, J. (ed.), *Useful Toil* (London; Allen Lane, 1974) is reproduced by permission of Taylor & Francis Books UK.

'The Dancers' from Clowns' Houses by Edith Sitwell reprinted by permission of Peters Fraser & Dunlop (www.petersfraserdunlop.com) on behalf of the Estate of Edith Sitwell.

Extract from *No Time Like the Present* by Storm Jameson reprinted by permission of Peters Fraser & Dunlop (www.petersfraserdunlop.com) on behalf of the Estate of Storm Jameson.

Chapter 7 Franchise and After: The Modern Woman? 1918–39

The publisher gratefully acknowledges the permission granted by Jenny Rathbone on behalf of the estate of Eleanor Rathbone to publish the extract from Rathbone, Eleanor, 'Equal Citizenship', 9 March 1920, in her *Milestones* (Liverpool: privately printed, 1929).

Price v Rhondda District Council, [1923] 2 Ch.372 is covered by the Open Government Licence: http://www.nationalarchives.gov.uk/doc/open-government-licence/version/3/.

Hansard, HC Deb, 11 Dec 1929 is covered by the Open Parliament Licence: http://www.parliament.uk/site-information/copyright-parliament/open-parliament-licence/.

The publisher gratefully acknowledges the permission granted by Juliet Nicolson on behalf of the estate of Harold Nicolson to publish the extract from Nicolson, Harold, *Diaries and Letters, 1930–39* (London: Collins, 1966).

Hansard, HC Deb, 24 Aug 1939, cc 47–50 is covered by the Open Parliament Licence: http://www.parliament.uk/site-information/copyright-parliament/open-parliament-licence/.

Chapter 8 War and Reconstruction, 1939–51

A Pacifist's War; diaries, 1939–45 by Frances Partridge. Published by Hogarth Press, 1978. Copyright © Frances Partridge. Reproduced by permission of the author's estate c/o Rogers, Coleridge & White Ltd, 20 Powis Mews, London, W11 1JN.

The publisher gratefully acknowledges the permission granted by Persephone Books to publish the extract from Vere Hodgson, *Few Eggs and No Oranges. A diary showing how unimportant people in London and Birmingham lived through the war years* (London, D. Dobson, 1976; repr Persephone Books, 1999).

The publisher gratefully acknowledges the permission granted by Helen Jones to publish the extract from Jones, Helen (ed.), *Duty and Citizenship. Correspondence and papers of Violet Markham* (London: Historians' Press, 1994).

Beveridge, William, *Social Insurance and Allied Services* (London: HMSO, 1942) is covered by the Open Government Licence: http://www.nationalarchives.gov.uk/doc/open-government-licence/version/3/.

Women's Group on Public Welfare (England), *Our Towns. A Close-Up* (Oxford: OUP, 1943) is reproduced by permission of Oxford University Press.

Hansard, HC Deb, 28–29 Mar 1944 is covered by the Open Parliament Licence: http://www.parliament.uk/site-information/copyright-parliament/open-parliament-licence/.

Sackville-West, Vita, *The Women's Land Army* (London, Imperial War Museum, 1944), pp. 7–8, 14 is reproduced with permission from Curtis Brown Group Ltd, London on behalf of The Estate of Vita Sackville-West. Copyright © Vita Sackville-West 1944.

Bowen, Elizabeth, *The Heat of the Day* (London: J. Cape, 1949; repr. London: Vintage, 1998), pp. 325–9 is reproduced by permission of the Random House Group Ltd and Curtis Brown Group Ltd, London on behalf of Elizabeth Bowen. Copyright © Elizabeth Bowen 1949.

Hansard, HC Deb, 8 Mar 1945, cc 2276–85 is covered by the Open Parliament Licence: http://www.parliament.uk/site-information/copyright-parliament/open-parliament-licence/.

Hansard, HC Deb, 30 Apr 1946, cc 85–91, 111–116 is covered by the Open Parliament Licence: http://www.parliament.uk/site-information/copyright-parliament/open-parliament-licence/.

The publisher gratefully acknowledges the permission granted by Wiley to reproduce the extract from Young, Michael, 'The Distribution of Income within the Family', *British Journal of Sociology*, 3, 1952, (London: Routlege & Kegan Paul). © 1952 London School of Economics.

Chapter 9 The Fifties and Sixties

The publisher gratefully acknowledges the permission granted by the Mistress and Fellows of Girton College, Cambridge to reproduce the extract from Wootton, Barbara, *In A World I Never Made: autobiographical reflections.*

Recommendations on prostitution, *Report of the Committee on Homosexual Offences and Prostitution (Wolfenden)* (London: HMSO, 1957) is covered by the Open Government Licence: http://www.nationalarchives.gov.uk/doc/open-government-licence/version/3/.

Hansard, HL Deb 5 May & 9 June, 1959 is covered by the Open Parliament Licence: http://www.parliament.uk/site-information/copyright-parliament/open-parliament-licence/.

15 to 18 (Crowther Report) (London: HMSO, 1959) is covered by the Open Government Licence: http://www.nationalarchives.gov.uk/doc/open-government-licence/version/3/.

Weldon, Fay, *Auto Da Fay* (London: Flamingo, 2002), pp. 352–7. Copyright © Fay Weldon, 2002. Reproduced by permission of Fay Weldon c/o Georgina Capel Associates Ltd., 29 Wardour Street, London, W1D 6PS.

The publisher gratefully acknowledges the permission granted by Tess McKenney on behalf of the estate of Sheila Kitzinger and the Orion Book Group to reproduce the extract from Kitzinger, Sheila, *The Experience of Childbirth* (London: Gollancz, 1962). Copyright © Shala Kitzinger 1962.

The extract from Whitehouse, Mary, *Cleaning-up T.V.: from protest to participation* (London: Blandford Press, 1967) is reprinted with kind permission of the executors of the estate of Mrs Mary Whitehouse.

Hansard, HL Deb, 8 Nov 1967, cc 421–8 is covered by the Open Parliament Licence: http://www.parliament.uk/site-information/copyright-parliament/open-parliament-licence/.

Children and their Primary Schools (Plowden Report) (London: HMSO, 1967), vol1 is covered by the Open Government Licence: http://www.nationalarchives.gov.uk/doc/open-government-licence/version/3/.

The publisher gratefully acknowledges the permission granted by David Higham to publish the extract from Castle, Barbara, 'No Kitchen Cabinet', in Maitland, Sara (ed.), *Very Heaven: looking back at the 1960s* (London: Virago, 1988).

The publisher gratefully acknowledges the permission granted by the Trades Union Congress to publish the extract from *Report of the 100th Annual Trades Union Congress, 1968* (London: TUC, 1968).

Nothing Sacred by Angela Carter. Published by Virago 1982. Copyright © Angela Carter. Reproduced by permission of the author's estate c/o Rogers, Coleridge & White Ltd, 20 Powis Mews, London, WII IJN.

Chapter 10   Women's Lib to Post-Feminism? 1970–2000
The publisher gratefully acknowledges the permission granted by Michelene Wandor to publish the extract from Wandor, M (ed.), *The Body Politic. Writings from the Women's Liberation Movement in Britain, 1969–72* (London: Stage 1, 1972).

Finer Report on One-Parent Families (London: HMSO, 1974) is covered by the Open Government Licence: http://www.nationalarchives.gov.uk/doc/open-government-licence/version/3/.

The publisher gratefully acknowledges the permission granted by David Higham to publish the extract from Castle, Barbara, *The Castle Diaries, 1974–6* (London: Weidenfeld & Nicolson, 1980).

The 1975 Sex Discrimination Bill is covered by the Open Government Licence: http://www.nationalarchives.gov.uk/doc/open-government-licence/version/3/.

The publisher gratefully acknowledges the permission granted by the Trades Union Congress to publish the extract from *Report of the 110th Annual Trades Union Congress, 1978* (London: TUC, 1978).

The publisher gratefully acknowledges the permission granted by the Trades Union Congress to publish the extract from *Report of the 115th Annual Trades Union Congress, 1983* (London: TUC, 1983).

The publisher gratefully acknowledges the permission granted by Taylor & Francis Ltd. to publish the extract from Purvis, June, 'Diana, Princess of Wales', editorial in *Women's History Review*, 6, 1997 (Wallingford: Triangle Journals, 1997).

Hansard, HC Deb, 8 June 1998, cols 695–6. Report of the Hansard Society Commission on Women at the Top (1990) is reproduced with permission from the Hansard Society.

Fairness and Freedom: the Final Report of the Equalities Review (London: HMSO, 2007) is covered by the Open Government Licence: http://www.nationalarchives. gov.uk/doc/open-government-licence/version/3/.

Index of Persons

Subject Index

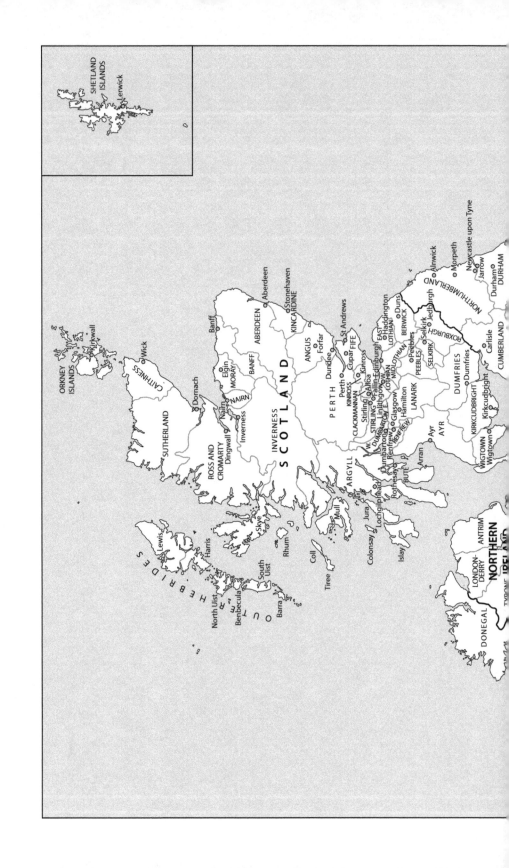